WITHDRAWN

LITERARY AFTERSHOCKS
American Writers, Readers, and the Bomb

TWAYNE'S

LITERATURE
&
SOCIETY

SERIES

Leo Marx, General Editor
Massachusetts Institute of Technology

Previously published

Imagining Columbus:
The Literary Voyage
Ilan Stavans

Epidemics in the Modern World
Joann P. Krieg

Tales of the Working Girl:
Wage-Earning Women in American Literature,
1890–1925
Laura Hapke

Vietnam in American Literature
Philip H. Melling

LITERARY AFTERSHOCKS

*American Writers, Readers,
and the Bomb*

Albert E. Stone
University of Iowa

Twayne Publishers • *New York*
MAXWELL MACMILLAN CANADA • TORONTO
MAXWELL MACMILLAN INTERNATIONAL • NEW YORK OXFORD SINGAPORE SYDNEY

Literary Aftershocks

Albert E. Stone

Copyright © 1994 by Twayne Publishers

Twayne Publishers
Macmillan Publishing Company
866 Third Avenue
New York, New York 10022

Maxwell Macmillan Canada, Inc.
1200 Eglinton Avenue East
Suite 200
Don Mills, Ontario M3C 3N1

Library of Congress Cataloging-in-Publication Data

Stone, Albert E.
    Literary aftershocks : American writers, readers, and the bomb / Albert E. Stone.
        p.   cm. — (Twayne's literature & society series : no. 5)
    Includes bibliographical references (p.   ) and index.
    ISBN 0-8057-8853-0 (alk. paper)
    1. American literature—20th century—History and criticism.
    2. World War, 1939–1945—United States—Literature and the war.
    3. Books and reading—United States—History—20th century.
    4. Nuclear warfare and literature—United States—History. 5. War stories, American—History and criticism. 6. War poetry, American—History and criticism. 7. Atomic bomb—United States—History.
    8. Atomic bomb in literature. I. Title. II. Series.
PS228.W37S76   1994
810.9 358—dc20   94-20030
                                                              CIP

The paper used in this publication meets the minimum requirements of American National Standard for Information Sciences—Permanence of Paper for Printed Library Materials. ANSI Z3948–1984. ∞ ™

10 9 8 7 6 5 4 3 2 1 (hc)

Printed in the United States of America

For
Ned, Rebecca, Douglas, and Dylan
Members of the next two generations
of the nuclear age,
if they and we are lucky

CONTENTS

FOREWORD

Each volume in the Literature and Society Series examines the interplay between a body of writing and a historical event. By "event" we mean a circumscribable episode, located in a specific time and place; it may be an election, a royal reign, a presidency, a war, a revolution, a voyage of discovery, a trial, an engineering project, a scientific innovation, a social movement, an invention, a law, or an epidemic. But it must have given rise to a substantial corpus of interpretive writing.

The idea of elucidating the relations between writing and its historical context is not new. In the past, however, those relations too often have been treated as merely ancillary, static, or unidirectional. Historians have drawn on literary works chiefly in order to illustrate, corroborate, or enliven an essentially socioeconomic or political narrative; or, by the same token, literary scholars have introduced a summary of extraliterary events chiefly in order to provide a historical setting—a kind of theatrical "backdrop"—for their discussions of a body of writing.

In this series, however, the aim is to demonstrate how knowledge of events and an understanding of what has been writtten about them enhance each other. Each is more meaningful in the presence of the other. Just as history can only be created by acts of interpretation, so any written work invariably bears the marks of the historical circumstances in which it was composed. The controlling principle of the Literature and Society Series is the reciprocal relation between our conception of events and the writing they may be said to have provoked.

Leo Marx

ACKNOWLEDGMENTS

Many individuals and institutions have materially contributed to make this book possible. Though I wish first to thank my Iowa colleagues Richard Horwitz, Brooks Landon, John Raeburn, Lauren Rabinovitz, Wayne Franklin, Kathleen Diffley, and Ed Folsom, I also want particularly to thank my students in American Studies and English at the University of Iowa. The 1990–1991 members of American Studies 90, "American Culture since Hiroshima," proved invaluable stimuli to my thinking and reading in the early stages of this project. Tom Karson and James Scott gave freely of their bibliographical and visual media expertise and enthusiasm. Finally, my wife Grace has discharged tactfully and lovingly her usual task of keeping me focused and, if possible, less wordy.

Librarians at the following institutions have provided generously of their time and services: University of Iowa Library; Hawthorne and Longfellow Library, Bowdoin College; Sterling Library, Yale University; Widener Library, Harvard University; Ladd Library, Bates College; Curtis Library, Brunswick, Maine; and Patten Free Library, Bath, Maine.

Another version of chapter 4, "Children, Literature, and the Bomb," appears in *Prospects: An Annual of American Cultural Studies* 19 (New York: Cambridge University Press, 1994).

Permission to quote from works cited in this book has been generously granted by the following publishers:

American Library Association (50 E. Huron St., Chicago, Ill. 60611): excerpts from *Nuclear Age Literature for Youth*, ISBN 0–8389–0535–8. Copyright © 1990 by American Library Association.

J. G. Ballard and Mr. Ballard's agent, Robin Straus Agency, Inc.: excerpts from *The Terminal Beach* by J. G. Ballard. Copyright © 1964, 1992 by J. G. Ballard.

Don Congdon Associates, Inc.: excerpts from *The Martian Chronicles* by Ray Bradbury (New York: Bantam Books, 1950). Copyright © 1950, © renewed 1977 by Ray Bradbury.

Harlan Ellison and Mr. Ellison's agent, Richard Curtis Associates, Inc., New York: quotations from "I Have No Mouth, and I Must Scream" and "A Boy and His Dog" by Harlan Ellison. Copyright © 1967, 1968, 1969 by Harlan Ellison. All rights reserved.

HarperCollins: 31 lines from "Plutonian Ode," from *Collected Poems, 1947–1980* by Allen Ginsberg. Copyright © 1984 by Allen Ginsberg.

HarperCollins: excerpt from "Nagasaki Days (Boulder, Summer 1978)," from *Collected Poems, 1947-1980* by Allen Ginsberg. Copyright © 1984 by Allen Ginsberg.

Henry Holt & Co.: excerpts from *Warday: And the Journey Onward* by Whitley Strieber and James W. Kunetka. Copyright © 1984 by Wilson & Neff, Inc. and James W. Kunetka.

Houghton Mifflin Company: excerpt from "The Fundamental Project of Technology," from *The Past* by Galway Kinnell. Copyright © 1985 by Galway Kinnell. All rights reserved.

Indiana University Press: excerpts from *Writing and Rewriting the Holocaust: Narrative and the Consequences of Interpretation* by James E. Young. Copyright © 1988 by James E. Young.

Alfred A. Knopf, Inc.: excerpts from *Hiroshima* by John Hersey. Copyright © 1946 and renewed 1974 by John Hersey.

Alfred A. Knopf, Inc.: excerpts from *Fiskadora* by Denis Johnson. Copyright © 1985 by Denis Johnson.

Alfred A. Knopf, Inc.: excerpts from *The Fate of the Earth* by Jonathan Schell. Copyright © 1982 by Jonathan Schell. Originally appeared in the *New Yorker*.

Alfred A. Knopf, Inc.: excerpts from *Wolf of Shadows* by Whitley Strieber. Copyright © 1985 by Wilson and Neff, Inc.

Lothrop, Lee & Shepard Books, a division of William Morrow & Co., Inc.:

excerpts and three illustrations from *Hiroshima No Pika* by Toshi Maruki. Copyright © 1980 by Toshi Maruki.

David Mura: "The Survivor," from *After We Lost Our Way* (E. P. Dutton, 1989). Copyright © 1989 by David Mura.

The editors of *Northwest Review*: excerpts from *Warnings: An Anthology on the Nuclear Peril* (Northwest Review Books, 1984). Copyright © 1984 by *Northwest Review*.

Random House, Inc.: excerpts from *New and Selected Poems 1923–1985* by Robert Penn Warren. Copyright © 1985 by Robert Penn Warren.

Carolyn See: excerpts from *Golden Days*, a novel (New York: McGraw, 1980). Copyright © by Carolyn See.

Simon & Schuster, Inc.: excerpts from *The Making of the Atomic Bomb* by Richard Rhodes. Copyright © 1986 by Richard Rhodes.

Norman Spinrad: excerpt from "The Big Flash," from *Beyond Armageddon: Twenty-one Sermons to the Dead*, edited by Walter M. Miller and Martin Greenberg (New York: Primus Books, 1985). Copyright © 1985 by Primus Books.

The Spirit That Moves Us Press, Inc.: excerpts from *Nuke-Rebuke: Writers and Artists against Nuclear Energy and Weapons*, edited by Morty Sklar and published in 1984 by The Spirit That Moves Us Press (Jackson Heights, Queens, N.Y.). Copyright © 1984 by The Spirit That Moves Us Press, Inc.

The estate of William Stafford: excerpt from "At the Bomb Testing Site," from *Stories That Could Be True: New and Collected Poems* (New York: Harper & Row, 1971). Copyright © 1977 by William Stafford.

University Press of New England: excerpts from *No Place to Hide* by David J. Bradley. Copyright © 1983 by David J. Bradley.

Viking Penguin, a division of Penguin Books USA Inc.: excerpts from *Praises and Dispraises* by Terrence Des Pres. Copyright © 1988 by the Estate of Terrence Des Pres.

Viking Penguin, a division of Penguin Books USA Inc.: "How to Survive Nuclear War," from *The Long Approach* by Maxine Kumin. Copyright © 1985 by Maxine Kumin.

Albert A. Whitman & Company: Illustrations and excerpts of text from *Nobody Wants a Nuclear War* by Judith Vigna. Copyright © 1986 by Judith Vigna. All rights reserved.

Eleanor Wilner: excerpts from *Sarah's Choice* (University of Chicago Press, 1989). Copyright © 1989 by Eleanor Wilner.

Philip Wylie: excerpts from *Tomorrow!* (New York: Rinehart, 1954). Copyright © 1954 by Philip Wylie renewed © 1982 by Karen Pryor.

PREFACE

In Carolyn See's *Golden Days*, one of the postholocaust novels discussed in this book, the exuberant narrator, in defense of a story that is by turns graphic and fantastic, exclaims: "But if you think you aren't going to care about this story, hold on. It's the most important story in the Western world!"[1] Such hyperbole may be difficult to take seriously in the mid-1990s. Yet this book risks similar skepticism from readers.

Some readers will suppose that, given the collapse of the Soviet Union and détente overtures, the nuclear age is fast becoming mere history, an important but no longer urgent era of the recent past. But much ominous evidence exists to contradict the assumption that nuclear threats of mass devastation are all but over. Even after American and ex-Soviet missiles are dismantled, some nuclear armaments—and hence the continuing danger of accidents or deliberate attacks—will surely be retained. Keeping some kind of nuclear arsenal in place will be prudent policy, some argue, given the proliferation of nuclear arms in the Middle East, the Indian subcontinent, and the Far East.

Terrorism and its devices magnify such dangers and extend the arena to all corners of the globe. At the same time, nuclear power plants and radioactivity are permanent facts of life. As Jonathan Schell points out in *The Fate of the Earth*, "[S]cience is a tide that can only rise. . . . [W]e do not know how, as a species, to *deliberately* set out to forget something."[2] Humankind can never forget Hiroshima and what it has come to symbolize for the fragile fabric of our postnuclear and postholocaust existence over the past half-century and more. (In this book, the term "postnuclear" denotes discovery, while "postholocaust" denotes deployment, either past or future.) Hence the headline in the 1992 issue of *Nuclear Texts and Contexts*, "Farewell to the First Atomic Age." This book takes seriously that adjective *first* and invites readers of history and literature to do the same.

If the nuclear age has a murky future, it likewise has a past both ill understood and avoided by many. Even when represented in fiction, poetry, or nonfictional narratives—discourses that necessarily simplify, symbolize, or, at times, defuse the realities of the Bomb's destructive power—the past is a bitter memory. Readers can choose to refuse to encounter its horrors and responsibilities even through vicarious imaginative encounters. Just as some evade the nuclear past as mere history, so others escape involvement by reading but then dismissing literature as mere fiction, mere poetry. Then when, as will be shown in chapter 4, children's literature is discovered to contain some powerful and graphic depictions of Hiroshima or postholocaust survival, parents, teachers, and librarians sometimes shield young readers from the very books written for their moral education. Literature's power as social instrument of information and indoctrination is thereby confirmed.

This book is written to demonstrate such power and to argue for that social function. Nonfiction works like John Hersey's *Hiroshima* and Schell's *Fate of the Earth* will be familiar to many, as will be a number of nuclear novels like Ray Bradbury's *Martian Chronicles* and Walter Miller's *Canticle for Leibowitz*. A few famous poems about the Bomb, such as Allen Ginsberg's "Plutonian Ode," will likewise find knowledgeable receptors. So, too, science fiction aficionados will surely find here some familiar magazine stories and a few Hugo or Nebula Prize–winning novels. At the same time, much of the nuclear literature published since August 1945 would, I suspect, prove less familiar to the bulk of American readers.

This sometimes neglected repository of stories, descriptions, myths, images, metaphors, and didactic and critical messages constitutes an impressive record of the imagination's confrontations with an awesome reality that will not—cannot—go away. I have arranged my treatment of this surprisingly extensive literature according to two conventions: first, chronological sequence in many instances; and then literary genres as the focus and framework of the several chapters. These conventional arrangements, as I see it, are readily recognized by the general reader. As the final chapter also seeks to establish, a growing number of 1980s literary and cultural critics have made this structure and agenda clearer. The ineluctable reality of the Bomb, I assert, determines both content and formal strategies of representation in this body of real-time and fantasy fictions, lyric and narrative poems, children's books, and nonfiction essays and narratives.

As my subtitle signals, readers are treated as essential participants in the social transactions between authors, texts, history, and the nuclear referent. Given constraints of space, therefore, this book will limit analysis almost entirely to readers, not viewers or listeners, of imaginative creations and criticisms of Hiroshima, the Bomb, and the era. Only passing notice is paid to films, plays, still photographs, radio, or television documentaries or docudramas. These modes and genres are, of course, important components of the nuclear dialogue within—and beyond—American culture. For similar reasons, non-American texts will not receive the attention here that some have earned and others deserve. (A pair of important exceptions appear in chapter 4.)

In cold war society over the past four decades, the nuclear topic has often been shrouded in official secrecy, misinformation, and censorship. Despite press coverage and efforts by activists in the nuclear freeze movement to air the dangers and deceptions of nuclear war policies, suppression of facts and implications continues to the present. At the same time, public discourse has for long been debased by "nukespeak," the deliberately misleading manipulation of language (for example, naming a missile "Peacemaker") to cloak realities, exaggerate benefits of nuclear power, or encourage wishful thinking. Such abuses of language sharpen the need for imaginative writing of all kinds. Even surreal plots, extraterrestrial settings, mythic characters, and exotic imagery may sometimes educate and inspire readers more responsibly than, say, a government civil defense manual. Thereby the cultural work of fiction, poetry, prose, and even criticism is performed through affective and effective language, so that readers are shown and told what they need to know about nuclear subjects, how to think and feel about them, and even on occasion how to act on them. Basic values and attitudes respecting life and death; localism, nationalism, and global consciousness; the "future of immortality," in Robert Jay Lifton's phrase, and the fate of the earth, in Schell's; the nature and usefulness of war; the causes of disarmament and world peace; all are expressed and criticized.

Because I believe literature still enacts such cognitive, emotional, and moral roles for readers of all ages and classes in these last years of the first atomic age, I admit to pushing an ideological agenda. "To write about nuclear weapons is inevitably to adopt a cause," writes Richard Falk in *Indefensible Weapons.*[3] *Literary Aftershocks* frankly endorses the traditional humanist values that literature has espoused for centuries: the illumination and celebration of life, hope, nature, and spirit. It is not, I trust, a simplistic condemnation of science and technology—or of their separation from literature, art, and religion, of *eros* divorced from *thanatos*—but a reminder of literature's complex nature as cultural communication. In the words of Terrence Des Pres, literature delivers to hearts and minds "right language," as a crucial help in "hard moments."[5] The struggle that literature participates in sustains our humanity in the face of potential (and man-made) oblivion in this moment in world history.

What follows, then, are discussions of various modal traditions in written expression and communication about the Bomb: first, popular and influential nonfiction works like John Hersey's *Hiroshima* and Jonathan Schell's *Fate of the Earth*; then fictional stories and novels, especially those that appeared during the crucial decades of the 1950s and 1980s; next, recent writings, chiefly fictional, for children; followed by poetry, both adults' and children's, that reflects feelings and formulations of the nuclear age; and finally, cultural criticism written in the 1980s that helps serious readers frame this rich and complex literature and the epoch of which it is a vital part.

1

The Common Medium and the Unique Event: Three Prose "Masterpieces"

The masterpieces cannot be timeless if time itself stops.
Jonathan Schell (*The Fate of the Earth,* 163)

EVEN AFTER THE TRIUMPH OF TELEVISION IN THE DECADE
and a half after Hiroshima, American society may still be characterized, in
revealing shorthand, as a communications network based on the elementary
skills of its members as readers and writers. In particular, reading newspapers,
magazines, school textbooks, paperbacks, and library volumes remains for
many a regular activity and valued social skill. It provides economic opportunities for large segments of the population.

In homes, offices, schools, and public libraries, the common currency of
written communication is nonfiction prose, through which the major cultural
work of informing and indoctrinating members of society is carried on. Especially for better educated citizens and their offspring who participate actively
in community life, skill in the uses of denotative discourses is expected and,
even in an era of overburdened educational systems, encouraged. Though

altered by the rise of electronic media, the widespread practice of prose in traditional modalities remains a powerful cement for a literate culture. Through its forms, genres, and usages, the institutions of journalism, law, education, medicine, and religion—to cite but the most obvious fields—are maintained and interrelated. The historical records preserved in public archives are likewise predominantly encoded in this genre. Hence the cultural historian commonly explores the past and interprets its messages and meanings through nonfiction prose narratives. Even the poetry, fiction, drama, art, music, religious incantations, and visual media that compose the "literature" of culture are interpreted via prose descriptions and critiques. In the process, when certain prose works get published, preserved, read, taught, and attacked or defended, they can over time come to be defined as "classic," "masterpieces," and endowed with "superior," "permanent," "iconic," or "transcendent" value.

These truisms lend more than plausibility to my decision to open this literary history of the atomic age by discussing nonfiction writing, especially three contemporary classics. For one thing, the beginning of the nuclear age has often been dated from the 495-word letter that Albert Einstein sent to President Franklin Roosevelt in August 1939, urging the establishment of what became the Manhattan Project.[1] And one of the leading scientists in that project, Niels Bohr of Denmark, later addressed a memorandum to the president laying out in eloquently understated English prose some of the political implications of nuclear energy and weaponry. "It is still the only comprehensive and realistic charter for a postnuclear world," Richard Rhodes declared in 1986.[2]

As for public prose discourse, many signals from readers who once lived through the remarkable events and transformations of postnuclear America suggest a more publicized point of departure. The first book to appear after 1945 that illustrated the American communications culture at work creating a "classic" was John Hersey's *Hiroshima* (1946). Furthermore, Hersey's journalistic history of six Hiroshima survivors' experiences was the most widely read account of nuclear holocaust during the early years of the new era, and his enduring work has continued to influence American imaginations and consciences. Reconstructing this seminal text's original message of 1946 and some of its later permutations and impacts leads, therefore, in two directions: sideways into the surrounding contexts and conflicts of the immediate post-Hiroshima moment, and forward into later moments and circumstances during which this narrative has played meaningful roles. "A quarter of a century has gone by since 'Hiroshima' was published," Hersey wrote in 1971, "and generations of school children have read it, and the letters I still get in considerable numbers suggest that the book *has* had a moral impact."[3] Later, in 1985, when *Hiroshima* was published in a revised paperback edition with a new section 5 entitled "The Aftermath," the historian Paul Boyer underlined the book's continuing relevance: "[I]t is true that during the periods of intense engagement with the nuclear threat that have occurred at intervals since 1945, *Hiroshima* has always been rediscovered as a primary text."[4] And a few years later still, Spencer Weart added that the spate of "realistic" or nonfiction works of nuclear literature is, as it were, anchored at both ends by two monuments, including "Jonathan Schell's *The Fate of the Earth*, the first non-fiction book about nuclear war to become a best-seller since Hersey's *Hiroshima* [of 1946]."[5]

These claims give rise to three closely linked inquiries. First, what factors explain this work's success in the immediate postwar situation? What new or repeated circumstances have perpetuated *Hiroshima*'s claim on the attention of readers and participants in nuclear debates, especially during the 1980s? And finally, what relationships exist between the language, literary form, and narrative strategies employed by Hersey and the cultural work performed for different groups of readers to meet their cognitive and emotional needs?

Answers to these fundamental queries start with consideration of the work's social-economic production and reception. *Hiroshima* exemplifies American literary culture after World War II in part because its double appearance, first as a long article in the *New Yorker* in the summer of 1946 and subsequently in book form, coincided with a period of intense public and private curiosity and concern over the meanings of the Hiroshima and Nagasaki bombings.[6] Hersey's timing was indeed fortuitous. For as Boyer, Michael Yavenditti, and other scholars make clear, American public expression had, by that summer, generated most of the military, political, and moral issues that have persisted to the present day. The chief social and intellectual groups debating these questions had identified themselves. Therefore, the linked matters of the sociology of knowledge and the relative influences of elite and popular attitudes—who knew what facts about the Bomb and its recent use, whose views affected public policy and popular sentiment—can be addressed. Concerns about secrecy and publicity, nationalism and internationalism, patriotic pride and vindictiveness in tension with private misgivings, can be explored, although only within the admittedly narrow context of a single set of author/text/audience transactions. This should prove profitable if we recognize *Hiroshima* as simultaneously a *personal expression*, a *social history* (under the umbrella of journalism), and a *cultural critique* of American and Japanese value systems. To identify these aspects of the inquiry is to recognize the complex status of this exemplary document of the early nuclear age.

As a 1946 best-seller and critical success, *Hiroshima* benefited from the passage of a year since the momentous events it records had arrested world attention. Hersey's version joined a host of other nonfiction messages in newspapers, magazines, and on the radio that reported, reflected on, and to some extent dispelled the secrecy surrounding the Bomb's creation and deployment. Dissipated, too, to some extent by August 1946 were the public's immediate emotions of elation, awe, and mystery. In *Life* and *Time*, *Reader's Digest* and *Saturday Review*, *Atlantic Monthly* and *Harper's*, and in all the major religious journals, including *Christian Century*, *Commentary*, *Commonweal*, and *America*, a public and often heated debate ensued. As Weart later observed,

"Hiroshima inspired more debate than the rest of the war's destruction put together. It was as if all the other recent massacres could be set aside and the entire moral problem of modern war could be concentrated in this one question" (107).

In this periodical literature, opinion preponderantly supported America's use of the atomic bomb to end the war and save American lives. These views closely mirrored official governmental propaganda. Indeed, the *Harper's* and *Atlantic Monthly* essayists were MIT's Karl Compton, a member of several key wartime boards, and Henry L. Stimson, Truman's secretary of war. Military justification of past decisions and political fears of future dangers (already in 1945 and 1946 focused on the Soviet Union and world communism) were persuasive for the majority of Americans. Nonetheless, strong moral and religious objections and questions were voiced. Not unexpectedly, this dissent was often couched in biblical language and imagery.

Religious language, however, also served pro-Bomb arguments. From President Truman down to letters to the editor from almost illiterate citizens, the Christian and Jewish heritages and vocabularies were invoked. "It is an awful responsibility which has come to us," the president announced. "We thank God that it has come to us instead of to our enemies, and we pray that He may guide us to use it in His ways and for His purposes" (Boyer, 6). While *Life* printed unforgettable images of the awful beauty of the mushroom cloud and the equally awesome devastation of the flattened city, the languages of the Old Testament, the book of Revelation, and Greek myths were deployed to define public feelings and forebodings. At the same time, racial prejudice and nationalist fervor against the Japanese were freely expressed. In editorials, essays, and cartoons, writers and their audiences came to share the belief that a brutal enemy had deserved American retribution. (Indeed, majority opinion four decades later seems not to have shifted decisively, as reflected in polls and political statements like President George Bush's on the fiftieth anniversary of Pearl Harbor. The persistence of this belief is a continuing literary factor as well.)

Still another ingredient in the political and moral ferment surrounding *Hiroshima*'s initial appearance was the American public's knowledge—derived from often scanty and belated journalists' and scholars' reports—of details of America's wartime embrace of strategic bombing, or "total" aerial warfare. Like its gradual awareness of the Nazi Holocaust, the actual extent and possible implications of the wholesale nighttime firebombing of Hamburg, Dresden, and Tokyo, among other cities, came differentially to segments of the reading public. The principal vehicle of that knowledge at all times, however, whatever the audience, was nonfiction prose, a discourse that was arguably much more difficult than novels and films to discount or ignore. Wartime censorship followed by cold war secrecy affected all modes of communication about the subject of nuclear warfare. It would be a painstaking task for a historian or sociologist, even today, to plot in detail the spread of information (and misinformation) on, for example, the firebombing of Dresden through the maze of government press releases, newspaper and magazine discussions, past the gaps and cryptic remarks in textbooks, and, years later, into imaginative depictions of the same event in Kurt Vonnegut's novel (1969) and Stanley Kubrick's film (1972), *Slaughterhouse Five*. Summarizing such transactions in postwar American culture underscores the importance of *relatively* reliable nonfiction discourses like Hersey's *Hiroshima*.

Though many events and issues are ignored or oversimplified by the above summary, it suggests the necessity of starting with modest queries about Hersey's own motives and his journalist's sense of his readers' concerns in 1946. In *Hiroshima* the most palpable of his personal feelings are awe, bewilderment, and confusion as to the actual nature and extent of atomic destruction of the two Japanese cities. Probably these responses, at once cognitive and affective, were shared by the *New Yorker* readership and those among the 848,000 members of the Book-of-the-Month Club who later received free copies of *Hiroshima*, as well as by radio listeners who heard the four-part reading of the book over ABC airwaves in 1946. To lump these early audiences together is not to discount real differences of response as affected by social and educational background or political commitment. Yet the basic need to learn more about the Bomb's impact—which increasing numbers of Americans now understood in terms of civilian more than military victims—soon embraced both the sophisticated, predominantly East Coast clientele of the *New Yorker* and the more diverse and far larger body of Hersey's readers nationwide who snapped up 15 reprintings during the book's first year of publication.

An allied issue frequently debated elsewhere but only obliquely treated in *Hiroshima* was whether the Bomb was just another (albeit more powerful) military weapon, as Winston Churchill, President Harry Truman, and military spokesmen averred, or a qualitatively different instrument of mass destruction. Coming to terms with this issue involved learning not only the full extent of urban obliterations, including accurate casualty figures (long shrouded in official secrecy), but, perhaps more ominous, the nature and extent of radiation sickness and its long-term effects. The most pervasive of American anxieties thus appeared: the growing fear that "this could happen to me!" Hiroshima's fate might someday be Denver's or Atlanta's. Of the books and articles addressing these concerns, *Hiroshima* became the centerpiece as soon as it appeared in book form. If by 1946 or 1947 most Americans could not yet *see themselves* as survivors of a Bomb—after all, only we possessed one—they were at least beginning to imagine and fear future repetitions of nuclear holocaust. Such fears were compounded on 24 September 1949 when it was announced that the Soviet Union had recently tested an atomic bomb. The first stage of the atomic age was over.

To the task of dealing with his countrymen's doubts and dread Hersey brought a background of experience and moral concern unusually rich and apt for such a youthful author. Born in China in 1914 and educated at Yale, he shared some early experiences and cultural values with two older, influential Americans: Henry Luce of *Time-Life* and Thornton Wilder, the playwright and novelist. Besides his familiarity with the Far East, Hersey's early Christian missionary education and careers in both journalism and fiction writing proved valuable assets. During World War II he was a correspondent in the South Pacific, narrowly missed death more than once, and wrote three books. Each depicted soldiers or civilians enduring and often conquering wartime hardship. Shortly after the surrender of Japan, he went on a fact-finding journey to China and Japan, underwritten by *Life* and the *New Yorker*. After resolving to write about Hiroshima and its survivors, he visited the city, interviewed nearly 40 persons, and read extensively in military and scientific sources, including the *United States Strategic Bombing Survey*. Sustaining him through this encounter with Hiroshima, which he later confessed "was a kind of horror" (Yavenditti, 35), was the personal conviction that war had confirmed: "[I]n both journalism and fiction, I have been obsessed, as any serious writer in violent times could not help being, by one overriding question, the existential question: What is it that, by a narrow margin, keeps us going, in the face of our crimes, our follies, our passions, our sorrow, our panics, our hideous drives to kill?" (Yavenditti, 33).

This challenge led the young realist first to choosing a point of view for the narrative, which originally was to be a feature-length article but which grew much longer at the urging of the *New Yorker*'s editors. He borrowed a strategy from Wilder's *Bridge of San Luis Rey* (1927), one later employed by the so-called New Journalists of the 1960s: exploring in turn the personal fates and perspectives of different victims of a common disaster. The contrast between the collapse of a mountain bridge in Peru and the nuclear devastation of a large modern city reveals the distance that history had placed between the worlds of Wilder and Hersey. Unexceptionable as this attempt now seems, at the time *Hiroshima* was one of the first American recordings of the outbreak of the nuclear age from the viewpoint of Japanese *hibakusha*, a term Hersey was to make familiar to millions. Here was a central issue and insight: the challenge to the post-Hiroshima writer to make victorious American readers *see* the horrifying details of nuclear devastation from the viewpoint of the victims, the enemy others. Meeting this challenge involved finding ways to encourage readers to come to grips with their own vulnerability and responsibility. In *Hiroshima* Hersey chose six *hibakusha* who, though not typical residents or survivors, did collectively embody key features of the cataclysmic event. They also expressed representative afterthoughts and postwar behaviors, for Hersey was determined to inform his American readers about not only the immediate physical and psychic shocks but also some of the long-term aftermaths of Hiroshima's monumental victimization.

One way to engage understanding and empathy, Hersey's background and outlook told him, was not to avoid realistic description but to contain horror within a reassuringly religious—indeed, specifically Christian—moral framework. This decision explains his initial focus on survival over suffering. The choice was rendered plausible by the cast of characters, which includes two Christian clergymen and two medical doctors—one pair that specializes in salvation, the other in healing or easing deaths. Of the six *hibakusha*, moreover, three spoke languages other than Japanese. And not surprisingly, as the nuclear literature of the succeeding decades would echo, four of the six were men.

If a decidedly skewed selection of protagonists unconsciously pleased future American readers, it fitted several historiographical imperatives as well. These are signaled first by Hersey's titles. *Hiroshima* as a title is tersely, even ominously direct in uniting geography, history, and individual biography. Narratively deployed, the city's immediate fate is epitomized in the six simultaneous and typical episodes of "A Noiseless Flash" and "The Fire," followed chronologically by "Details Are Being Investigated" and "Panic Grass and Feverfew." Long-term consequences—specifically, radiation as a decades-long reminder of the Bomb and a tenacious threat to rebuilt lives—are dealt with in "The Aftermath," added retrospectively in 1985. Thus a historical sequence is placed around the images, descriptions, and statistics, which are at once precise and symbolic. Silence at the solar-bright epicenter was surrounded at once by deafening noise, then by fiery violence sweeping outward and across the city in the deceptive guise of a "natural" disaster. "Details Are Being Investigated" points to information and its contested control by government, the military, science, even journalism. At issue here is the sociology and politics of knowledge. The common Asiatic weeds and grasses that sprang up soon in the city's ruins are signs of nature's resilience, highlighting Hersey's major theme—*life* in death. Finally, "The Aftermath" folds the fates of the six *hibakusha* into the cyclical history of the earth as individual horrors and cripplings are resolved by death or forgetting.

Each survivor starts his or her story at the same minute. Each awakens, that August morning, in a set of circumstances that leads to miraculous or simply lucky survival. Yet each of the six—Miss Toshiko Sasaki, the office clerk; Dr. Fugii, a successful older doctor; Mrs. Nakamura, the poor tailor's widow; Father Kleinsorge, a German Jesuit missionary; Dr. Sasaki, a young surgeon at the central hospital; and the Rev. Mr. Tanimoto, the American-educated Methodist pastor—enacts a different drama of escape. Hersey weaves a patchwork of details that both particularize and universalize each character's fate.

As befits nonfiction prose writing, each minibiography is couched in language that directly reflects historical records rather than the metaphoric imagination of the author. Miss Sasaki, for example, was at the moment of the explosion seated at her desk in the personnel office of the East Asia Tin Works. A split second before the flash, she turned her head away from the windows. "She was paralyzed by fear, fixed still in her chair for a long moment (the plant was 1,600 yards from the center). Everything fell, and Miss Sasaki lost consciousness. The ceiling dropped suddenly and the wooden floor above collapsed in splinters. . . . The bookcases right behind her swooped forward and the contents threw her down, with her left leg horribly twisted and breaking underneath her. There, in the tin factory, in the first moment of the atomic age, a human being was crushed by books" (16).

This passage typically combines vivid detail and generalizing statement as it dramatically concludes the opening section. The little clerk's fate and her horribly mangled leg will be traced forward into "The Aftermath." On the way, Hersey's comment about bone-breaking books reverberates with implications. Later, for instance, Father Kleinsorge and his fellow priests each grab something to rescue from the wreckage. A theology student bewails the loss of two right shoes. " 'It's funny,' he observes, 'but things don't matter any more. Yesterday, my shoes were my most important possessions.' . . . Father Cieslik said, 'I know. I started to bring my books along, and then I thought, "This is no time for books" ' " (36). Later, we learn from Dr. Sasaki that the Hiroshima that rose from the ashes would soon contain "seven hundred and fifty-three bookstores and two thousand three hundred and fifty-six bars" (109). By this point, Father Kleinsorge, suffering a series of nuclear-related maladies, has narrowed his life down to essentials. He now reads only the Bible and railroad timetable books—"the only two sorts of texts, he told Yoshiki-san, that never told lies" (117). Then, "one day, he called Yoshiki-san, greatly excited. He had found an error [in a timetable]. Only the Bible told the truth!" (118). Such simple patterning shows Hersey's trust in homely metaphoric minutiae when confronting unimaginable horrors. Books are a convenient way to draw attention to civilization itself and the perhaps dubious role writers of books play in truthfully describing cataclysmic breakdown.

Common to several of these verbal games is the theology student's remark, "But things don't matter any more." Clearly, certain things do matter very much, even in the midst of catastrophe. Two everyday possessions suddenly endowed with poignant significance are Father Kleinsorge's papier-mâché suitcase and Mrs. Nakamura's Sankoku sewing machine. The priest's luggage, hidden beneath a desk when the flash came, miraculously survived intact: it "stood handle-side up, without a scratch on it, in the doorway of the room, where he could not miss it. Father Kleinsorge later came to regard this as a bit of Providential interference, inasmuch as the suitcase contained his breviary, the account books for the whole diocese, and a considerable amount of paper money belonging to the mission, for which he was responsible" (22). Mrs. Nakamura's sewing machine, less miraculously preserved, was equally valuable in the poor widow's survival. Too heavy to be carried far, it was first dumped in the cement water tank in front of her ruined house. Her "symbol of livelihood" reposed for weeks in "the symbol of safety" (20). Rescued, cleaned up, and used to keep her family alive, the machine was eventually sold to pay Mrs. Nakamura's mounting medical bills. "She came to think of that act as marking the lowest and saddest moment of her whole life" (92). However, with characteristic zeal for happy endings, Hersey notes that this cheerful *hibakusha* eventually conquered "A-bomb sickness," raised her three children, and lived to receive as a present from her son a new sewing machine.

Behind this small domestic parable hovers the question of spiritual or religious belief. In the following interpretation, Hersey reaches for a personal and cultural perspective on the Bomb that may also, and conveniently, salve some American consciences.

> As Nakamura-san struggled to get from day to day, she had no time for attitudinizing about the bomb or anything else. She was sustained, curiously, by a kind of passivity, summed up in a phrase she herself sometimes used—"*Shikata ga-nai*," meaning loosely, "It can't be helped." She was not religious, but she lived in a culture long colored by the Buddhist belief that resignation might lead to clear vision . . . and the hell she had witnessed and the terrible aftermath unfolding around her reached so far beyond human understanding that it was impossible to think of them as the work of resentable human beings, such as the pilot of the *Enola Gay*, or President Truman, or the scientists who had made the bomb—or even, nearer at hand, the Japanese militarists who had helped to bring on the war. The bombing almost seemed a natural disaster—one that it had simply been her bad luck, the fate (which must be accepted) to suffer. (93)

Passages like this, with its loaded words like *impossible, resentable, luck, fate,* and *natural disaster*, suggest an American apologist as well as responsible journalist placing words in the mouth of the lowborn Japanese woman. In fact, *Hiroshima*'s critical and commercial success did not prevent some readers from accusing its author of, if not ideological manipulation, at least skirting some ticklish political and moral issues. Here, Mrs. Nakamura's quite credible fatalism in the face of "almost . . . a natural disaster" sounds like a cultural attitude disguised as one seamstress's testimony. In any case, the seamstress is never directly quoted. Indeed, surprisingly little direct quotation characterizes this text. As a result, hewing closely to the perspectives of the survivors does not entail reporting their exact words. Sometimes, of course, direct quotation does occur. Impressionistic evidence suggests that the English speakers (or, in the case of Mr. Tanimoto, letter writers) are quoted more often than those confined to their native language. If so, this privileges males and the better-educated of Hersey's protagonists. The much-noted "impartiality" and "flatness" of *Hiroshima*'s discourse is, in these terms, a literary attribution with decidedly ideological overtones.

Involved here is not only the issue of careful historical documentation (not necessarily a standard to hold Hersey and the *New Yorker* to) but the issue of censorship. Was nuclear journalism in 1946 still forced to stay within official wartime parameters? In general, readers absolved Hersey of doing so voluntarily. In a later interview, however, he acknowledged that his manuscript underwent "close editing" in the magazine's offices—a comment elucidated by *Time* magazine's report on 9 September 1946 that Harold Ross, the *New Yorker*'s editor, was "afraid that Hersey's sympathetic piece on the Hiroshima Japanese might sound a little anti-American—so he got Hersey to explain why the U.S. dropped the bomb" (Yavenditti, 36).

In "Details Are Being Investigated," Hersey apparently did, in fact, feel obliged to explain American military thinking directly to readers—since his Japanese subjects did not, in August 1945, know what an atomic bomb was or (he said) why it had been used on them.

> [N]or is it probable that any of the survivors happened to be tuned in on a shortwave rebroadcast of an extraordinary announcement by the President of the United States, which identified the new bomb as atomic. . . . Those victims who were able to worry at all about what had happened thought of it and discussed it in more primitive, childish terms—gasoline sprinkled from an airplane, maybe, or some combustible gas, or a big cluster of incendiaries, or the work of parachutists; but, even if they had known the truth, most of them were too busy or too weary or too badly hurt to care that they were the objects of the first great experiment in the use of atomic power, which (as the voices on the shortwave shouted) no country except the United States, with its industrial know-how, its willingness to throw two billion gold dollars into an important wartime gamble, could possibly have developed. (49–50)

Readers of *Hiroshima* have always had reason to wonder how literally to take this explanation. Though the writer may have been soothing editorial fears by selective paraphrase, ironic emphasis is also possible. Nonetheless, if not here at least subsequently, Hersey sounds like an American booster, as in this description of cleanup operations after the devastation: "Utilities were repaired—electric lights shone again, trams started running, and employees of the waterworks fixed seventy thousand leaks in mains and plumbing. A Planning Conference, with an enthusiastic young Military Government officer, Lieutenant John D. Montgomery of Kalamazoo, as its adviser, began to consider what sort of city the new Hiroshima should be. The ruined city had flourished—and had been an inviting target—mainly because it had been one of the most important military-command and communications centers in Japan, and would have become the Imperial headquarters had the islands been invaded and Tokyo been captured" (80). The segue from comforting statistics on restored city plumbing, to the helpful American officer (shades of *A Bell for Adano?*), to Hiroshima's wartime status as "mainly" a military center and a legitimate target, is smoothly accomplished in three sentences. Left unmentioned, however, are contrary opinions and speculations circulating already in 1946—such as that Hiroshima was one of several cities (Kyoto being another) deliberately spared bombardment late in the war so as to present a favorable site on which to demonstrate the power of the atomic bomb. If Hiroshima was, in fact, "one of the most important military-command and communications centers," would it not have been attacked sooner? Further, the fact that the *Enola Gay*'s bomb was detonated 1,900 feet above the ground, not directly on a ground target, suggests that heavy civilian casualties and radioactive fallout were acceptable from the start. Such issues seemed in line with the 1945 military policy of inflicting heavy losses on the Japanese people so as to avert heavy losses of American soldiers (Rhodes, 713, 698).

If Hersey ever planned to go into such complexities—including the question of what was known and not known, what was planned and what was accidental—"The Aftermath" was surely an appropriate place to do so. However, except for one new feature, this chapter simply continues the stories of six lives, six fates. New italicized sections interpolated in the book's final 16 pages provide historical counterpoints to the postholocaust careers of, for example, the Rev. Mr. Tanimoto: *"On July 1, 1946, before the first anniversary of the bombing, the United States had tested an atomic bomb at the Bikini Atoll. On May 17, 1948, the Americans announced the successful completion of another test"* (136). To be sure, Hersey's account of the later experiences of the six *hibakusha* mentions postwar Japanese politics, including peace movements and Hiroshima's symbolic role therein. He continues to devote much more space, though, to private lives than to, for example, the military and political aspects of the Occupation. What we learn about Toshiko Sasaki's postholocaust life is typical. In affecting detail, the consequences of her cruelly deformed leg, her gradual conversion to Roman Catholicism, and her career as a professional caregiver as a nun are traced. Her life of physical pain and saintly service is credited "to all she had learned about herself in the hours and weeks after the bombing" (123). As for peace activists and parliamentary debates on *hibakusha* rights, the aging nun held to "an opinion that was unconventional for a hibakusha: that too much attention was paid to the A-bomb, and not enough to the evil of war" (121).

One of Hersey's protagonists, then, arrives at the same conclusion that, in 1946, was already preached in American pulpits and expressed in other quarters. But the trajectory of this postholocaust life of suffering service is one that, emotionally and spiritually focused on an individual, circles back to the ruins of Hiroshima and Toshiko Sasaki's original ordeal. There, the author insists, lies the deepest meaning of this woman's life. Its cultural significance is not simply ideological but imaginal. Her moment of transfiguration is, therefore, a characteristically low-key but unmistakable climax of the *New Yorker* narrative:

> Much later, several men came and dragged Miss Sasaki out. Her left
> leg was not severed, but it was badly broken and cut and it hung askew
> below the knee. They took her out into a courtyard. It was raining. She
> sat on the ground in the rain. . . . "Come along," a torn-up woman said
> to her. "You can hop." But Miss Sasaki could not move, and she just

waited in the rain. Then a man propped up a large sheet of corrugated iron as a kind of lean-to, and took her in his arms and carried her to it. She was grateful until he brought two horribly wounded people— a woman with a whole breast sheared off and a man whose face was all raw from a burn—to share the simple shed with her. No one came back. The rain cleared and the cloudy afternoon was hot; before night-fall the three grotesques under the slanting piece of twisted iron began to smell quite bad. (32–33)

Michael Perlman in *Imaginal Memory and the Place of Hiroshima* (1988) does not cite this particular scene as a prime imaginal legacy bequeathed by Hersey's book to world consciousness.[7] Yet for Western readers familiar with Gustav Doré's illustrations of Dante's *Inferno*, with Hieronymus Bosch, or with Nativity scenes, not to mention Goya or Hemingway, Miss Sasaki's suffering in the rain resonates with artistic and spiritual meaning as well as historical immediacy. Like the rescue efforts of Mr. Tanimoto and Father Kleinsorge on the Ota River bank and in Asano Park, this moment creates inexpungible memories of sites, sounds, and smells. They become "memories" for readers completely unfamiliar with nuclear catastrophe.

A primary image is of Father Kleinsorge carrying water to victims in the park:

When he had given the wounded the water, he made a second trip. This time the woman by the bridge was dead. On his way back with the water, he got lost on a detour around a fallen tree, and as he looked for his way through the woods, he heard a voice ask from the under-brush, "Have you anything to drink?" He saw a uniform. Thinking there was just one soldier, he approached with the water. When he had penetrated the bushes, he saw there were about twenty men, and they were all in exactly the same nightmarish state: Their faces were wholly burned, their eyesockets were hollow, the fluid from their melted eyes had run down their cheeks. (They must have had their faces upturned when the bomb went off; perhaps they were anti-aircraft personnel.) Their mouths were mere swollen, pus-covered wounds, which they could not bear to stretch enough to admit the spout of the teapot. So Father Kleinsorge got a large piece of grass and drew out the stem so as to make a straw, and gave them all water to drink that way. One of them said, "I can't see anything." Father Kleinsorge answered, as cheerfully as he could, "There's a doctor at the entrance to the park. He's busy now but he'll come soon and fix your eyes, I hope." (51–52)

In scenes like this, Hersey's tendency to see survival and transcendence as the twin lessons of Hiroshima gives way to an equally candid recognition of suffering and death as the event's inescapable message as well. Much of the time, though, Hersey's text affords comfort (as in Toshio Nakamura's matter-of-fact essay for his primary school that ends the *New Yorker* account) rather than such strong doses of almost pure psychic suffering. Indeed, Hersey's ambivalence mirrors the mixed feelings he attributed (with good reason, it seems) to his readers of 1946 as well as to later readers. Attraction and repulsion, recognition and evasion, initiation and innocence are long-term responses that *Hiroshima* has received and confirmed, if not actually generated. Miss Sasaki under her iron canopy and the 20 sightless soldiers in the Asano woods are primal images of the age that announce the world's new status of death-in-life. However, Hersey knew his readers also needed more reassuring readings of the Bomb's historical significance. Hence, there are two conclusions to the latest edition of *Hiroshima*. First comes Toshio's childish prose: "I saw a light. I was knocked to little sister's sleeping place. When we were saved, I could only see as far as the tram. My mother and I started to pack our things. The neighbors were walking around burned and bleeding. . . . We went to the park. A whirlwind came. . . . We stayed in the park one night. Next day I went to Taiko Bridge and met my girl friends Kikuki and Murakami. They were looking for their mothers. But Kikuki's mother was wounded and Murakami's mother, alas was dead" (90). Forty years later, American readers of the new paperback took leave of Hersey's *hibakusha* in an even more reassuring description:

> Kiyoshi Tanimoto was over seventy now. The average age of all *hibakusha* was sixty-two. The surviving *hibakusha* had been polled by *Chugoku Shimbun* in 1984, and 54.3 per cent of them said they thought that nuclear weapons would be used again. Tanimoto read in the papers that the United States and the Soviet Union were steadily climbing the steep steps of deterrence. He and Chisa both drew health-maintenance allowances as *hibakusha*, and he had a modest pension from the United Church of Japan. He lived in a snug little house with a radio and two television sets, a washing machine, an electric oven, and a refrigerator, and he had a compact Mazda automobile, manufactured in Hiroshima. He ate too much. He got up at six every morning and took an hour's walk with his small woolly dog, Chiko. He was slowing down a bit. His memory, like the world's, was getting spotty. (152)

Compassionate identification, the prime aim of *Hiroshima* in both editions, is made easier by the author's comforting conclusions. Even Toshio's childish "alas" testifies to the power of convention to diminish to safer levels the psychic aftershock of the Hiroshima flash. The domestication of "woundedness" is even more palpable in the summary of Mr. Tanimoto's retirement and approaching senility.

Nonetheless, Hersey's impact on American thought and feeling (and possibly public policy) extended further than the phrase "compassionate identification" suggests. In short-term effects, as Michael Yavenditti has shown, *Hiroshima*'s best-seller success and marked influence on high-minded antimilitarist readers (chiefly clergymen, educators, and some scientists) did not translate into large-scale protests or political proposals. "Americans could, with no apparent inconsistency, appreciate Hersey's work," Yavenditti declared from his viewpoint of 1974, "without also engaging in a collective *mea culpa* or demanding scientific or governmental scapegoats to salve their own consciences. The bomb *had* ended the war, and in the absence of persuasive evidence to the contrary, few Americans were disposed to reverse their initial approval" (46). At least during the safety period before the Soviets developed their atomic bomb, "Hersey's work aroused many readers but incited few of them" (48). As a collective conscience emerged, as it did much later, more troubled and better-informed readers would demand different strategies of enlightenment and emotional indoctrination than *Hiroshima*, even in its 1985 version, afforded.

Apathy, not just ignorance or proximity to wartime emotions, also accounts for what some Americans, early and late, have called the failure of Hersey's best-seller as political critique. One source of postwar anxiety and apathy was the Bikini Atoll tests from 1946 to the early 1950s. As a public relations event designed to show the world convincing proof of American nuclear power, Tests Able and Baker, as the first two explosions were called, were, at first, qualified flops. The detonation of bombs above and beneath the fleet of obsolete American, Japanese, and German warships anchored in the Bikini lagoon was witnessed and photographed by hundreds of journalists and international observers. But owing to governmental secrecy and the explosions' apparent failure to produce spectacular destruction (for instance, sinking dozens of vessels in an instant, or blowing a hole in the ocean floor), the tests were mishandled by the press and misunderstood by many. The tests' broader significance became more widely appreciated in 1946, when the second early popular prose work of nuclear literature, David Bradley's *No Place to Hide*, was published.

Like its predecessor, *No Place to Hide* quickly (though only temporarily) reached the best-seller list; also a main selection of the Book-of-the-Month Club, it was excerpted in *Reader's Digest* and the *Atlantic Monthly* (Boyer, 91–92). Part of its instant appeal derived from the fact that Bradley, a young doctor, participated in the tests and helped monitor the radiological results. After the public relations aspects of Bikini subsided, the sobering news of radiation contamination and sickness among the Marshall Islanders jolted American pride and complacency. The doctor's log and deceptively offhand report played a role in the ensuing escalation of concern.

The Bikini tests were collectively named "Crossroads," a prophetic, public relations–type title that Bradley plays with effectively. "What happened at Crossroads was the clearest measure yet of the menace of atomic energy," he writes in the prologue. "Less spectacular perhaps than Hiroshima and Nagasaki, the Bikini tests give a far clearer warning of the lingering and insidious nature of the radioactive agent which makes it such an ideal weapon for use on civil populations. . . . What was learned at Bikini of a scientific or military nature may have been of value. Unfortunately much of it is disguised in the esoteric idiom of the scientist. The really great lessons of that experiment, however, belong to no special group but to all mankind. The atomic era, fortunately or otherwise, is now man's environment, to control or adapt himself to as he can."[8]

Bearing such epochal meanings, Bikini demanded from Bradley a literary response that could be readily grasped by the average reader. Hence his choice to cast his narrative in a personal, almost folksy voice, as well as to include 14 dramatic photographs. Although he does not play up the plight of the Marshall Islanders or the experimental animals aboard the target ships, Bradley does attempt to make readers see and feel the deeper meanings of events widely underestimated, indeed, almost trivialized, by the American press. In deliberate counterpoint to the photographs is Bradley's arresting description of the detonation on Baker Day:

> I have seen two hundred pounds of T.N.T. go off at night from a distance of half a mile, but this shot in broad day, at fifteen miles, seemed to spring from all parts of the target fleet at once. A gigantic flash—then it was gone. And where it had been now stood a white chimney of water reaching up and up. Then a huge hemispheric mushroom of vapor appeared like a parachute suddenly opening. It rapidly filled out in all directions until it struck the level of the first layer of clouds, about 1,800 feet. Here, as though striking a layer of plate glass, this shock wave (or more strictly speaking, this cloud of vapors which formed in the vacuum phase behind the shock wave) spread out by leaps and bounds beneath the clouds. I remember being alarmed lest our plane be overtaken and smashed by it.
>
> By this time the great geyser had climbed to several thousand feet. It stood there as if solidifying for many seconds, its head enshrouded in a tumult of steam. Then slowly the pillar began to fall and break up. At its base a tidal wave of spray and steam arose, to smother the fleet and move on toward the islands. (92–93)

To augment the impact of the still-novel scene for 1940s readers, Bradley provided readily understandable summaries of basic scientific data and medical findings. He also pointed out American sailors' amazed ignorance of radioactivity. He compared measures taken to protect the personnel checking damage aboard the surviving ships with civilian efforts to cope with a similar explosion over an American city. "We were in a position similar (though infinitely better probably) to that of a city bombed out with atomic weapons. No such rigamarole as rubber boots and gloves and oxygen rebreathing masks could conceivably be used if San Francisco were atomized, its population struggling to escape from the blazing debris, the smoke, and the terror of the unseen emanations" (145). Then he drove home the full extent of the danger. "We can't predict to what degree the balance of nature will be thrown off by atomic bombs. We certainly have little idea what the long-range effects on our lives would be from an all-out atomic war, devastating our shores, our fish, and our agricultural industries. But at least at this time we do know that Bikini is not some faraway little atoll pinpointed on an out-of-the-way chart. Bikini is San Francisco Bay, Puget Sound, East River. It is the Thames, the Adriatic, Hellespont, and misty Baikal. It isn't just King Juda and his displaced native subjects about whom we have to think—or to forget" (149).

In conclusion, Bradley continues his pointed and personalized arraignment of American complacency. "We were surprised at first to find so little interest in the Bikini tests," he observes of his fellow scientists alighting at a California airport. "But we really had no right to be. Atomic energy was an uncomfortable subject. Things like John Hersey's *Hiroshima* were rough. How much more pleasant to consider the coming miracles of healing, the prolongation of life, the days of sunny leisure which people were everywhere promising" (167–68). In an epilogue written for the 1984 reissue, Bradley spells out again the unconsoling lessons that younger readers in particular could now grasp:

1 atomic bomb = 1 city
1 hydrogen bomb = 1,000 Hiroshima bombs (173, 174)

He condemns American obliviousness to nuclear aftereffects with equal directness. The Marshall Islanders who returned to their atolls were told in 1957 that eating the food and staying there was safe. Later, after the magistrate and his son had suffered leukemia and thyroid operations, they and the others were belatedly warned to leave. "Bikini is empty again. The children have wandered among the deserts of their tropical paradise for nearly 40 years and there is no end" (181). Then, bringing the message home anew, Bradley lists targeted American and Soviet cities with comparable populations. This not so subtle reference to deterrence and mutual assured destruction (MAD) is followed by a brief comment on stockpiling. "*If all our megatonnage were in Hiroshima-sized bombs, we could drop one a day since the time of Christ and still not run out. The Russians could do the same*" (186). Then, as if to underscore the contrast between his epilogue and Hersey's "The Aftermath," Bradley includes two up-to-date appendices on radioactivity. He observes that the building blocks of matter were fairly well understood in 1946; "now I read of leptons and quarks, hadons, muons, gluons, down, up, strange, and charm and wonder whether this is physics or a new book by Lewis Carroll" (209). Yet faced with such proliferating knowledge, we must not lapse into apathy or despair. The lessons of Bikini—and, by implication, of thermonuclear weapons, neutron bombs, Chernobyl, and the Strategic Defense Initiative (SDI)—remain humankind's responsibility, not simply that of physicists, RAND strategists, and the Pentagon. "In the long run," he concludes, "the one thing more dangerous than informed governments abroad will be an uninformed American opinion" (165). As these warnings again underline, Bradley remains a concerned physician and scientist whose book has as its repeated targets the American ostrich attitudes that emerged in 1946 and flourished still, he seems to believe, in 1984. *No Place to Hide*, a narrative of firsthand experiences and observations at Bikini, established and continues to authenticate Bradley's lifelong role as an informed Cassandra.

"We are all survivors of Hiroshima and, in our imaginations, of future nuclear holocaust. The link between Hiroshima and ourselves is not simply metaphorical, but has specific psychological components which can be explored in relation to the general psychology of the survivor."[9] So wrote Robert Jay Lifton in *Death in Life: Survivors of Hiroshima*. As a National Book Award winner, the psychiatrist's 1967 account of his interactions with a sizable number of *hibakusha* reached wide circles of concerned Americans. In the longer view, Lifton's is the second major prose work of the American atomic age. So it was inevitable that comparisons would be drawn with Hersey's still-popular pioneer account. Lifton, in fact, underlines continuities with his predecessor while developing a different and in many respects deeper, more demanding and thought-provoking approach and agenda. One link that Lifton hoped to make was reaching Japanese as well as American readers, as *Hiroshima* had done. Writing from the perspective of 1962 (the year most of his interviews with survivors took place), Lifton observes that, "when Americans have combined humanitarian concerns about *hibakusha* with strong convictions concerning the control or elimination of nuclear weapons—as have John Hersey and Norman Cousins—they evoke less ambivalence, because *hibakusha* can make common cause with them in a way that renders the atomic bomb experience meaningful, and therefore diminishes anxiety and resentment" (337). Here the academic physician, psychiatrist, and social psychologist from Yale announces his political agenda and allegiances. These were well known, at the time and later. In fact, Lifton's early success at getting suspicious *hibakusha* to talk candidly to an American was attributable in part to his reputation as an outspoken antinuclear activist. The interviews thus facilitated also demonstrate a perhaps surprising fact to American readers: literate Japanese of the *hibakusha* generation knew and admired a number of American writers. One such pro-Western intellectual was a Hiroshima professor with liberal prewar sympathies and a background in American and European literature. "But with the defeat his longstanding Western identification was reawakened in connection with atomic bomb problems. He thus played an important part in introducing John Hersey's *Hiroshima* into Japan, told me 'how deeply moved' he was by the humanism inspiring the book, and gave me the impression that *he* had learned much from *it* concerning how one should feel and think about the A-bomb experience" (331).

Though such imputation of two-way influences may simplify the professor's ambivalent responses, it surely reflects Lifton's own hopes for his book and for the continuing influence of Hersey's. He believed both books had

significant roles to play in reconciliation via moral as well as scientific education. So he dared to hope that by encouraging the individual *hibakusha* to
"[come] together with an American in common concern, he was at least moving
in the general direction of healing the A-bomb—inflicted 'wound in the order
of being.' But although the death-linked resentments which *hibakusha* brought
to the encounter could be directly or indirectly aired, modified, or lessened,
they could hardly be eliminated—involved as they were with lifelong struggles
to absorb and master, by giving inner form to, the entire atomic bomb experience" (365).

If such healing was difficult for *hibakusha* and other Japanese victims of
American military power, the common task was a formidable psychological
problem for Americans as well. Lifton's cultural work became, therefore, a
triple task: to discuss the specific historical and social circumstances affecting
hibaskusha memories and emotions; to define cultural differences between all
Japanese and all Americans; and, finally, to assert basic psychological affinities
linking all survivors of extreme experience. Unlike Hersey, the journalist-
novelist of religious faith and imagination, Lifton was a social scientist and
secular humanist who, like his mentor Erik Erikson, sought universal psychosocial and psychohistorical principles. "The mythological metaphors usually employed to suggest this idea—the genie let out of the bottle or Pandora's box
opened—do not seem adequate for the phenomenon. That of man threatened
by his Frankenstein comes closer, but this more recent myth, though technolog-
ically based, humanizes and keeps finite its monster. We need new myths to
grasp our relationship to the cool, ahuman, *completely* technological deity
which began its destructive reign with Hiroshima" (13).

What Lifton, by way of narrative structure and explanatory paradigm,
puts in place of classic Western myths and imagery like Pandora's box and
Frankenstein's monster is an equally classic psychic journey of vicarious experience. Through literature and psychology—in his case, a prose case history
of personal exposure to others' memories and feelings—he leads American
readers through a three-part process. First comes an immersion in death so
deep as literally to reverse Hersey's hopeful life-in-death construct. Second is
a reintegration of self, community, and history through psychological detoxifi-
cation of violence. The last step is transcending even the recognition that "we
are all *hibakusha*" (ineluctable and essential as that recognition is) by means
of a vision of human life extending *into* and *through* death.

Lifton's 555-page record of nuclear death and postholocaust denial, fear,
anxiety, resentment, disintegration, and recovery is explicitly psychoanalytic
in principle and procedure. Yet his interviews and interpretations only tangen-
tially focus on childhood trauma and sexuality, two hoary preoccupations
of conventional Freudianism. Instead, he emphasizes throughout the adult
struggles to understand and cope with terrible recent memories and actual
wounds. "In every age man faces a pervasive theme which defies his engagement and yet must be engaged," he concludes with grim hopefulness. "In

Freud's day it was sexuality and moralism. Now it is unlimited technological violence and absurd death. We do well to name the threat and analyze its components. But our need is to go further, to create new psychic and social forms to enable us to reclaim not only our technologies, but our very imaginations, in the service of the continuity of life" (541).

Developing personal imagination through collective awareness and politics begins with the frank recognition voiced by a young Japanese short-story writer, a non-*hibakusha* Lifton met in Hiroshima, who observed that he was also interested "in the differences between those who went through the historical experience and those who did not" (433). Here is a prime feature of *Death in Life* as literary text. It is about and is addressed to a widening circle of different readers, carefully distinguished from one another. The first audience addressed is the *hibakusha* themselves. Then Lifton turns to non-*hibakusha* Japanese. He next singles out American readers. Identified last is the worldwide audience that shares vicariously in the pasts and presents of the other groups and is now able to say, "We are all *hibakusha*." "In a large sense history itself is a series of survivals, but in our century the theme of survival is more immediate and more ominous" (540).

The common task, then, of late twentieth-century peoples is mental, emotional, and moral comprehension—in the Gospel of John's sense of "to see around"—of the massive immersion in death visited upon humanity on 6 and 9 August 1945. Lifton's exploration of the descent/reintegration/return process is necessarily complex. But it is rendered understandable by the author's use of fairly untechnical language, a strongly personal narrative voice, copious illustrative quotations, and wide-ranging references and allusions. Given such richness, an adequate rehearsal of the book's full argument is impossible here. Indeed, Lifton's readers may often feel overwhelmed by the multiple demands of text and subject matter. Because Lifton realizes he is not writing for Erikson, Bruno Bettelheim, or Robert and Jane Coles, he provides frequent summaries of the unfolding discussion. Here is a key instance, in a description of a representative *hibakusha*:

> His death imprint is complicated by a sense of continuous encounter with death—extending through the initial exposure, the immediate post-bomb impact of "invisible contamination," later involvement with "A-bomb disease," and the imagery surrounding the *hibakusha* identity. Death guilt, stimulated at each of these stages, is reinforced by group patterns within a "guilty community," and further reawakened by every flexing of nuclear weapons—whether in the form of threatening words or weapons testing—anywhere in the world. Psychic closing-off is extraordinarily immediate and massive, and later psychic numbing, inseparable from radiation fears, gives rise to a particularly widespread form of psychosomatic entrapment. Suspicion of counterfeit nurturance is markedly strong, and lends itself readily to guinea-pig imagery. Contagion anxiety is similarly great because of the radiation-intensified

death taint. Formulation is made profoundly difficult, both by the
dimensions of the original experience, and by the complexity and threat
surrounding the general nuclear problem. And here we arrive at another
quality of atomic survival not unique to it but of unique importance:
we all share it. (540)

Most of the author's essential terms for describing the descent into death
and disintegration are here and are readily recalled by persevering readers
willing to run real emotional risks by traversing an intensely unpleasant landscape. Perhaps the most widely discussed term—and by some most fiercely
denied—is "psychic numbing." Closely allied to denial as a conscious and
unconscious response to extreme experience, psychic numbing actually serves
vital restorative purposes. By short-circuiting cognitive and emotional reactions to mass death and dying, Lifton argues, numbing at first protects survivors
from complete helplessness. Avoidance or denial of emotional participation is
a temporary means of resisting total and permanent change (500). All too often,
however, psychic numbing "turns into a deadly pathological force. . . . [It]
begins as a defense against exposure to death, but ends up by inundating the
organism with death imagery" (503). Furthermore, numbing has a long afterlife.
For "at still further remove from the experience (for non-Japanese, and particularly for Americans) there may be a near-total emotional separation from the
Hiroshima experience through relatively easily accomplished psychic numbing" (506).

Weart in *Nuclear Fear* (1988) later corroborates from domestic American
evidence Lifton's bold treatment and extrapolation of this presumably circumscribed psychological process: "[S]ince the early 1950s acute observers had
noted that many citizens were refusing to face the issue of nuclear war, and
by the mid-1960s the defense mechanism was ubiquitous. It almost made sense
to close one's eyes, the way sensible children cover their faces in a horror
movie. As a young adult said in 1965, 'If we lived in fear of the bomb we couldn't
function.'. . . Somebody who denied an idea would also thrust away everything
reminiscent of the idea; [refusal] to feel, to think, or to contemplate action
could spread outward indefinitely. One of the great unanswered questions of
our age is how far denial of nuclear dangers has promoted such numbing"
(266–67).

Responding to this ongoing psychosocial danger, Lifton offers "formulation," a technical term perhaps a bit harder to grasp than "psychic numbing."
"By formulation I do not mean detached theories about the atomic bomb, but
rather the process by which the *hibakusha* re-creates himself—establishes
those inner forms which can serve as a bridge between self and world. Ideology
and 'world view'—often in their unconscious components—are central to the
process, and by studying their relationship to A-bomb mastery, we gain a sense
of their significance for mental life in general" (367). Here Lifton's debt to
Erikson's lifetime engagement with the problem of identity[10] is evident, espe-

cially in his explanation of the necessary steps toward self-formulation: "the *sense of connection*, of organic relationship to the people as well as non-human elements [for example, nature] in one's life space." Then comes "the *sense of symbolic integrity*, of the cohesion and significance of one's life, here including some form of transcendence of the A-bomb experience." Finally emerges "the *sense of movement*, of development and change, in the continuous struggle between fixed identity and individuation" (367).

Formulation requires not only knowledge (of self and the world of violence) but also intuitive insight into the images and memories out of which confrontation and integration must be built. In Lifton's experience, men are better equipped with cognitive and articulation capacities, and women often excel at organic thinking. Both unite in aesthetic expression. Lifton's range as social psychologist and cultural critic is nowhere better shown than in his extensive discussions of nuclear novels, poems, films, and even paintings and musical compositions. But for others to share such reidentifications, aesthetic and emotional aids need to be accompanied by historical consciousness. Survival, though an exquisitely threatening component of twentieth-century experience, has, of course, been present in earlier ages and personal histories. Thus historical formulation can help Third World peoples, African-Americans, and others to empathize with the disintegrations in Hiroshima by analogizing them to such disasters as colonialism, slavery and the shipboard horrors of the Middle Passage, and the Civil War. Lifton does not cite these American extreme events, preferring instead to mention the Black Death and the Nazi Holocaust as pertinent and striking Western parallels to Hiroshima.

Detoxifying past nuclear destruction and future fears cannot, however, take place through isolated aesthetic or historical exercises. Identifying deeply with *hibakusha* may come to American readers of Masuji Ibuse's *Black Rain* (1969) or, from another direction, by immersion in the Civil War photographs of Matthew Brady or Walt Whitman's wartime memoir *Specimen Days* (1882). But if vicarious transformation is to succeed, specific nuclear images, emotions, and responses must become linked to Hiroshima itself. Readers must see and feel *this* event as our age's archetypal embodiment of terror and absurd death. To this end, Lifton quotes freely from *hibakusha* experiences and memories.

One effective and powerful picture is in the following recollection by a Hiroshima technician in a war factory:

> And one thing that has never disappeared from my mind, even today, a miserable thing was . . . a girl in the rain of about eighteen or nineteen years old, and she had no clothing on her body except half of her panties, which did not cover her. She took a few steps toward me but as she was ashamed of her situation, she then crouched on the ground and she asked me for help—putting her hands in a position of prayer. And when I looked at her hands I saw the skin was burned off as if she were wearing gloves. Her hair was disheveled and her breast was red

from burns. . . . Since she was the first to ask me directly for help, I
wanted to do something for her, but she was stark naked . . . and the
company order—which was really like a military order—was supreme
to me . . . so I was at a loss. . . . I told her she better stay under the
eaves of the destroyed house and that I would come back to help her
later. (50–51)

Then, unlike Hersey the journalist, Lifton the psychiatrist carefully ana-
lyzes the scene's multiple messages, noting "that powerful feelings of death
guilt can combine with existing psychic inclinations toward perverse sexual
and aggressive fantasies" (50). His conclusion embraces Americans as well as
Japanese. "Such psychic inclinations were particularly strong in this man, but
they are universal, and that is why it is probably accurate to say that all
hibakusha were in some degree drawn to these grotesque scenes" (51).

Coping and surviving, then, are subsequent movements of *hibakusha*
psyches made possible, first, by immersion experiences deeply endured and
later interrogated, and then, by restorative social processes and institutions.
Though disintegration and reintegration are built upon universal psychic processes and residues, they inevitably take specific historical and cultural forms.
Whether American readers can fully enter into the entire postholocaust progress depends upon their recognizing the differences between Japan and the
United States. These are, of course, comprehensive and involve distinctions or
divergences respecting war, militarism, defeat, authority, family, nature, ritual,
native place, literary tradition, and even historical monuments. Yet Lifton
seems confident that intelligence, imagination, and intuition can bridge such
barriers. *Knowledge* of the Bomb and its consequences; *fantasies* of revenge
and *identification* with the destructive other; the *inspiration of nature* and
love for a particular place, to which one returns after the violent event; *telling
one's version of the common story; burying and remembering the dead*—
these are the chief modalities of reconstitution of a survivor self.

In the struggle, success is capped only when the *hibakusha* identity is itself
transcended. Realization of transcendence takes several forms: awareness that
survivors throughout history have experienced similar breakdowns in the
human matrix and then restoration of order and meaning; remembering that
institutions like Christianity and communism are living forms of survival of the
deaths of their founders; knowing that one may overcome psychic numbing to
become, in one's own eyes and in those of others, something more than
hibakusha. Death and end-of-the-world consciousness can give new meaning
to life when each is a part of the other. Whether "absurd death," in some
imminent or postponable nuclear holocaust, will bring an end to history and
to humanity's dreams of immortality are issues only pointed to but not discussed in *Death in Life*. These issues became the burden of Lifton's writings
in the years after 1967, including *The Future of Immortality* (1987).[11]

Weart is not the only nuclear critic to relate the reawakened concerns of

Americans in the late 1970s and 1980s to, among other factors, the widening influence of Robert Jay Lifton. "In addition to whatever permanent political effects there may have been, the real meaning of the old nuclear ideas and images became better understood. For example, widespread use of Robert Lifton's term 'numbing' pointed to a recognition of the psychological mechanisms of denial, learned helplessness, and so forth. . . . Deepened insight also emerged in a burst of excellent poems, paintings, short stories, and novels that began where earlier artistic works on bombs had stopped" (386). In the chapters that follow on nuclear fiction, we shall explore further the different responses to the complex of concerns raised by the author of *Death in Life*, the era's seminal study of survivorship.

Late in February 1982 (the year of *Death in Life*'s reissue), an editorial writer for the *Nation* tugged the sleeves of that venerable journal's readers, urging them to read "a remarkable series of articles" that had appeared in three issues of the *New Yorker* earlier that month. "You should make a point to read them, even if you've heard it all before." By no means a faint praiser, the editorialist added that Jonathan Schell's *Fate of the Earth* was one of the most striking examples of "a new nuclear eschatology," an outlook "that seeks to make the unwitnessable extinction visible." Citing British, Soviet, and other American authors, the *Nation* writer identified their common target as "our bone-weary numbness" in the face of the recent nuclear escalations by the superpowers. This passivity was "precisely what Schell is passionately crying out against."[12] Two months later, the magazine devoted virtually an entire issue to survival politics and the nuclear freeze movement. Prominent among its contents was a long, searching, and favorable review by Neil Schmitz of *The Fate of the Earth*.

By that spring, Schell's articles had been published as a paperback book, which rapidly circulated nationwide and across Europe. On its cover, *The Fate of the Earth* bore even more impressive endorsements than either edition of Hersey's *Hiroshima*. "Jonathan Schell puts to us in an absolutely uncompromising way the great test of human intelligence that is coming in the next few months and years. Something has to turn us around. This book may," Hersey himself wrote in one blurb.[13] His enthusiasm was echoed by a blue-ribbon galaxy of liberal politicians, scientists, and opinion-molders, among them, W. Averill Harriman, Walter Mondale, Walter Cronkite, Studs Terkel, Barry Commoner, and Jerome Weisner. "THIS IS A BOOK THAT WILL CHANGE YOUR THINKING ABOUT THE STATE OF THE WORLD," exclaimed Victor Weisskopf of MIT. "*The Fate of the Earth* is the most important and profound book on the nuclear predicament that I have read," said a writer for London's *New Statesman*. Scant surprise, then, that Schell's book became a 1982 bestseller and Book-of-the-Month Club main selection.

What explains the apparently sudden and dramatic success of a book almost too depressing and terrifying for many to read? Answers to this conundrum begin with recognizing a few similarities between Schell, Hersey, and Lifton as nuclear prophets. All three seminal studies emerged from social and political contexts in which numerous readers' emotional and intellectual needs pressed for release and satisfaction. In addition, each work represents the successful fusion of subject, style, and range of implication that makes content inseparable from language and imagery. Of Schell's argument and intent, Harriman asserted, "If it forces people to think, to discuss and to act, it will have served a most valuable purpose." Schell shared these aims with his predecessors and tried to realize them by fusing social criticism, education, political instigation, and literary force.

Contextual location of Schell is offered by Max Lerner in his careful review of *The Fate of the Earth* in the *New Republic*.[14] A bombshell book is placed clearly within the framework of contemporary tensions and confusions in both domestic and international politics. Schell's readers, Lerner asserts, are acutely aware of opposing belief systems and political agendas—the new administration's aggressive escalation of nuclear capabilities and threats confronted by burgeoning peace movements in Europe, Japan, and the United States. President Ronald Reagan and Secretary of Defense Caspar Weinberger were presenting the United States, in rhetorical terms at least, as simply responding to the latest Soviet threat, the invasion of Afghanistan in 1979; should this Soviet equivalent to America's Vietnam incursion lead to a military thrust into Iran and the Persian Gulf, then the stage could be set for World War III. For President Jimmy Carter (the most pacific of recent American presidents) had already warned the Soviets that such actions would "be repelled by any means necessary, including military force" (Schell, 212). A leak subsequently let it be known that the use of nuclear weapons would in such circumstances be considered. Indeed, this conflicted period was marked by a significant increase in public knowledge of how many times since the Berlin airlift of 1947 nuclear threats had been secretly worked by American presidents. As for the peace and disarmament movements in the early 1980s, the actions of SANE, the Union of Concerned Scientists, women's groups, and others represented renewed mobilizations by older 1960s activists as well as new endeavors by the young. All ages and affiliations were alarmed by the cost and dangers of nuclear stockpiling and by the failure of arms reduction talks. Fueling confrontations between the two political and cultural forces was the partial relaxation of governmental secrecy regulations, under the pressure of legal challenges, investigative reporting, and the availability of the government's own publications. Such relaxation underscored a point that Schell makes at the outset: "[I]n order to discuss something one should first know what it is" (4). This necessity leads the author to buttress his arguments with data from scientific and governmental reports of the recent past, including *The Effects of Nuclear War* (1979), *The Effects of Nuclear Weapons* (1977), *Hiroshima and Nagasaki* (a Japanese report of 1981), *Long-term Worldwide Effects of Multiple Nuclear Weapons Detonations* (1975), and *Survival of Food Crops and Livestock in the Event of*

Nuclear War (1970). "Drawing on these and other printed sources, and also on interviews that I conducted recently with a number of scientists, I have attempted to piece together an account of the principal consequences of a full-scale holocaust" (4–5).

Schell then accosts readers as another Cassandra armed with up-to-date data and detailed reasons for heeding his warnings. But although the fate of the earth hangs by a slender thread, pulled nearly to the breaking point by the lethal weight of weapons astronomically more destructive than those that fell on the Japanese cities, knowledge of these grim facts is only the first of Schell's objectives. The first chapter, "A Republic of Insects and Grasses," tells readers about the physical effects of present and future thermonuclear warfare. "The Second Death" and "The Choice" then focus on the emotional and moral implications of environmental and social disaster and on the practical choices Americans must make to avert catastrophe. But *The Fate of the Earth* is no mere handbook of current nuclear affairs. Indeed, the overall thrust is plain: information leads to ideological formulations, as embodied in individual outlooks and collective actions. But in the later pages, which drew the sharpest criticism from many reviewers, Schell moves well beyond social analysis and practical politics. This section constitutes a philosophical, even theological speculation on humanity's postnuclear condition. As the *New Statesman*'s writer points out, this ambitious nonspecialist has produced "literature of a high order," a synthesis of "political, military, ecological, moral, scientific, religious, artistic, psychological and philosophical" issues.[15]

Schell's desire to serve as middleman between expert and layperson is developed through three narrative devices for combining information, idea, and ideology. The simplest of these is the iteration of key words around which problems and levels of argument are arranged. Readers should find it easy to recall these as contrasting signs (often italicized, as below) to denser descriptions and prescriptions. On one side are *fate, doom, catastrophe, destruction, war, violence, holocaust, extinction, nothingness, immersion, predicament, death, insanity, numbing, fatalism, sovereign state, deterrence, radical evil.* And on the opposite side of the thermonuclear coin are inscribed *life, knowledge, coherence, communication, civilization, choice, science, survival, concern, future, morality, reality, idealism, history, time, creation, preservation, peace.* Schell's four titles—"The Fate of the Earth," "A Republic of Insects and Grasses," "The Second Death," and "The Choice"—deploy this basic glossary of terms as coherent (though sometimes repetitious) arguments and descriptions.

A signal feature of these orchestrations of repeated key terms is Schell's second literary technique: the use of aphorisms, pithy phrases, memorable sentences, and brief quotations. College students, for instance, reviewing for examinations might use yellow highlighters to assemble a useful outline and anthology of memory bites from *The Fate of the Earth*. Here is one impressionistic version:

A nuclear holocaust [is] widely regarded as "unthinkable" but never as "undoable" (8).

The amount of mass expended in the destruction of Hiroshima was about a gram—or one-thirtieth of an ounce (11).

The right vantage point from which to view a holocaust is that of a corpse but from that vantage point, of course, there is nothing to report (26).

There is no hole big enough to hide all of nature in (61).

Science is a tide that can only rise. . . . [W]e do not know how, as a species, to *deliberately* set out to forget something (105).

We have only to learn to live politically in the world in which we already live scientifically (108).

[E]xtinction is the death of death (119).

We must become the agriculturalists of time (174).

[O]ur failure to acknowledge the magnitude and significance of the peril is a necessary condition for doing the deed. We can do it only if we don't quite know what we're doing (186).

Violence can no longer . . . produce victory and defeat; it can no longer attain its ends. It can no longer be war (191).

Thus, in today's system the actual weapons have already retired halfway from their traditional military role. They are "psychological" weapons. . . . We need to make the weapons *wholly* cerebral. . . . We need to destroy them (222).

Knowledge is the deterrent (223).

It is no more realistic than idealistic to destroy the world (225).

No one will ever witness extinction, so we must be witness to it before the fact (227).

Indifferent to the future of our kind, we grow indifferent to one another. We drift apart. We grow cold. We drowse our way to the end of the world (230).

A third mode of popular narration of an unpopular and often arcane subject is the succinct summary, of which Schell, like Lifton, is a master. Since *The Fate of the Earth* is less than half the length of *Death in Life* but also attempts formidable tasks of explanation and argumentation, its author needs to bring readers quickly up to 1982 levels of understanding and feeling. Here is how he does so by summarizing thermonuclear war's effects on the world's environment:

Bearing in mind that the possible consequences of the detonations of thousands of megatons of nuclear explosives include the blinding of insects, birds, and beasts all over the world; the extinction of many ocean species, among them some at the base of the food chain; the temporary or permanent alteration of the climate of the globe, with the outside chance of "dramatic" and "major" alterations in the structure of the atmosphere; the pollution of the whole ecosphere with oxides of nitrogen; the incapacitation in ten minutes of unprotected people who go out into the sunlight; the blinding of people who go out into the sunlight; a significant decrease in photosynthesis in plants around the world; the scalding and killing of many crops; the increase in rates of cancer and mutation around the world, but especially in the targeted zones, and the attendant risk of global epidemics; the possible poisoning of all vertebrates by sharply increased levels of Vitamin D in their skin as a result of increased ultraviolet light; and the outright slaughter on all targeted continents of most human beings and other living beings by the initial nuclear radiation, the fireballs, the thermal pulses, the blast waves, the mass fires, and the fallout from the explosions; and, considering that these consequences will all interact with one another in unguessable ways and, furthermore, are in all likelihood an incomplete list, which will be added to as our knowledge of the earth increases, one must conclude that a full-scale nuclear holocaust could lead to the extinction of mankind. (93)

To be sure, extracted from its narrative and topical context, this doom-tinged litany of effects betrays, more strikingly than is quite fair, Schell's penchant for piling up the extreme instance and the direst consequence. Yet skeptical readers who object that these deadly consequences are predicated upon detonations of "thousands of megatons of nuclear explosives," not a very likely event in light of four decades of "peace," are arrested at every page by learning the actual scale of nuclear power in the thermonuclear era and the increasing unlikelihood of its never being used. Furthermore, Schell's basic "what if?" argument aims to awaken emotional and moral responses as well as mere cognitive judgment.

That said, the opening chapter is directly addressed to readers' minds. A rehearsal of recent data, it is deliberately intended to surprise and dismay. Past history, too, is reviewed for its abiding lessons. "The Hiroshima people's experience, accordingly, is of much more than historical interest," he declares.

It is a picture of what our whole world is always poised to become—a backdrop of scarcely imaginable horror lying just behind the surface of our normal life, and capable of breaking through that normal life at any second. Whether we choose to think about it or not, it is an omnipresent, inescapable truth about our lives today that at every single moment each one of us may suddenly become the deranged mother looking for her burned child; the professor with the ball of rice in his hand whose wife has just told him, "Run away, dear!" and died in the flames; Mr. Fukai running back into the firestorm; the naked man standing on the blasted plain that was his city, holding his eyeball in his hand; or, more likely, one of millions of corpses. (46–47)

This vivid synecdoche of Hiroshima imagery derives from sources other than Hersey, of course. Schell taps Japanese accounts—Dr. Michihiko Hachi-ya's *Hiroshima Diary* (1955), Yoko Ōta's stories, the scientists' *Hiroshima and Nagasaki*—to give such imaginal memories a bitter authenticity sometimes softened by the older American journalist.[16] The first *New Yorker* writer looks back and sees survival under the often consoling sign of Western religion; the second *New Yorker* writer looks backward, too, but views the same scene from a corpse's perspective and writes under the aegis of Western science. One reason for their divergences is simply the intervening four decades. "What happened at Hiroshima was less than a millionth part of a holocaust at present levels of world nuclear armament" (45), Schell declares flatly. Discoveries like the electromagnetic pulse are realities postdating—and dating—*Hiroshima*. In Schell's eyes, this makes qualitative differences.

Schell's intellectual and moral ties to Robert Jay Lifton are closer, more explicit, and yet contradictory. As his title suggests, Schell broods on issues raised in *Death in Life*—chief among them, radical evil, the Nazi Holocaust, extinction, the "end of civilization," and psychic numbing. But the 1980s author is less interested in getting at these issues via individual case histories and psychoanalytic principles. His science of choice is ecology, not psychology. Specific manifestations of, and dangers from, depletion of the ozone layer are of more moment than ego defenses like avoidance and denial. Psychic numbing is, however, an exception to this generalization. Lifton openly urges "immersion in death" as essential to *hibakusha* readers, but Schell leaves more room for various adaptations to nuclear reality. "Because denial is a form of self-protection," he argues, "if only against anguishing thoughts and feelings, and because it contains something useful . . . anyone who invites people to draw aside the veil and look at the peril face to face is at risk of trespassing on inhibitions that are part of our humanity" (8). Yet numbing is so transparently and vitally a social and historical phenomenon that Schell joins other 1980s critics in using Lifton's term—without, however, rehearsing its psychic dynamics. He is rather preoccupied with the political and military exploitation of a benumbed populace in support of dangerously outmoded policies like tactical nuclear deployments and a "winnable war." In such possibilities, desensitizing goes hand in hand with abstract thinking of the sort practiced by Herman Kahn and other influential ideologues. As a man of his age, Schell inhabits this wider 1980s context rather than the Hiroshima-centered territory that Lifton and Hersey explore.

Schell's fully developed agenda emerges, at the end, as cosmic and potentially transcendental in scope. Leaving behind debts to and arguments with Hersey and Lifton, he even goes beyond national politics of war and peace, elite and popular knowledge and decision-making, and even ecological and environmental implications for the whole earth. Ultimately, a vast vision of postnuclear existence is offered readers of *The Fate of the Earth*. In articulating "the choice" between life and extinction, Hannah Arendt is invoked as the most pertinent moral philosopher for the nuclear age. Though she does not deal directly with thermonuclear violence, Arendt is pertinent because she has dealt imaginatively with totalitarianism and the Nazi Holocaust. She has formulated a post-terror "common world" that humanity can and must affirm, a global community composed "of all institutions, all cities, nations, and other communities, and all works of fabrication, art, thought, and science, and it survives the death of every individual" (Schell, 118). As our sole timeless reality, this common world, now imperiled by the Bomb, overcomes death through its social manifestations: the "public realm" and the "publicity" that language gives to human achievements, as well as to "the preëxisting, biological immortality of our species and of the life on the planet" (Schell, 119). Exemplary individuals like Christ, Socrates, and Gandhi have variously shown the way of self-sacrifice, which preserves and enriches the common life, which is, Schell believes, mankind's only eternity. *Self*-sacrifice, however, must never justify sacrificing *others*. Thus Schell fiercely attacks Christian fundamentalists who imagine and welcome God's Apocalypse coming in a mushroom cloud.

This attack masks, as Ira Chernus points out, Schell's limited transcendentalism, his belief that humanity is bound within "a radically finite realm of experience." Schell's "highest value is endless continuation of human biological and social life," Chernus declares. But the Bomb threatens just such finitude, which may not be timeless. For the Bomb really offers philosophically and theologically attuned imaginations the challenge Schell would implicitly deny: the need to face the extinction imagery that lies at the heart of the nuclear threat. Indeed, psychologists would probably agree with Chernus when he asserts that Schell is "a spokesman for the rational ego, and the ego must stop short when there is simply nothing to imagine. It can not teach us how to imagine nothing, nor can it find a reason for learning that lesson. The need to face formlessness as a dimension of infinitude is beyond its ken."[17]

From a different direction, Schell's final section, "The Choice," is also sharply criticized by Neil Schmitz in his *Nation* review. Decrying the "soft foolish solemn language" Schell too often falls into at book's end, Schmitz laments the author's failure to lay out specific steps toward a postnuclear world modeled on Arendt's precepts. Schmitz terms the book's political prescription—first a freeze, then nuclear disarmament, followed by conventional weapons disarmament, an international government, and universal peace—"a mystification, the certain sign of an aversion." What Schell avoids is any succinct analysis of the present American nuclear complex, which over the decades has proved, as Schmitz sees it, the most dangerous threat to the world: "a bristling, imperial nation-state [under] tight control by certain Americans." Schell, a too careful liberal, seems not to wish to antagonize the powerful American right by mounting a critique based upon "a precise remembering of history."[18] Thus, for example, Schell makes no mention anywhere in *The Fate of the Earth* of Edward Teller and says little specifically about deterrence as the postwar mode of American imperialism. This, Schmitz concludes, is the unspeakable message lurking still within Schell's version of the unthinkable subject, one many of his readers in 1982 seemed all too willing to evade as well.

Though cogent, Schmitz's criticism shortchanges somewhat the aims and achievements of *The Fate of the Earth*. Schell wants Americans to confront many daunting aspects of the unthinkable besides those Schmitz mentions. Extinction as the second death; the implications of American public surrender of nuclear policy to the military, politicians, and think-tank experts; widespread ignorance of thermonuclear and environmental realities; above all, a fresh and unconsoling look at what survival means as a postholocaust possibility—this is by anyone's standard an ambitious and prophetic agenda. *The Fate of the Earth*, though incomplete, anticipates a number of later 1980s works of nuclear criticism and culture, including the National Conference of Catholic Bishops' *The Challenge of Peace* (1983), Boyer's *By the Bomb's Early Light* (1985), Grace Mojtabai's *Blessèd Assurance* (1986), Weart's *Nuclear Fear* (1988), and Rhodes's *The Making of the Atomic Bomb* (1986).[19]

Though Boyer's and Weart's are incisive cultural histories (as we shall point out more fully in chapter 6), the successor to *The Fate of the Earth* that best constitutes "a precise remembering of history" *and* a moral treatise that does not sidestep difficult political, military, and scientific realities is Rhodes's monumental work. In this 790-page history of American nuclear science and technology, Rhodes intersperses trenchant moral reflections arising out of historical developments and decisions. One such is his discussion of Niels Bohr's heroic and prescient efforts to convince Roosevelt, Churchill, and George Marshall to share scientific and military knowledge, and thus nuclear responsibility, with the Soviet Union. "Within any community it is only possible for the citizens to strive together for common welfare on the basis of public knowledge of the general conditions of the country," Bohr told Marshall after the end of the war. "Likewise, real co-operation between nations on problems of common concern presupposes free access to all information of importance for their relations. Any argument for upholding barriers of information and intercourse, based on concern for national ideals or interests, must be weighed against the beneficial effects of common enlightenment and the relieved tension resulting from such openness" (Rhodes, 535). Here and in other prose messages to key leaders and to the United Nations, Bohr enunciated powerfully prophetic statments that anticipated Arendt's "common world" ideal and the central role in its realization of public knowledge.

Rhodes reflects on this moment and this moral man's place in it. "Bohr had searched the forbidding territory of the atom when he was young and discovered multiple structures of paradox; now he searched it again by the dark light of the energy it released and discovered profound political change" (532). Rhodes then meditates on this turning point in light of four decades of profound political and historical change:

Nations existed in a condition of international anarchy. No hierarchical authority defined their relations with one another. They negotiated voluntarily as self-interest moved them and took what they could get. War had been their final negotiation, brutally resolving their worst disputes.

Now an ultimate power had appeared. If Churchill failed to recognize it he did so because it was not a battle cry or a treaty or a committee of men. It was more like a god descending to the stage in a gilded car. It was a mechanism that nations could build and multiply that harnessed unlimited energy, a mechanism that many nations *would* build in self-defense as soon as they learned of its existence and acquired the technical means. It would seem to confer security upon its builders, but because there was no sure protection against so powerful and portable a mechanism, in the course of time each additional unit added to the stockpiles would *decrease* security by adding to the general threat until insecurity finally revealed itself to be total at every hand.

Then Rhodes continues this line of reasoning as it appeared to the thoughtful Dane:

Bohr saw that far ahead—all the way to the present, when menacing standoff has been achieved and maintained for decades without formal agreement but at the price of smaller client wars and holocaustal nightmare and a good share of the wealth of nations—and stepped back. He wondered if such apocalyptic precariousness was necessary. He wondered if the war-weary statesmen of the day, taught the consequences of his revelation, could be induced to forestall those consequences, to adjourn the game when the stalemate revealed itself rather than illogically to play out the menacing later moves. It was clear at least that the new weapons would be appallingly dangerous. (533)

Bohr's early recognition of "the complementarity of the bomb" (Rhodes, 528)—its precarious status as both opportunity and threat for the future—is another manifestation of the so-called soft humanistic, idealistic imagination that this brilliant scientist shared with J. Robert Oppenheimer. Rhodes describes in some detail Oppenheimer's loving familiarity with literature and Oriental religion. But in general, *The Making of the Atomic Bomb* shares with *The Fate of the Earth* a preference for scientific, rational, and pragmatic issues. Despite brave words about the place of language and literature as foundations of our common world, Schell remains suspicious of fiction as a medium of insight. He declares that "some analysts of nuclear destruction have resorted to fiction, assigning to the imagination the work that investigation is unable to do. But then the results are just what one would expect: fiction" (25). Lifton, Boyer, and Weart, among Schell's immediate successors, all pursue wider (and, in fact, deeper) paths across the map of nuclear history and culture. They share with Michael Perlman and Ira Chernus a need to examine sympathetically the artistic imagination as a necessary instrument for grasping the psychological and spiritual recesses of *hibakusha* existence. Nuclear art, they recognize, is both social and historical record *and* spiritual seismograph of humanity's enforced encounter with extinction. Their histories and critiques show that since at least the early 1950s, fiction and poetry, films, television, and occasionally drama have contributed to our intuitive and cognitive understandings of the full extent of the new world order created by the Bomb. Indeed, as I hope to demonstrate in the chapters that follow, popular and elite modes of fictional discourse developed by the 1980s into major sources, along with nonfiction criticism, of insight and instigation. The shadow of Hiroshima—and for younger readers it became just that, a monstrous but remote shadow—fell across many ambitious imaginations fired now by realization of the challenge of Schell's warning: "The masterpieces cannot be timeless if time itself stops."

2

Fictions of the Age of Anxiety,
1945–1963

"IF THERE IS ANYTHING THAT MODERN MAN REGARDS AS INFI-
nite it is no longer God," Gunther Anders declared in 1956, midway through
the historical epoch called the Age of Anxiety by critics and historians. "Since
we are in a position to inflict absolute destruction of each other, we have
apocalyptic powers. It is we who are the infinite . . .; we are Titans, as long as
we are omnipotent without making *definitive* use of this omnipotence of ours."[1]
Hiroshima, that is, has radically revised history. There are today three valid
divisions in human experience. One can but trace the progression from a world
of "all men are mortal" to that of "all men are exterminable," arriving now, in the
era of the H-bomb, at the stage wherein "mankind as a whole is exterminable." It
is an actuality truly monstrous. Mankind now knows more than we can imagine,
psychically and morally. "What are the boundaries of our emotional capacity
in a post-nuclear age?" Anders therefore wonders. In despair almost, he challenges readers to close this terrifying gap between ourselves as producers of
annihilation and as critics of annihilation. These two sides, he concludes,
scarcely know of each other's existence. Hence we are connected by the

thinnest of threads—"knowledge of this split and [of] there [being] no internal principle integrating these halves" (155).

The consequence of this bleak diagnosis for writers and readers is simple yet formidable. As Jacques Derrida later declared, these facts of postnuclear reality render the subject "fabulously textual." For, quite literally, "one can only talk and write about it."[2] Yet in the same issue of *Diacritics* in which Derrida made this assertion, none of the other contributors mentioned any specific nuclear texts, thereby confirming Thomas M. F. Gerry's 1987 accusation that "literary criticism has regularly ignored the nuclear fact."[3] In light of the critics to be discussed in chapter 6, Gerry's charge may seem dated or over-stated. The same reservation will, I think, prove true of the ensuing analysis of first-generation nuclear fiction in light of recent critical treatments.

Central to this assertion about writers, readers, and critics who belie the charge of indifference or avoidance is the field of science fiction. In fact, "it was a novel, among other things, which originated the atomic bomb," Peter Schwenger has asserted.[4] By "novel" he means to invoke the century-long tradition of modern science fiction, whose principal pioneer, H. G. Wells, in 1914 used the term "atomic bomb" in *The World Set Free*, dramatized world war as catastrophe, and mentioned radioactivity, world government, and possible peaceful uses of atomic power. "SF has offered us crucial insights into the sources, dangers, and dimensions of our nuclear nemesis," H. Bruce Franklin concludes in a 1986 issue of *Science Fiction Studies* devoted to "Nuclear War and Science Fiction." Indeed, Franklin proceeds to correct Boyer's claim that virtually all the basic features of the nuclear debate emerged in the months after Hiroshima. He claims an even more prophetic role for science fiction of a century ago. "Each stage of the American quest for security after Hiroshima is characterized by delusions expressed in American fiction, 1880–1917."[5] Frank Stockton, Jack London, and Hollis Godfrey were novelists who debated apologists for technology like Thomas Edison and Nicholas Tesla over the issue of whether men or machines would be used in future wars. Ever since, Franklin avers, popular and elite fictions have created imaginary worlds in which planetary travel and alien invasions are themes tied to lethal weaponry in the hands of aggressive earthlings. "Stories of global catastrophe, the end of the world, and the end of man—anticipated, fulfilled, or averted—constitute the mean among works of science fiction," David Ketterer declared in 1974.[6] The spate of novels, short stories, and films preceding and following his statement confirms its accuracy and importance. Science fiction now composes the purest form of apocalyptic romance, a genre hallowed by nineteenth-century greats like Melville, Poe, and Mark Twain. Canonization likewise has extended to works in modern literature linked to science fiction, especially those published during the 1950s and 1960s. Familiar titles in the unofficial SF pantheon include Ray Bradbury's *Martian Chronicles* (1950), Arthur C. Clarke's *Childhood's End* (1953), William Golding's *Lord of the Flies* (1954), Nevil Shute's *On the Beach* (1957), Helen Clarkson's *Last Day* (1959), Walter M. Miller, Jr.'s *A Canticle for*

Leibowitz (1959), Mordecai Roshwald's *Level 7* (1959), Robert A. Heinlein's *Stranger in a Strange Land* (1961), and Kurt Vonnegut's *Cat's Cradle* (1963). Less well known or critically acclaimed are a number of other nuclear novels: Judith Merril's *Shadow on the Hearth* (1950), Philip Wylie's *Tomorrow!* (1954), Pat Frank's *Alas Babylon* (1959), Eugene Burdick and Harvey Wheeler's *Fail-Safe* (1962), Peter George's *Dr. Strangelove, or, How I Learned to Stop Worrying and Love the Bomb* (1963), and Philip K. Dick's *Dr. Bloodmoney, or, How We Got Along after the Bomb* (1965).[7]

Nuclear extinction today, however, is not just a trendier or scarier version of earlier imaginary apocalypses in American and European fiction. Los Alamos and Hiroshima afford chillingly new contexts for reading potboilers, like F. H. Rose's *The Maniac's Dream* (1948), that were not available to early audiences of, say, Hollis Godfrey's *The Man Who Ended War* (1908) (Brians [1987], 292, 205–6). Furthermore, science fiction today is a complex cultural and literary activity, one enmeshed in wide networks of communication through interlocking social and commercial enterprises like magazines, paperback clubs, newsletters, prizes, and conventions. Though some of this activity is cultish exploitation, science fiction's leading journals—*Astounding Science Fiction*, *Galaxy*, and *Wonder Stories*, among them—discuss vital issues and routinely publish stories and letters to the editor that articulate a serious critique of American society and post-Hiroshima practices of avoidance and psychic numbing. Thus many science fiction writers, editors, and critics discharge an important social responsibility to inform and entertain. They serve readers who are asking what they need to know and how to feel—perhaps how to behave—regarding nuclear realities and prospects.[8]

With a pre–World War II audience once characterized by Alexei Panshin as "intense, but limited in size and composed mainly of fans, engineers, and bright fifteen-year-olds" (Clareson, 329), science fiction (and mainstream fiction sharing its nuclear themes and techniques) now addresses with increasing directness the psychological concerns of new generations of readers. These needs were identified in 1982 by Michael J. Carey. His interviews, published in the *Bulletin of Atomic Scientists*, reveal a group of young to early middle–aged readers genuinely puzzled by the nuclear phenomenon they called the "mystery of the age." Despite exposure in school to "duck-and-cover" and government film clips, they were still surprisingly ignorant of key facts about nuclear weapons and the terms used to describe or cloak nuclear power. They were convinced, however, that the Bomb could devastate a world—and not just a city or two. "The diverse attributions to the Bomb's psychological impact," Carey concluded, "suggest that discovering the bomb's importance to the American psyche is as much a matter of conviction, expectation, passion and intuition as it is a question of facts. . . . This generation has a collection of memories, images, and words that will not disappear, even for those who profess not to be troubled." Hence Carey named the era the Age of Anxiety.[9]

From other evidence, both popular and sophisticated fiction are common sources and diagnoses of American *hibakusha* attitudes and anxieties. Novels, short stories, films, and, toward the end of this early era, television offer invaluable access to public and private feelings and thoughts on the nuclear referent. Historical study, moreover, suggests that the 1950s was a key period in the formation of social attitudes and values through literature, especially fiction. Literature contributed support to the emerging nuclear culture, as it did to its criticism and opposition. The entire social fabric thus stitched together came perilously close to destruction in the Cuban Missile Crisis in the fall of 1962, a fact that makes 1963 or 1964 the plausible terminus, temporary and arbitrary to be sure, of a historical period. By 1964, it may be argued, so many Americans had come to the anguished realization of the fragility of their world that Gunther Anders's gap in consciousness had perhaps narrowed a bit. If so, fiction, and science fiction in particular, assisted in the process and reflects it.

For literate Americans, in the years before television became the source of leisure, entertainment, and information transmittal for the majority of the population, the short story was a major mode of popular reading matter. Readily available by magazine or even newspaper purchase or subscription, or by access to a public library, the short story still serves several functions for a range of serious and casual readers. By its brevity and battery of literary devices, stories deliver often powerfully compressed messages. With almost the immediacy and impact of poems, stories can generate and fix images. Their authors, who are sometimes novelists as well, develop acute antennae for picking up the public's cognitive concerns and emotional needs. Because their work is published in periodicals, short-story writers can respond quickly to changes in readers' agendas caused by public events. No chain of events has been more disturbing or mysterious than those associated with the Bomb.

As many of its devotees and critics delight in pointing out, science fiction was in the vanguard in helping to form new patterns of awareness in the wake of the news from Los Alamos, Hiroshima, and Nagasaki. Long before 1945, in fact, an American literary descendant of H. G. Wells, Pierrepont B. Noyes, anticipated in *The Pallid Giant: A Tale of Yesterday and Tomorrow* the advent of the nuclear age and the dread it would engender. The "pallid giant" was not the Bomb itself but atomic fear. First published in 1927, Noyes's book (retitled *Gentlemen, You Are Mad!*) was reissued in 1946. In the interim, short stories like Cleve Cartmill's "Deadline" (1944) and Philip Wylie's "The Paradise Crater" (1945) were briefer imaginative anticipations of coming events (Brians [1987], 345).

Despite these bellwether publications, science fiction, whether short or long, is not exactly prophesy, as Robert Heinlein points out in *Expanded Universe* (1980). Rather, it is a form of imaginative extrapolation. "It means continuing a curve, a path, a trend into the future, by extending its present direction and continuing the *shape* it has displayed in its past performance.[10] Therefore science fiction stories differ from ordinary brief fictions; they are neither "realistic" slices of imagined experience nor pure fantasy. As Mark Rose summarizes, science fiction is a "form of the fantastic that denies it is fantastic" (20). Relying on readers who are familiar with this tightrope act, some science fiction writers, Rose adds, stress unelaborated ideas or concepts largely unsupported by adequate character development, plot, or metaphoric patterning. Both Cartmill and Wylie conform to this pattern, one typical of early nuclear fiction. Later writers—especially those invading science fiction domains from other literary sectors—depart from this shorthand reliance on striking ideas, moving instead toward interiorization (for example, psychological states) and metaphor (such as mythic and poetic utterance).

Resistance to the fantastic and symbolic, as opposed to "fact" or plausible prophesy, runs throughout the history of science fiction as postnuclear phenomenon. Information early outweighed imagination in this field. Thus, even as fantasy writers like Theodore Sturgeon ("August Sixth, 1945" [1945] and "Thunder and Roses" [1947]) and Ray Bradbury ("Million-Year Picnic" [1946]) caught Americans' attention in the immediate aftermath of Hiroshima, other "realistic" or "documentary" story writers were crowding into the field. The latter mode's most striking success was no doubt *Life* magazine's "36-Hour War" (Brians [1987], 319, 143, 245). This article hit the newsstands on 19 November 1945. Neither pure nor even impure science fiction, the *Life* article might best be termed imaginative journalism. Yet the editors freely used fictional techniques to tell millions of readers the gist of General Henry "Hap" Arnold's report on missiles and their possible effects if used on the United States. "The destruction would be so swift and terrible that the war might well be decided in 36 hours," they wrote, backing up the shocking possibilities with illustrations bearing highly imaginative captions.[11] Doubtless the most sensational and memorable of these captioned pictures (actual photographs of Hiroshima being conspicuously absent) was the large drawing of Fifth Avenue in ruins. Above the caption—"By the Marble Lions of New York's Public Library, U.S. Technicians Test the Rubble of the Shattered City for Radioactivity" (*Life*, 35)—the stone statues gaze down on the shattered street and white-garbed experts. The imagined scene clearly symbolizes American national survival of a nuclear attack. Yet the absence of crisped corpses, in both text and picture, also represents, more obliquely, the evasions *Life* was practicing in communicating an accurate picture of likely effects. As one of the first fictional messages telling Americans "it could happen to us," "The 36-Hour War" was an exercise in sanitized sensationalism.

A very different sort of short fiction appearing in the immediate wake of Hiroshima and Nagasaki was that of Langston Hughes. The creator of Jesse B. Semple ("Simple"), a vernacular Harlem figure, Hughes wrote in the didactic tradition of Mark Twain and Finley Peter Dunne. Though his audience was far smaller than *Life*'s, he was widely syndicated in such black newspapers as the *Chicago Defender*, and his sketches were later published by prominent New

York and London publishers. He began his satiric commentary from a Harlem viewpoint a few days after Nagasaki and continued it throughout the Age of Anxiety. In "Simple and the Atomic Bomb" (18 August 1945), Hughes was one of the first to voice the widely shared attitude of blacks and some whites that it was no coincidence the Bomb was first used against yellow-skinned Japanese, not white Germans (Brians [1987], 223). During the Bikini test years, Simple spoke out with a witty irony not very different, at times, from that of the nightclub satirist Tom Lehrer.[12] Typical of his down-home humor in the 1950s is "Bones, Bombs, Chicken Necks." In this story, Simple's wife chides him for carrying chicken bones away from the dinner table to gnaw on at the front window. "White folks might not gnaw bones in windows," he retorts, "but they sure do some awful other things. . . . It looks like to me it would be better to gnaw a bone than to singe them Marshall Islanders. . . . Bone-gnawing, to my mind, is better than bomb-bursting. Atom bombs is low-rating the tone of the whole world."[13]

Hughes's Simple satire not only serves the special needs of black readers by ironically balancing their perennial concern with racism against new fears, but suggests both the racist and supraracial dimensions of the new age. In neither direction, though, does Hughes push fantasy as far as did E. B. White. Written long before *Dr. Strangelove*, White's 1950 *New Yorker* story "The Morning of the Day They Did It" imagines a pair of astronauts on a satellite launching an atomic bomb out of sheer boredom (Brians [1987], 335–36). The dominant wisdom, however, of the early years of the cold war was: "Fantasy, yes, but humor, generally not—too dangerous." Since a genuine and pervasive fear of the mysteriously dreadful lay always near the surface of the era's emotional history, it is scarcely surprising that the Hughes/Lehrer/White strain was a distinctly minor note in short fiction.

Much more prevalent was the social realist mode. Through Simple, Hughes could amuse and chide but not educate Americans about the history, nature, or effects of Nagasaki and Bikini. But writers like Poul Anderson, Edgar Pangborn, Arthur C. Clarke, and J. G. Ballard, to mention several among many, achieved more jolting effects—and possibly more effective education—by not letting readers off the hook with jokes, parodies, or absurd fantasies. Their cultural work became fleshing out, in brief but convincing social and scientific detail, their stories, which addressed Americans' central nightmare: megawar at home and chances of survival. Indeed, these short-story writers anticipated the themes, plots, and even imagery of later novelists in the variety and power of their versions of what Jonathan Schell deemed the major new myth of the age—life after the Bomb.

As both echo and anticipation, Poul Anderson and F. N. Waldrop's "Tomorrow's Children" epitomizes as succinctly as any science fiction the potential this literature possessed to simultaneously extrapolate, alarm, and educate. Appearing in *Astounding Science Fiction* in March 1947, this early tale was often reprinted, as eventually in Walter M. Miller, Jr., and Martin Greenberg's admirable anthology *Beyond Armageddon: Twenty-one Sermons to the Dead* (1985). There Miller underscores the topicality of "Tomorrow's Children." "To me the story still has the smell of 1946 about it, right after World War II . . . when much of the Old World, east and west, was picking itself up out of the rubble, under the auspices of conquering overseers."[14]

In fact, Anderson and Waldrop imagine a post–World War III situation exponentially more desperate than Berlin or Leningrad in 1945–46. Almost unflinchingly—there are a few palliatives—they expose American fears of worldwide holocaust and American faith in military leaders to reorder a devastated continent. Hugh Drummond and General Robinson are anything but "conquering overseers." They are finite actors in a small-scale drama of survival. In a plot that anticipates Whitley Strieber and James Kunetka's *Warday: And the Journey Onward* (1984) (see chapter 4), the narrator looks over Drummond's shoulder as he flies across the nuclear-blasted continent, "the lone man in the solitary stratojet" (Miller and Greenberg, 147). Upon returning to the nation's temporary capital, Taylor, Oregon, he reports the destruction's dimensions to Robinson. "Our culture hasn't lost its continuity," the upbeat general replies, "but it's had a terrific setback. We'll never wholly get over it. But—we're on our way up again" (Miller and Greenberg, 152). On another flight, Drummond visits a tiny Minnesota community. Its bearded leader exemplifies American pioneer toughness. With brutal directness, he has suppressed the religious fundamentalists in his flock, who foresee more apocalypse in the deformed births now plaguing people, animals, plants. "'It's God's jedgment, I tell you!' The woman was shrilling again. 'The end o' the world is near.'. . . The woman shrank back, lips tight. The room filled with a crackling silence. One of the babies began to cry. It had two heads" (Miller and Greenberg, 164). "It's wrecking our culture," Drummond asserts to Robinson upon his return this time. "People are going crazy as birth after birth is monstrous. Fear of the unknown, striking at minds still stunned by the war and its immediate aftermath. Frustration of parenthood, perhaps the most basic instinct there is. It's leading to infanticide, desertion, despair, a cancer at the root of society. We've got to act" (Miller and Greenberg, 166). At first the general advocates a radical cure, sterilization of all mutants. But when his own wife is brought to the birthing bed, he must confront the attending physician. " 'You're a brave man,' said the doctor. . . . 'You'll need your courage. . . . ' A nurse brought out the little wailing form. It was a boy. But his limbs were rubbery tentacles terminating in boneless digits" (Miller and Greenberg, 171). "You were right," Robinson remarks hopelessly. "We should never have created science. It brought the twilight of the race." But Drummond has the last word. "I never said that. The race brought its own destruction, through misuse of science. Our culture was scientific anyway, in all except its psychological base. It's up to us to take that last and hardest step. If we do, the race may yet survive. . . . I still think you've got a good kid" (Miller and Greenberg, 173).

Hugh Drummond of "Tomorrow's Children" as stalwart survivor anticipates another dutiful American officer enduring a nuclear holocaust. Commander Dwight Towers of Nevil Shute's *On the Beach* (1957) is also a loyal officer who has lost wife and children in the sudden devastation. But whereas Shute has space in a 278-page novel to elaborate Towers's delusion that he will be reunited with his Connecticut family, Drummond is more pithy, realistic, and eloquent. *"Barbara, maybe it was best you and the kids went as you did. Quickly, cleanly, not even knowing it. This isn't much of a world. It'll never be our world again"* (Miller and Greenberg, 160–61). While Shute's Australians and Americans staunchly but resignedly await the end of the world, Drummond and Robinson struggle against the odds to survive. Abetting Drummond's humanity is his newfound global consciousness. "Ten miles up, it hardly showed. Earth was a cloudy green and brown blur, the vast vault of the stratosphere reaching changelessly out to spatial infinities, and beyond the pulsing engine there was silence and serenity no man could ever touch" (Miller and Greenberg, 146–47). A similar, even more stratospheric perspective, combined with sympathy for the young survivor, is also exhibited in Arthur Clarke's "If I Forget Thee, Oh Earth" (1951), but this later story, safely set on another planet, is marked (and marred) by a nostalgia, a quality almost wholly kept under control by Anderson and Waldrop (Brians [1987], 159).

Nostalgia and the wrenching gap between the generations that nuclear holocaust can bring are components of several science fiction tales published after these early achievements. None is more carefully or convincingly realized than Edgar Pangborn's "A Master of Babylon." Originally titled "The Music Master of Babylon" when it appeared in *Galaxy* in November 1954 (Brians [1987], 278), Pangborn's is a longer, more detailed survival fable than either "Tomorrow's Children" or "If I Forget Thee, Oh Earth." New York City after a nuclear attack is the Babylon over which an aged, once-famous pianist presides from the upper stories of New York's Museum of Human History. The rest of the metropolis is flooded. By contrast with Hugh Drummond, who is quintessentially a military man but morally attuned to living humanely in a world of mutants, Brian Van Alda is remarkably sensitive to natural and artistic experience but out of touch with social and generational problems. His is a dream-filled and watery existence in a Poe-esque metropolis of the dead. Not a living soul else survives on Manhattan or Long Island, as far as he can tell. "Such things, places and dates, were factual props, useful when Brian wanted to impose an external order on the vagueness of his immediate existence" (Miller and Greenberg, 198). Physically and psychologically self-sufficient, he shoots deer on the Palisades with bow and arrow, plays sonatas in the hall of the museum, and can even joke at his own loneliness. "For twenty-five years no one came" is the story's memorable opening line. Above all, music sustains him. "It would never have occurred to Mozart, Brian thought, that a world could die" (Miller and Greenberg, 206).

Into Van Alda's time-warped world come two young survivors from the

South. They are a postholocaust Adam and Eve. Rudiments of the old order survive in their desire for a ritual blessing of their mating, their syncretist religion, and their language, which the old man can barely understand. But they fear the old man's awkward arrogance when he insists that they listen to a piano sonata before being married. The thunderous notes frighten them, and they flee in their canoe. Pursuing them vainly, Van Alda shouts across the fast-flowing Hudson: *"Damn it, hasn't MY world some rights?"* (Miller and Greenberg, 222). But instead of receiving a human reply, he finds himself drifting silently, helplessly toward the ocean. " 'Why,' he said aloud, detachedly observing the passage of his canoe beyond the broad morning shadow of the Museum, 'Why, I seem to have killed myself' " (Miller and Greenberg, 223).

In this postholocaust romance, Pangborn testifies to humanity's persistence in the face of technological violence. But his isolato (Melville's term for the loner seems apt here) cannot communicate his ancient art to these wild children who are surviving to start a fresh and, in the old man's eyes, savage culture. However, more than most 1950s science fiction stories, "The Master of Babylon" exhibits a wide range of literary concerns and conceits. Biblical and American transcendental romance traditions are reenacted by an American Adam and Eve now out on a frontier of time, not space. Pangborn's setting reestablishes within Darwinian and geological frames the legendary timelessness of Poe, Cooper, and Melville. Yet the protagonist's memories of nuclear dates and devastation hover in the background as horrifying, inescapable realities. Tensions thus remain between science and technology, on the one hand, and religion, music, and art, as residues of a humane, beleaguered civilization, on the other. A new pastoralism emerges, ironically enacted in the ruins of America's greatest metropolis. Despite science's onslaughts, nature remains and sustains. Radioactivity is never mentioned. Nevertheless, nature cannot unite the old ones and their wild grandchildren in this stricken society.

As neutral but inexorable setting and force, nature also presides over the fate of another postholocaust survivor—Traven, the protagonist of J. G. Ballard's brief masterpiece, "The Terminal Beach" (1964). Like Shute, Clarke, and Roshwald, Ballard is a non-American whose subsequent novels—*The Atrocity Exhibition* (1964), *Crash* (1973), and *Empire of the Sun* (1984)— were as popular with American readers as this first story. From internal evidence, Ballard appears to be as aware of American literary antecedents as of English ones. Such cross-cultural sensitivity makes "The Terminal Beach" a fitting synecdoche of nuclear short fiction in the 1950s and 1960s (Brians [1987], 124).

The title, for one thing, plays on the image popularized in Shute's *On the Beach* and was destined to reappear in numerous subsequent texts. The last shore in this nuclear fable is not, however, humanity's final destination but only one symbolic man's end zone. Traven was once a military pilot and, like Hugh Drummond and Dwight Towers, has lost a wife and child. He comes to Eniwetok some years after the Bikini tests, at a time when, for "the two decades, 1945–1965," as he believes, the world is "suspended from the quivering volcano's lip of World War III" (Miller and Greenberg, 127). His motives, a mysterious mixture of guilt, curiosity, and desire to escape the past and future, all center on the H-bomb, whose birth Traven associates with this Pacific atoll. His imagination seizes upon the sterile landscape of sand, empty military and scientific installations, and other residues of the thermonuclear tests. The island thus is Ballard's ironic alternative to Pangborn's Museum of Human History. Yet while Van Alda's surroundings are outward signs of an interior nostalgic consciousness, for Traven the empty nuclear site defines and controls *him*; "if primitive man felt the need to assimilate events in the external world to his own psyche, twentieth-century man had reversed this process—by this Cartesian yardstick, the island at least *existed*, in a sense true of few other places" (Miller and Greenberg, 127). Traven's new identity, however, is a deserted spot, willed into oblivion by others who wish to forget the landing strip, concrete bunkers, Super Fortresses in the sand, and plastic dummies. This final home, he believes, is "the tomb of the unknown civilian, *Homo hydrogenesis*, Eniwetok Man" (Miller and Greenberg, 138). When his boat is wrecked on landing, he becomes a latter-day Robinson Crusoe in a surreal, postholocaust setting. But to the doctor and nurse who come to rescue him, he is merely "a strange derelict figure, hiding in a bunker in a deserted interior of the island. He is suffering from severe exposure and malnutrition, but is unaware of this, or, for that matter, of any other events in the world around him." Laced with ironies, the outsiders' report concludes: "August 6. He has the eyes of the possessed. I would guess he is neither the first, nor the last, to visit the island" (Miller and Greenberg, 135–36). To the doctor and others, Eniwetok represents simply a "nightmarish chapter of history . . . gladly forgotten" (Miller and Greenberg, 127). But in Traven's supersensitive imagination (he is apparently diagnosed by the doctor as harboring a death wish), the atoll, "this minimal concrete city" of dead planes, no people, and abandoned bulldozers, sits at "thermonuclear noon" in human history's brief day (Miller and Greenberg, 126). It represents objectively what Traven feels: we all now live in a quantal world of segmented time sensations and hallucinatory private imagery.

Chief among these images of the island of death is the dessicated corpse of a mysterious Japanese visitor—not a leftover soldier but a doctor or lawyer gripping a leather map-case. Literarily, of course, Crusoe has found his man Friday, just as, psychologically speaking, Dr. Yasuda is Traven's alter ego in a grimly updated Conradian tale. A surreal colloquy takes place between the dying man and the corpse. It is the moving story's powerful climax. Presided over by a single buzzing fly, now the island's single other living thing—and an echo of Emily Dickinson's famous lyric on death—the exchange between the Westerner and the Asian, both survivors of World War II, trades insights into their common existential situation. Yasuda seems to have come here to mourn the death of two nieces in the World War II firebombing of Osaka. His other role, though, is to provide "rich liqueurs and distillations" from his dead eyes to sustain the fly's life. Unthinkingly, Traven moves to kill the fly but desists. "I'm sorry I tried to kill it," he remarks. "These ingrained habits, you know, they're not easy to shrug off." East and West seem to agree to maintain their own and the fly's identities. As Yasuda says, "After all, each one of us is little more than a meagre residue of the infinite unrealized possibilities of our lives. But your son and my nieces are fixed in our minds forever, their identities as certain as the stars" (Miller and Greenberg, 143). Then Yasuda suggests Traven's truer American identity, that of an obsessed hunter "for the white leviathan, zero" (144). This signals the Ahab role that has brought him to Moby-Dick's old ocean. Instead of seeking nothingness or cosmic unity, Yasuda says, Traven should escape his guilt-ridden post-Hiroshima past, "finding here among the blocks . . . the image of yourself free of time and space. This island is an ontological Garden of Eden; why try to expel yourself into a quantal world?" (Miller and Greenberg, 144). The fly symbolizes that primal world. As nature's diversity, it is the opposite of the beach. "The beach is a dangerous zone; avoid it," Yasuda advises. "Have a proper humility; pursue a philosophy of acceptance." But the dying American prefers empty concrete bunkers to the buzzing, living fly.

Traven: Then may I ask why you came here, Doctor?

Yasuda: To feed this fly. "What greater love—?"

Traven: (*still puzzling*): It doesn't really solve my problem. The blocks, you see. . . .

Yasuda: Very well, if you must have it that way. . . .

Traven: But, Doctor—

Yasuda: (*peremptorially*): Kill that fly!

Traven: That's not an end, or a beginning. (*Hopelessly he kills the fly. Exhausted, he falls asleep beside the corpse.*) (Miller and Greenberg, 144)

Only by pondering the implications of this action can the puzzled reader grasp the story's real ending. For Traven—apparently honoring the Japanese's acceptance of life and death—drags his corpse and sets him up as guardian against the sterile rows of white concrete bunkers. Then images of his dead wife and son return. "Patiently Traven waited for them to speak to him, thinking of the great blocks whose entrance was guarded by the seated figure of the dead archangel, as the waves broke on the distant shore and the burning bombers fell through his dreams" (Miller and Greenberg, 145).

As the above survey of the short story attests, science fiction was in the vanguard of American imaginative writing on the Bomb and its aftershocks during the Age of Anxiety. Flourishing in these two decades together with this rich and varied short fiction and its magazine venues were nuclear novels and full-length romances. A number, in fact, hit the best-seller charts here and abroad and, like Hersey's *Hiroshima*, have remained steadily in circulation. Some were translated into foreign languages; some were made into successful films. Though only spottily absorbed into school and college curricula (Golding's *Lord of the Flies* was a temporary exception), novels on nuclear themes reached sizable audiences and influenced important mainstream writers who unashamedly borrowed settings and themes from science fiction. Neither the separate field of full-length science fiction nor the early works of so-called mainstream authors—John Barth, Jorge Luis Borges, Thomas Pynchon, and others—will be explored here. Instead, I shall concentrate on several crossover texts that occupy the middle ground between science fiction and elite, often experimental mainstream fiction dealing with the nature of postnuclear reality. This midterritory became a fascinating and frightening zone during these decades, one suffused in readers' imaginations with the potentiality of sudden destruction and the extinction of human life and culture.

One feature of the curiosity and dread experienced by many American readers of the 1950s and 1960s continued to be the mystery and secrecy mantling the history of the bombing of Hiroshima and Nagasaki. Even the advent of the hydrogen bomb and the Bikini tests, though widely trumpeted, did not clear the clouds of silence and misinformation surrounding these manifestations of American power and policy. As Martha Bartter later pointed out, "[C]ulture hides its secrets more effectively from its own members than from outsiders, and fiction can express (often metaphorically, obliquely) these blind spots."[15] Neither *Life*'s "36-Hour War" nor Bradley's *No Place to Hide* overcame—much less clearly identified—governmental efforts to thwart or manipulate such needs to know. Indeed, "nearly three decades passed without any technically accurate and widely seen portrayal of hydrogen bomb war," wrote the author of *Nuclear Fear* (Weart, 237).

As information-starved and nervous audiences of the late 1940s and 1950s grew in number and concern, an immediate market for popular domestic fiction likewise appeared. This public included more women than the science fiction market had previously attracted. (The world of *Astounding Science Fiction* consisted overwhelmingly of male writers and male readers.) So it should be no surprise that one of the first novels to bring Hiroshima home to the American suburb was by a woman. Judith Merril, later a prolific writer and critic of science fiction, made one of the early and oft-reprinted contributions to nuclear fiction in "That Only a Mother," a story published in *Astounding Fiction* June 1948 (Brians [1987], 260). But it was her novel *The Shadow on the Hearth*, issued by Doubleday in 1950, that began the treatment of nuclear danger in the social realist mode (however limited) of popular fiction. Following in the wake of Merril's novel was Philip Wylie's *Tomorrow!* (1954) and, at decade's end, Pat Frank's *Alas Babylon* (1959). These works are not science fiction proper, for they do not deal with monsters, mutants, flights to Mars, or end-of-the-world apocalypses. Yet each is explicitly a nuclear romance of survival.[16]

In place of a military pilot or submarine commander, Merril's protagonist is Gladys Mitchell, a timid housewife in Westchester County, New York. On a fateful day, she sends her husband Jon off to the city and happily contemplates her postwar situation. With a husband, two daughters, and a comfortable suburban home, she wonders, like many of her real-life postwar cohorts, "[H]ow long could things go on, getting better all the time?" Suddenly a siren sounds. An air attack and evacuation plans for New York City are announced over the radio. When the reality of nuclear attack is verified, the governor reassures the citizenry: "Our enemies shall learn now to fear the eagle in its nest" (28). Damage is done, however, though it occurs safely away from Gladys's suburban retreat. The neighborhood is not safe enough, though, to avoid radioactive fallout. There follow some brief but vivid scenes at the local hospital showing glimpses of nuclear wounding—a little hairless boy, for instance, with bloody pus seeping from his bandaged arms.

From a later perspective, such sanitized versions of nuclear devastation seem as timid as the protagonist witnessing them. They are accurate prophecies, on the other hand, of the paperback teenage adventure stories later written by Gloria Miklowitz (see chapter 4). The parallel is apt, for Barbie, the Mitchells' teenager, is something of a heroine. She outshines her mother and several other adults in demonstrating intelligence, courage, and competence in a nuclear crisis. Barbie's maturity underlines her mother's fictional status as a thoroughly dependent domesticated woman, a stereotype later criticized in Betty Friedan's *The Feminine Mystique* (1963).[17] Constantly yearning for her absent husband's protection, Gladys maintains a policy of denial and silence on the nuclear realities that her daughters plainly see. As the ordeal begins, Gladys celebrates family closeness with cups of tea in the kitchen. "Later Gladys remembered it, relived every one of those minutes in the warm, bright kitchen, with both her girls trusting her, secure, mysteriously confident in her power to fix things, somehow" (40). When not weakly apathetic, she is fiercely protective of her private world, unlike two male characters, a doctor and an antiwar activist. "I never really believed any nation would *use* it this way," Gladys complains. "*We* did," the doctor replied harshly. "We used it in 1945. In Japan. Why wouldn't somebody else use it on us?" (57).

That the conventions of domestic romance outweigh candor and historical accuracy in a post-Hiroshima world emerges in the conclusion to *The Shadow on the Hearth*. By then, Merril's title is in danger of becoming *The Shattered Hearth*. Still, the family's suffering ends abruptly, almost magically, when the radio suddenly blares, "The war is over! The enemy conceded at 5:37 a.m., EST, just five minutes ago. Ladies and gentlemen, the national anthem!" (275). Husband Jon, wounded while homeward bound from the blasted city, is carried in on a stretcher. The doctor warns Gladys that "he may turn out to be another radiation case. The Geiger wouldn't show that. If he is, I'm afraid there's no hope" (277). But she is sure he suffers only shock and minor injuries. Thus, though sobered by a few explicit dialogues on fallout and radiation sickness, the book's readers are carefully consoled by this upbeat ending. "It's Jon, you know. He came home" (277) is the final note. The minor one, though, is the more guarded reflection preceding Gladys's triumphant relief: "Would anything ever be safe again?" (275).

A topical subtheme in this suburban survival romance is the author's running critique of a blindly anticommunist official who, in the midst of nuclear devastation and evacuation chaos, is more concerned with catching liberal dissenters than with effective disaster work. These scenes, though, are few. By contrast, Philip Wylie's *Tomorrow!* contains more than 200 pages of often savage satire on the political and social prejudices of the inhabitants of his two imaginary midwestern cities—leaving less than 70 pages in his best-seller for dramatizing the nuclear attack that disrupts and destroys River City and Green Prairie. Such satiric sniping, aimed at weak-kneed liberals, bellicose anticommunists, and governmental dispensers of misleading or simply inadequate civil defense pamphlets, carries over into Wylie's fictional depiction of nuclear attack. Again unlike *The Shadow on the Hearth*, *Tomorrow!* brings Hiroshima home with a graphic force unexcelled by any other 1950s fiction. One character speaks of "the Hiroshima effect," a term that, combined with other evidence of careful research, suggests the presence of Hersey's *Hiroshima* in Wylie's imagination of disaster. (Indeed, if English translation of Ōta Yoko's *City of Corpses* [1950] had not been forbidden by U.S. Army of Occupation policy, one might suspect a Japanese influence as well.) In any case, authorial approval of one character's vigorous assertion is clear: "Our nation is founded on the theory that the majority of the people, if informed, will make appropriate decisions. That, in turn, implies—it necessitates—the one freedom that underlies all others: freedom to know, intellectual liberty, the open access of all men to all truth" (105). This is the outburst of a popular novelist preaching openly and vociferously to readers and fellow citizens.

Wylie's message, until the very end, is a grim one about the price America pays for a spurious security system based on military might, official secrecy, and paper civil defense. When "Big Eddie" (ham radio operators' code for the atom bomb) arrives, national and local defense plans are suddenly disrupted. Pandemonium turns streets into mayhem and savage gridlock. One admirable character is then shown standing directly on ground zero:

> *There it is*, he thought strangely.
> It was quite long, dark, but with a flare of fire at the tail end that shone palely against the winter sky. . . .
> Then, where it had been, almost overhead by that time, a Light appeared.
> It was a Light of such intensity that Coley could see nothing except its lightness and its expanding dimensions. It swelled over the sky

above and burst down toward him. He felt, at the same time, a strange physical sensation—just a brief start of a sensation—as if gravity had vanished and he, too, were a rushing thing, and a prickling through his body, and a heat.

And he was no more. (209)

This arresting addition to American imaginal memories is one of Philip Wylie's real achievements as nuclear historian. With good reason Paul Brians later asserted, "[I]n the three decades which have passed since the publication of *Tomorrow!*, no author has equalled this description" ([1987] 42). This extraordinary accomplishment occurs in a popular satire peopled largely by stereotypical characters. Significantly, Coley, the victim here, is one of Wylie's more attractive mouthpieces. Like God's rain, the Light falls on the just and the unjust. Perhaps, too, Wylie realizes that he has spared Coley a worse fate— becoming a short-term survivor. *Tomorrow!* is thus a doubled-edged title: the day *after* is, if anything, more horrible than the day the Bomb falls on the two cities. Nothing in *The Shadow on the Hearth* comes close to the explicitness of several scenes in *Tomorrow!* of individual suffering and mass hysteria. Wylie's familiarity with the Hiroshima material imparts a verisimilitude and historical resonance to an otherwise routine topical satire. Very likely, echoes of Asano Park and Father Kleinsorge's ordeal of merciful suffering are to be felt in, for example, the wintry "bloodscape" of shivering survivors near the frozen city lake. "The earth was humanity-covered," Wylie writes, "a litter of supine men and women and children, blanketed, quilted, dressed like hobgoblins, warming fires spaced between. The snow here had turned to mud. And here the roar of the fire storm was a mumble. The earth quivered only a little." Then comes the Dantean vision's atomic age climax: "Here the night was rent by one single shriek, one voice of a myriad in agony" (254). Here, too, readers of Hersey—and later of Ibuse's *Black Rain*—will note the unmentioned contrast between this noisy American scene of mass agony and the silent deaths of the Japanese amid the ruins of their metropolis.

Despite real accomplishments of political and historical education and social criticism within the economic and literary constraints of popular fiction, *Tomorrow!*'s ending is both implausible and sentimental. It caters blatantly to the wishes and false hopes for survival and victory of Wylie's least sophisticated and most ill-informed readers. In miraculously short order, for example, one sympathetic character returns to her battered home to find "a big white printed sign nailed on the door. 'Inspected' the sign said. 'Safe for occupancy. Use extreme caution. Beware of fire' " (266). Yet even such implausible warnings are forgotten as she enters her kitchen (a woman's sacred space, as Merril also attests). Most of her canned fruits and vegetables are still "on the shelves where she'd placed them, labeled and tidy" (267).

Also more tidy than likely is the story's even more far-fetched military and political victory over the Soviets. America's surviving leaders, rejecting surrender or atomic disarmament, dispatch the nuclear-powered submarine *Nautilus* to detonate a cobalt bomb in the Baltic. This counterblow will "demolish herself, and the foe" (272). This sacrifice occurs on Christmas night. "The rays, the temperatures, vaporized Finland's Gulf in a split part of an instant. The sea's bottom was melted. The Light reached out into the Universe. Finland was not. Lithuania, Latvia, Estonia, they were not. . . . The blast kicked up the ashes that once had been Moscow, collected the burning environs, and hurled their dust at the Urals" (272). Quite improbably, radioactive dust never reaches American shores. With one stroke of the popular writer's pen, "the Light" strikes the Soviet Union into surrender, and "the last great obstacles to freedom [are] removed from the human path" (274). Survival works. A winnable war is a real possibility. These are consoling final messages that readers take away from *Tomorrow!* Wylie's ideological messages, it now seems, are as contradictory as American public opinion evidently was in the 1950s. From a more disturbing point of view, Wylie's fictitious narrative comes close to providing what Susan Sontag in "The Imagination of Disaster" (1961) would later claim is the cultural and psychic work of science fiction films, namely, to provide morally acceptable fables that give expression to the cruel and amoral feelings normally repressed in American consciousnesses.[18]

Though no extraordinary sensory experience, *Tomorrow!* as a novel conforms to some expectations that American moviegoers had also developed by the late 1950s. We do not need, however, to wait until Susan Sontag's critique seven years later for a plausible and telling criticism of Wylie's performance as popular fiction writer. In the same year *Tomorrow!* appeared, Lewis Mumford articulated in *In the Name of Sanity* (1954) an equally trenchant diagnosis of current thought and behavior. He foresaw an increasing desire by Americans to resolve their nuclear anxieties and frustrations by resorting to "a final apocalypse of violence."

> The only purpose of such a war of extermination—a war that would, at the very least, liquidate civilization—would be to relieve by action the irrational terrors and antagonisms that have brought it about. At the end of such a conflict, the savage remnants of the same peoples would face each other, and infinitely worse problems would remain to be settled. But the courage and the hope and the good will that might have been invoked to keep such a war from starting would no longer be available to bring about peace.[19]

Mumford's prediction, happily, has not yet materialized. But as a 1950s statement, it is pertinent not only to *Tomorrow!* and its author and audiences but to U.S. nuclear diplomacy and arms policy. Mumford addresses his judgment also "to one's countrymen and oneself" (4). Similarly, Wylie aims the barbs in his popular hit at Americans generally. But if the nation was indeed ripe in 1954 for "an outbreak of irrationality," as Mumford asserts, then Wylie himself is implicated in the situation as well. His conclusion seems to confirm his entrapment in what Mumford calls the "one-dimensional world of the immediate present" (4). That his story's violent revenge action appealed widely to American anti-Soviet feelings helps perhaps to account for the success of both the original and paperback editions of *Tomorrow!*, as well as that of the one-hour radio dramatization narrated by Orson Welles on 17 October 1956 (Brians [1987], 346).

By contrast with *The Shadow on the Hearth* and *Tomorrow!*, Pat Frank's 1959 contribution to this popular fiction added little to the decade's formulaic treatments of domestic nuclear disasters. *Alas Babylon*, though a best-seller, created neither intimate portraits of domestic fears nor graphic urban demonstrations of mass terror and brutality. Nevertheless, what it did offer American readers must have touched nerves and imaginations, for it was quickly turned into a successful television play on "Playhouse 90" (1960) and reappeared in 1963 as a stage production—climactic moments in the Age of Anxiety (Brians [1987], 200). Perhaps the novel's pedestrian style and its plot's implausible outcome for the residents of Fort Repose, Florida, who survive "The Day," are sufficient reasons for this success. If so, suspense was not part of the formula. In a foreword, Frank, speaking autobiographically, recalls the circumstances of creation. "What do you think would happen if the Russkies hit us when we weren't looking?" he remembers being asked. His "horseback opinion" in reply gives away his story's outline and outcome. "Oh, I think they'd kill fifty or sixty million Americans—but I think we'd win the war" (8). Two hundred and fifty pages later—pages packed with family and community survival adventures— a rescue helicopter lands in the small town. After matter-of-fact exchanges of information, the book closes with these words:

> Randy said, "Paul, there's one thing more. Who won the war?"
> Paul put his fists on his hips and his eyes narrowed. "You're kidding! You mean you really don't know?"
> "No, I don't know. Nobody knows. Nobody's told us."
> "We won it. We really clobbered 'em." Hart's eyes lowered and his arms drooped. He said, "Not that it matters."
> The engine started and Randy turned away to face the thousand-year night. (253–54)

Since nothing follows by way of amplification, readers are left with both reassurance and mysterious dread. The final phrase, though it has a portentous ring, is not anticipated by the preceding action. These pages, although often filled with journalistic summaries of nuclear destruction of American cities and airfields (most far distant from Fort Repose), dramatize the relatively easy time the chosen small-town survivors have before peace is summarily restored. Whereas Wylie captures close-up and in terrifying detail a nuclear bomb's power to level cities and recounts with savage relish the victims' often animal-like behavior in the aftermath, Frank's superficial prose blunts larger truths while dwelling on smaller, mostly transitory difficulties. "When nuclear fireballs crisped Orlando and the power plants serving Timucuan County," he writes, in a representative passage, "refrigeration stopped along with electric cooking. The oil furnaces, sparked by electricity, died. All radios were useless unless battery powered or in automobiles. Washing machines, dryers, dishwashers, fryers, toasters, roasters, vacuum cleaners, shavers, heaters, beaters—all stopped. So did the electric clocks, vibrating chairs, electric blankets, irons for pressing clothes, curlers for hair" (121). Rich opportunities for effective irony, hinted at in Frank's rhyming pairs but most trenchantly present in the contrast between "crisped" Orlando and hair curlers as symbols of American consumerism, remain unexploited. Merril, too, chooses a restricted setting safely to the side of urban destruction. Hence her female protagonists are spared direct confrontation with the mass violence that Wylie shows is the likely shape of evacuation efforts. But Gladys Mitchell's inner landscape of timidity and avoidance is evoked with considerable subtlety. All three popularizers settle for happily upbeat endings; all three preach reassuring sermons on national victory in winnable wars, with personal survival as an apparent reward for resourceful courage. All three novels, therefore, support current governmental policies and confirm dominant psychological states. Yet as Michael Strada later pointed out of these years, this military-political outlook on nuclear war, though very influential, was but one among several competing formulations of postnuclear American attitudes. While dramatizing the terrifying differences between thermonuclear and conventional weaponry, Merril, Wylie, and Frank support more than criticize the dominant ideology.[20] Hiroshima offers American audiences, therefore, only a limited model and warning. Japanese devastation now seems to afford sensationalist excitement and safe horror more than it provides a signpost to be seriously contemplated. Gunther Anders, it seems, was dead right in 1956 when he asserted, "[A] city full of dead people remains a mere word to us" (152).

If the domestication of nuclear violence is both theme and anodyne in these popular fiction treatments of the 1950s, then Martha Bartter's later generalization seems much to the point. In such fiction, at least, "we still expect to 'renew' society by surviving the 'inevitable' atomic war, rather than by changing the conditions that lead to it" (149). If survival actions and winnable war scenarios are common to real-time narratives of social relationships, are they as prevalent at the other end of the literary spectrum? Here lies a fiction at once popular and highly sophisticated, dealing in postnuclear myths, fantasies, and romances. Three of the most noted—in terms of sales, public attention, and critical discussion—of such nuclear romances are Ray Bradbury's *Martian Chronicles*, Walter M. Miller, Jr.'s *A Canticle for Leibowitz*, and Kurt Vonnegut's *Cat's Cradle*. Punctuating the Age of Anxiety from 1950 to 1963, these fictions have often been held up as typically American nuclear tales worthy of comparison with the best of foreign writings by Huxley, Orwell, Golding, Shute, and Roshwald. These works entertain by separating the historical matter of Hiroshima some distance from real-time domestic settings. More unusual still are the techniques of dream, romance, and mythic narrative that these authors use to displace the language, concepts, and ethos of probabilistic science fiction into new nuclear frontiers of the imagination. Estrangement and defamiliarization result, to a degree unseen in Merril, Wylie, or Frank but closer to the vision of J. G. Ballard's "Terminal Beach." In attempting to blend verisimilar and visionary experiences, Bradbury, Miller, and Vonnegut break down barriers between traditional science fiction and what these writers suggest instead— a New Wave nuclear fiction freed of the limitations of strict extrapolation and short-term prophesy, wedded instead to science fiction's heritage of fantasy. Breaching these walls sharpens as well as obliterates the usual antitheses: science and technology versus religion, art, and psychology; machines versus spiritual consciousness; nation-state imperatives versus individual conscience.

"SF represents the normal form of mythology in our time," declared Michel Butor in 1967.[21] Though he later revealed his ignorance of many recent texts and trends in the field, the French critic here correctly identifies the cultural work that Bradbury and company were performing for post-Christian readers disenchanted with—indeed, scared of—science and lethal technology. Sharing fictional visions of strangely different places and times, readers willing to loosen their cognitive corsets were transported into extraterrestrial, remote time or surreal environments and experiences, even as they received messages about the causes and consequences of their present ignorance and anxiety. The result of this New Wave science fiction was a sporadic but often intense and searching interrogation of nuclear policy and the future, if any, of a thermonuclear world. In this 1950s dialogue among readers, writers, critics, and political leadership, no fictional text was more frequently invoked than *The Martian Chronicles*.[22]

As earlier noted, Bradbury's novel first swam into readers' ken in short-story form. "The Million-Year Picnic" initially appeared in *Planet Stories* in the summer of 1946; "There Will Come Soft Rains" (probably the most widely reprinted nuclear tale ever written) followed in *Collier's* in May 1950. Many readers of the novel, of course, would not have read both magazines and thus could hardly have comprehended the stories' new placements in the larger narrative. "Soft Rains" (now retitled "August 2026") forms the next-to-the-last section of *Chronicles*, and "Picnic" (with a new dateline, "October 2026") closes the 1950 novel (Brians [1987], 142–43). Thus, whether—or how—Bradbury's book *is* a unified novel becomes an issue even for casual readers. Similarly problematic are the dates and chronology of the new narrative, which contains 27 sections arranged in a linear—but also obliquely circular— structure. How complete is this apparent collection of stories?

"There Will Come Soft Rains," as the penultimate image of Bradbury's mythical postnuclear world, is not Martian at all. Instead, his California is the scene, and 4–5 August 2026 the moment, of the reader's introduction to an American wastescape. Allendale, California, is evidently part of the Los Angeles urban sprawl. The suburb has not escaped devastation. Only a single middle-class house stands amid the radioactive rubble. All its occupants, except for a sore-ridden dog, are gone. Earthlings on distant Mars can, however, glimpse the condition of the planet, a dead and dangerously glowing spot in the black sky. Watching a nuclear war break out, some of the space travelers have heeded the radioed message "COME HOME." "Soft Rains" shows what they have to come home to. The entire west face of the empty house, within which machines are busily and efficiently carrying on the life of the absent owners, is "black, save for five places. Here the silhouette in paint of a man mowing a lawn. Here as in a photograph, a woman bent to pick flowers. Still farther over, their images burned on wood in one titanic instant, a small boy, hands flung into the air; higher up, the image of a thrown ball, and opposite him a girl, hands raised to catch a ball which never came down."[22] Here a Hiroshima imaginal memory (scarcely five years before in the real past, and 81 years before in the author's fictional chronology) is Americanized to arresting effect. Moreover, literarily speaking, these family figures compose an ironic postholocaust echo of Keats's Grecian urn.

Yet the Bomb has not completely stopped terrestrial life. After the day's ironic reenactment of suburban routine organized completely around work-saving machines, nature reasserts herself. In a "natural accident" prophetic of the Coke bottle in Shute's *On the Beach*, the wind pushes a tree bough through a window and fire breaks out. Machines operate in vain to stem the fiery destruction. The remote-control devices set off a frenzy of ineffectual activity by clocks, vacuum cleaner, door opener, lawn mower, record player; it is a scene (though eerily without humans) out of a Charlie Chaplin or Buster Keaton movie. What gives unity to this "scene of manic confusion" (171) is the sound of a human voice on the recording machine reciting a Sara Teasdale poem from the 1920s:

> And not one will know of the war, not one
> Will care at last when it is done.
>
> Not one would mind, neither bird nor tree,
> If mankind perished utterly. (169)

In a wry mixture of despair and hope, then, Bradbury locates his fictional creation somewhere between Sara Teasdale's post–World War I world and Hiroshima. But, perhaps to afford readers the comforting belief that nature and art can survive Allendale's apocalypse, he concludes the novel with the Martian episode of "The Million-Year Picnic." This is the last of the ironic titles, suggesting as it does the inconceivably long time a human family must survive on Mars to be able perhaps to return to Earth. "Picnic" is, under the circumstances, as ironic a term, of course, as "Million-Year." This pleasing word indicates the way Dad has enticed his family to flee with him to Mars in the family rocket. (By this point in the *Chronicles*, readers will have had to grant Bradbury his unscientific assumptions; family rockets and endless supplies of earthly resources are no less incredible than the atmosphere on Mars, which the author by fantastic fiat has made breathable.) When Dad, Mom, and the boys fare forth in this final fable, it is as if they have left Allendale for a weekend in the Mohave Desert. Setting is, in fact, symbolic throughout, for, as Ketterer and other critics point out, Bradbury's fantastic satire posits a running parallel between the gentle Martians conquered by earthlings and Native Americans treated the same by pioneer Americans (Ketterer, 31–33). Invaders have murdered the inhabitants and trashed the Martian landscape, turning their stone canals and crystal cities into dead ruins reminiscent of the deserted pueblos in Arizona and Utah. Dad does not approve or accept this imperialist history, however. He lectures the boys on its cruelties: "[T]he people got lost in a mechanical wilderness, like children making over pretty things, gadgets, helicopters, rockets. . . . Wars got bigger and bigger and finally killed Earth. That's what the silent radio means. . . . Earth is gone. Interplanetary travel won't be back for centuries, maybe never. But that way of life proved itself wrong and strangled itself with its own hands" (180).

This bitter history picks up themes from several preceding stories, notably, "June 2001—And the Moon Be Still as Bright." This parable creates and kills Jeff Spender, the first rocketeer who understands and appreciates Martian civilization. While his fellow Americans ignore or desecrate the dead cities, Spender "filled the streets with his eyes and his mind" (56). Teaching himself the Martian language, he is visited and eventually taken over in body and gun by a spirit Martian. Spender, now both man and Martian, returns to the rocket to kill his fellow invaders. But in the ensuing gunfight (reminiscent of a Western movie), Spender is himself killed. However, the captain, who has come to appreciate Spender's vision of a beautiful, peaceful civilization, at once fabulous and real, resolves to take up the dead idealist's burden: "[T]hat's it. . . . I'm Spender all over again, but I think before I shoot. I don't shoot at all, I don't kill. I do things with people" (71). In similar parables, Bradbury fleshes out his moral symbolism: humans (read: Americans in particular) are both earthlings and Martians. On the one hand, they know all that is real—that is, material, objective, amenable to scientific, practical, mechanical exploitation. On the other hand, they could be more like Spender, sensitively blending mythic religion and art with science so as to achieve an almost timeless peace with nature and each other.

Imaginative history, however, like actual American experience in the conquest of North America, records the victory of the former over the latter. In one of the mordantly satiric sequels to Spender's tragedy, Parkhill, a veteran of the Fourth Expedition who loved to shoot tops off the fragile towers of Martian cities, has settled on Mars. In "November 2005: The Off Season," he has opened a prefab hotdog stand at the intersection of a major highway leading to the rich mines of Mars. He anticipates a spate of earthling tourists and prospectors. Standing with his wife beside his shop, he exults:

> "It sure makes you humble," he said among the cooking odors of wieners, warm buns, rich butter. "Step up," he invited the various stars in the sky. "Who'll be the first to buy?"
> "Sam," said Elma.
> Earth changed in the black sky.
> It caught fire.
> Part of it seemed to come apart in a million pieces, as if a gigantic jigsaw had exploded. It burned with an unholy dripping glare for a minute, three times normal size, then dwindled.
> "What was that?" Sam looked at the green fire in the sky.
> "Earth," said Elma, holding her hands together. (143)

"We don't want to know anything. . . . We already *know* it," say the first earthmen as their "rockets burned down to civilize a beautifully dead planet" (19, 104). The double entendre of "burned down" may at first go unnoticed as a way to describe these arrogant astronauts of space in the first half-century after Hiroshima. What earthmen have yet to learn is that reality itself includes others' hallucinations and dreams as well as their own artifacts like rockets and hotdog stands, which, too, are real hallucinations. Martian ghosts know what this wider reality is, though their manipulations of Earth objects like rockets can only go so far to control them. "Go away!" screams a Martian at the rocket whose crew he has just killed. "Contaminated," he whispers. "Carried over into me. Telepathy. Hypnosis. Now *I'm* insane. Now *I'm* contaminated. Hallucinations in all their sensual forms." Only one cure remains: the Martian turns the gun on himself. After the massacre, "the rocket reclined on the little sunny hill and didn't vanish" (30).

Bradbury's rocket, unvanished by Martian imagination or will, is a metaphor of the atomic bomb. Representing the power of Earth-American belief in science and machines, it embodies the terrible ironic danger earthlings cannot understand and so cannot master: their own deadly dreams. "[W]e're kids in rompers, shouting with our play rockets and atoms, loud and alive. But one day Earth will be as Mars is today" (55). Hence *The Martian Chronicles* dramatizes in myriad repetitions of image, word, and action the deepest dilemma its author sees for the post-Hiroshima globe in whose near-term future lay Sputnik and the first astronaut walking on the moon. "The amazing dream of reality" (43), projected by scientific beings in the ultimate shape of a bomb, explodes Earth at the moment Earth discovers and destroys Mars. The two imaginary planets thus personify the lethal possibilities and noble ideals of humanity. But Bradbury refuses to console readers of his romance by making the superior Martians survive. Though they represent idealized dreams of gentleness and beauty, his Martians can be killed by the equally "real" guns and rockets of the boisterous boys from Earth.

As perhaps the last escapees from Earth's holocaust, the picnickers at first seem to represent hope. The father's idealism has energized their escape; perhaps it will model a new start. Yet there are disturbing counterhints. One son's trusting hand on his father's arm feels "like a young tarantula." Another ominous sign is the same son's wondering efforts to grasp his father's altruism. "Timothy hadn't quite figured out what was ticking inside the vast adult mechanism beside him" (173). The mechanical trope, it seems clear, is the child's "natural" earthling idiom. This renders the postholocaust parable of a Martian Swiss Family Robinson ironic to the end. The seeds of imbalance and conflict between material science, idealist philosophy, and man's animal nature are already planted in Timothy's mechanistic metaphors of mind. *The Martian Chronicles*, then, is indeed a very different survival story from the earthlier ones of Merril, Wylie, and Frank.

Bradbury's book was a quick and steady success with two generations of readers. It struck responsive chords, too, with later writers, inspiring some to explore, through the forms and conventions of nuclear romance or fable, the ambiguous mixture of nightmare, desire, and brute scientific fact constituting post-Hiroshima reality. Like Bradbury, other writers made demands on their audiences' capacities to grasp perplexity and contradiction. Thus the apparently confusing chronology of the *Chronicles*, involving multiple holocausts at different dates in the sequence of stories—or conversely, the same holocaust taking place at different times—models a common task for New Wave fiction writers: to lead readers into familiarity with a fantastic world that may become true (that is, vanish) at a moment's push of a button. Counterfactual romance, then, infuses, disorients, and enriches the pseudoempiricism of traditional science fiction and popular fiction in the social realist mode.

The surreal time frame of Bradbury's narrative, in which 27 years in the twenty-first century can balloon into a million years, opened a fresh vista in 1950s fantasy-history, of which Walter M. Miller, Jr.'s *A Canticle for Leibowitz* became in 1959 the next "classic" example. Miller's romance extends Bradburyian time greatly in both directions: backward a thousand years into an imaginary dark ages, several thousand years forward into a science fiction world of spaceships and interplanetary escape. *A Canticle* thereby makes new demands on readers' attention and assent. It embodies a temporal, spatial, social, and spiritual fantasy made explicitly meaningful through the lives and mouths of a dozen or more representative characters. If *The Martian Chronicles* is an imaginative jigsaw exploding, like the stricken Earth, into 26 little pieces around the reader's inner ear, Miller's narrative sticks closer to nuclear epic. It is an intricately interconnected saga of pilgrims, warriors, mutants, and other victims and survivors.

Nearly twice as long as its predecessor, *A Canticle* also appeared serially as stories, in the *Magazine of Fantasy and Science Fiction* of April 1955,

August 1956, and February 1957 (Brians [1987], 260–61). The novel finally
published in 1959 reflects this history in its three long subsections, "Fiat Homo,"
"Fiat Lux," and "Fiat Voluntas Tuas." Miller's novel was adapted for the stage
in 1967 and for radio broadcast in 1983. If a Hugo Award in 1959 as the
outstanding science fiction of that year signaled the esteem of the SF community, the book's steady sales—more than a million copies sold by 1980—as
well as foreign translations and adaptations, testify to its broad reach and its
effect on literate America. With critics as well, this religious parable has won
abiding admiration, though some more severe judgments. In 1974, for instance,
David Ketterer called it "the most effective postcatastrophe story" in print at
that time (140). Subsequently, Robert Scholes and Eric Rabkin in 1977 praised
A Canticle, terming it "probably the finest work of religious science fiction
presently in the canon" (50). Darko Suvin, however, though admitting Miller
had opened the field to many new kinds of science fiction readers, condemns
Miller's heavy religious emphasis, one pushed well beyond historically plausible material toward explicit authorial endorsement of myth and ideology. This,
Suvin maintains, is counterscientific and counter-SF.[23]

In fact, Suvin's two critiques are closely related. As Mark Rose noted, *A
Canticle*'s appeal, especially during the 1960s, has been to readers caught
in contemporary postnuclear conflicts between scientific, technological, and
military priorities and policies and religious, antimilitarist, anti-imperialist protests (111–12). These cultural contradictions were raised, and debates often
raged, in the arena of the popular arts as well as more "serious" fiction. Films
like *Fail-Safe, Dr. Strangelove*, and *2001: A Space Odyssey* (1968) illustrate
popular uses of "realistic" representation, black humor, and postnuclear fantasy in waging such ideological warfare. Miller's book has always been prized
for being in the middle of this cultural dialogue, and through its patterns,
themes, and tropes, it still contributes imaginative fuel to the fires.

What is at once evident is that *A Canticle for Leibowitz* attacks 1950s
issues by postponing reenactment of Hiroshima until the final 10 pages of a
320-page story. As the last thermonuclear bomb falls upon the Abbey of the
Albertian Order of Leibowitz, its abbot, Dom Jethrah Zerchi, is pinned beneath
the masonry of its chapel. The monastery walls, symbolizing its social role,
have stood—changed but never obliterated—since the book's opening pages.
Zerchi is but the latest in a line of "memorizers and bookleggers" among the
spiritual leaders of the Catholic community whose historical function has been
to survive the Flame Deluge, Lucifer, and the demon Fallout.[24] The point of the
monks' tenacity is to preserve certain written records, called the "Memorabilia," of "a great and wise civilization" that, centuries before, destroyed itself.
The story of Zerchi's death occurs long after the novel's first episode; both take
place in the remote American Southwest. No major nuclear novel or short
story has imagined a broader time frame within which to dramatize nuclear
holocaust and survival.

Miller imagines, moreover, each stage or age in plausible historical terms.

In the first section, "Fiat Homo," for instance, the monastery residents and their language, way of life, and religious horizons recapture the ethos of the early Middle Ages in Western Europe. The simple piety and superstitious ignorance of the postulant Brother Francis Gerard of Utah is depicted with gentle authorial humor. Miller eschews the savage satire of Wylie, Bradbury, and Vonnegut. Though Brother Francis never understands the significance (either literal or symbolic) of the underground ruins of a fallout shelter in the desert of his pious retreat, he nevertheless becomes the savior of important relics of a long-defunct civilization—ours. These identify one of its obscure members, I. E. Leibowitz, a Jewish-American engineer, now become the unlikely patron saint of the Albertian Order.

The common elements and internal divisions of the spiritual-humanistic tradition are personified in the two religious men, both found amid masonry ruins, in the opening and closing episodes. The later victim, the wiser, more sophisticated Abbot Zerchi, understands, as Brother Francis does not, what their common fate means. Zerchi voices a very modern despair. "Listen, are we helpless? Are we doomed to do it again and again and again? Have we no choice but to play the Phoenix, in an unending sequence of rise and fall? Assyria, Babylon, Egypt, Greece, Carthage, Rome, the Empires of Charlemagne and the Turk. Ground to dust and plowed with salt. Spain, France, Britain, America—burned into the oblivion of the centuries. And again and again and again" (255). Brother Francis is represented just as aptly by the quaintly pious language of the Church's official version of holocaust, as read at refectory mealtime:

> And the prince smote the cities of his enemies with the new fire, and for three days and nights did his great catapults and metal birds rain wrath upon them. Over each city a sun appeared and was brighter than the sun of heaven, and immediately that city withered and melted as wax under the torch, and the people thereof did stop in the streets and their skins smoked and they became as fagots thrown on the coals. And when the fury of the sun had faded, the city was in flames; and a great thunder came out of the sky, like the great battering-ram PIK-A-DON, to crush it utterly. (180–81)

These two versions of secular history imply, at different levels, the persistence and witness of the Catholic faith throughout the rise and fall of human violence. A third, even more ancient figure in *A Canticle* is present at each paradigmatic moment. He goes by several names: Benjamin, the Wandering Jew, Lazar, Israel. Somewhat like the black obelisk in *2001: A Space Odyssey*, he is a recurrent symbol, a reminder of an older tradition whose prophets continually search the present for a future Messiah. Benjamin sides neither with the abbot and his fellow faithful nor with their secular opponent, the philosopher-scientist Thon Taddeo. Whether he will turn up aboard the spaceship bearing Brother Joshua and the band of Christian survivors to Alpha Centauri remains an unanswered question as the last nuclear holocaust falls, like Lucifer, upon mankind.

Unresolved, too, are other metaphysical and moral issues raised in the confrontations between religious and secular belief systems and spokesmen. One arena of struggle is the Albertian monastery library, sanctuary of the "Memorabilia" but also the laboratory in which, at one point, Brother Kornhoer, the order's amateur inventor, has installed a rudimentary wood-and-wire dynamo. Powered by novices' arms and legs on bicycles (a touch reminiscent of Mark Twain's *Connecticut Yankee in King Arthur's Court* [1889]), the crude machine produces "electrical essences" powering a few guttering arc lights. These strange lights shine next to the traditional candles representing "lux" to the rest of the scholarly community of manuscript copiers and librarians. When Thon Taddeo arrives to assess the "Memorabilia," he is astonished to find this practical invention—one that is "a standing broad-jump across about twenty years of preliminary experimentation, starting with an understanding of the principles" (193). After the thon explains the long-range implications of the arc lights, the abbot orders their dismantling. He and the order will have nothing to do with the advent of what the thon calls Truth, an advance sure to be marked "by violence and upheaval, by flame and by fury, for no change comes calmly over the world" (206).

This imaginary debate has clear resonances for 1950s and 1960s readers familiar with then-current discussions, by clergymen at seminaries, by physicists at Los Alamos, in the pages of the *Bulletin of Atomic Scientists*. "[Y]ou promise to begin restoring Man's control over Nature," the abbot asserts. "But who will govern the use of the power to control natural forces?" To which the arrogant thon retorts, with heavy sarcasm: "Keep science cloistered, don't try to apply it, don't try to do anything about it until men are holy. Well, it won't work. You've been doing it here in the abbey for generations" (215). Patently, the interactions of "homo" and "lux" carry entirely different meanings for the actors in this postmodern morality play, of which "Fiat Lux" is the second act.

In the third and final act, "Fiat Voluntas Tuas," Zerchi and his ancient community face Lucifer in the same desert where his ancestors did centuries before. "Generation, regeneration, again, again, as in a ritual, with blood-stained vestments and nail-torn hands, children of Merlin, chasing a gleam" (236), whispers the Christian apologist upon hearing that "Lucifer has fallen" again. But now his Bomb-threatened monastery has become a vastly different place. A superhighway bisects the grounds with automated vehicles gliding beside the abbey's chapel and library. When Lucifer falls, the Exposure Survey Team is located in the new glass and aluminum building. Its spokesman, Dr. Cors, is prepared to decide which victims will be treated, and which sent to the Eucrem (the euthanasia crematorium). "Radiation sickness. Flash burns. The woman has a broken hip. The father's dead. The filings in the woman's teeth are radioactive. The child almost glows in the dark. Vomiting shortly after the blast" (293). The priest, though, resists. Visiting a stricken mother and child, he offers the former a rosary and counsels her to refuse the red ticket to voluntary death. "Voluntas tuas" has very different meanings, though, for the dying woman and the priest. When the woman steps from the car to enter Mercy Camp No. 18, Zerchi wrestles briefly with the doctor to prevent her action. Present-day readers cannot fail to recall scenes not unlike this outside abortion clinics. On the other hand, they cannot recall any such science-religion faceoffs in *Hiroshima*, where Father Kleinsorge, a Roman Catholic priest, is an actor and spokesman.

But the battle between religion and medicine outside Mercy Camp No. 18 is not the final showdown in *A Canticle for Leibowitz*. Miller's relatively evenhanded depiction of the rival camps and value systems is strained to the utmost as the Bomb falls and Abbot Zerchi encounters his most perplexing moral and spiritual dilemma. It is embodied in Mrs. Grales. She is "the bicephalous old tomato woman" (252) who peddles vegetables at the abbey and begs its abbot to baptize the second head, which lolls (apparently comatose) on her shoulder. The monks refuse to accept that "Rachel" is another soul, though Zerchi is not so sure. "How many souls has an old lady with an extra head?" (262). To which Brother Joshua replies, "Rachel. She smiled. I thought she was going to wake up." When Mrs. Grales appears to make confession for her "naughties," the abbot, too, sees Rachel smile. At this moment, the Bomb explodes. Pinned in the rubble, the priest ponders this latest manifestation of Original Sin. Then—perhaps in delirium—he sees Mrs. Grales and Rachel seated amid the ruins, on which vultures already perch. While the old woman's face turns gray in coma, Rachel seems alive and reaching out to him. He struggles to crawl to her to baptize her. In turn, Rachel hands him a wafer from the ciborium and murmurs "love" to the dying cleric. "The image of those cool green eyes lingered with him as long as life. . . . He had seen primal innocence in those eyes, and a promise of resurrection. One glimpse had been a bounty, and he wept in gratitude. . . . Afterwards he lay with his face in the wet dirt and waited" (318).

This ends, almost, the postholocaust myth, or the pseudomyth that Suvin objects to as claiming for itself more than subjective or "historical" validity. Indeed, it is clear well before this point that Miller's narrator occupies a space closer to the religious characters than to the skeptical or secular actors. Such partiality persists to the coda. Making their escape in the starship, Brother Joshua and the others "sang as they lifted the children into the ship. . . . They sang heartily to dispel the fright of the little ones. When the horizon erupted, the singing stopped. . . . The last monk, upon entering, paused in the lock. He stood in the open hatchway and took off his sandals. '*Sic transit mundus*,' he murmured, looking back at the glow. . . . There came a blur, a glare of light, a high thin whining sound, and the starship thrust itself heavenward" (319). Though some present-day readers may wonder if a version of "the Rapture" that fundamentalist Christians believe will be God's deliverance of the redeemed from earthly damnation is here symbolized, Miller gives no hint that this is his intention. In fact, the succeeding image undercuts any such assumption. Even though a Catholic monk has just shepherded his flock to apparent safety in space, the very last image of life on the blasted postholocaust planet takes Miller's readers back to still another beach. "A wind came across the ocean, sweeping with it a pall of fine white ash," he writes. "The ash fell into the sea and into the breakers. The breakers washed dead shrimp ashore with the driftwood. Then they washed up the whiting. The shark swam out to his deepest waters and brooded in the cold clean currents. He was very hungry that season" (320). Like the buzzards in previous ages and episodes, the shark is anthropomorphized just enough by the words *his* and *brooded* so as to keep alive, perhaps, some hope in survival and some sort of evolutionary reenactment of consciousness over the millenia that both science and religion allow to human history. If so, a shark promises notably less of the green-eyed innocence of Rachel or the solicitous leadership of Brother Joshua without his radioactive sandals than it augurs the continuity of rapacious violence in the human animal.

Since the 1950s, *A Canticle for Leibowitz* and *The Martian Chronicles* have attracted newer readers of both science and mainstream fiction, and this continuing popularity reveals a steady demand for education and consolation as well as entertainment and escape. In such transactions, large doses of satiric invective, as in Wylie, Bradbury, and (more gently) Miller, have been tolerated, even welcomed. Real-time events and issues could not, however, be distanced as readily as could remote-time, alien, or other fantastic stories. In 1962 and 1963, for instance, the Cuban Missile Crisis added fresh levels of anxiety to memories already beset by images of Hiroshima, Nagasaki, Bikini, and Sputnik. The real devastation of American cities and society became a live possibility. Into this context of renewed and widespread fear, exacerbated by new scientific disclosures about thermonuclear warfare, came another striking expression of the nuclear imagination. Kurt Vonnegut's *Cat's Cradle* (1963) joined films like *Dr. Strangelove* and fictions like Robert Heinlein's *Strangers in a Strange Land* in capturing the admiration of a new generation of readers, especially those in the counterculture. Vonnegut spoke to and for an audience of concerned American *hibakusha*, some of whom, by the late 1960s, were learning from Robert Jay Lifton that they were indeed *hibakusha*.

In *Cat's Cradle*, both older and newer aficionados of science fiction encountered many of the themes, images, ideas, and emotions previously expressed by Bradbury, Shute, Golding, Miller, and Roshwald. But filtered through Vonnegut's antic imagination, these familiar elements—travel to strange places; an indeterminate future time frame; the mad scientist and conflict between science and religion, between empiricism and mythic transcendence; the child as victim and witness—were recombined in a disturbingly comic construct. It took familiarity with black humor, magical surrealism, and horror films to equip some 1960s audiences with the right handles for grasping Vonnegut's matter and manner as postnuclear fabulist. Even today, readers can find this author's send-up of conventional social, moral, and metaphysical truths to be both frustrating and exhilarating. Nonetheless, fabulist satire proves, in Vonnegut's case, a memorable source of cultural insight.

Setting up too rigid a schema for deconstructing *Cat's Cradle* is, however, sure to distort as well as clarify understanding. Negative truth, deliberate contradiction, and, above all, radical playfulness are essential modes of postmodern communication and meaning for Vonnegut. These approaches are all grounded in the book's title. Cat's cradle, a hand game with string enjoyed for centuries by children and adults, is the first metaphoric string to be unraveled. Other strings besides the string game itself are, first, the historical reality of the atomic bomb; then the confrontation of the science-technology responsible for Hiroshima with Bokononism, a made-up religion of the inhabitants of San Lorenzo, an imaginary Caribbean island nation; next, the various members of the Hoenikker family, chief of whom is Dr. Felix Hoenikker, "the father of the atomic bomb" and inveterate game-player; and finally, perhaps, the metaphor of writing this book by its narrator, whose first name is alternately John and Jonah but whose surname (never actually revealed in the text) was originally Vonnegut.

A cat's cradle appears first in the mouth of Newton Hoenikker, the scarcely four-foot-tall son of his distant physicist father, who one day suddenly tries to play a game of cat's cradle. Frightened by his father's austere demeanor and inexplicable game, Newt runs away, shrieking "no cat . . . no cradle." Later on in San Lorenzo, Newt paints a picture of a cat's cradle, one the narrator calls "small and black and warty. . . . The scratches formed a sort of spider's web, and I wondered if they might not be the sticky nets of human futility hung up on a moonless night to dry."[25] Though John/Jonah's own pessimism is here piled on Newt's, the picture's wider symbolism is plain: it represents all sorts of unloving, indecipherable communication between people, as well as a small son's special need for a caregiving father as "cradle" against life's mysterious disappointments.

Playing inappropriate and scary games, it soon appears, is Dr. Hoenikker's hallmark as both man and scientist. His work on the atomic bomb was affected by being interrupted by his latest pastime in the lab, studying turtles. "Father never said a word about the disappearance of the turtles," his daughter Angela recalls. "He just came to work the next day and looked for things to play with and think about, and everything there was to play with and think about had something to do with the bomb." Failing to connect her father's penchant for play with the destruction of two Japanese cities, Angela, an adoring daughter, slaps little Newt when he calls their father "ugly." "How dare you say that about your father? . . . He's one of the greatest men who ever lived! He won the war today" (20). Not surprisingly, this family spat took place on 6 August

1945. Another clue to amoral innocence is Hoenikker's remark at Alamogordo to a fellow scientist watching the first bomb test. "Science has now known sin," the other remarks. "What is sin?" Hoenikker replies (21).

As literary signal, the cat's cradle also represents the activity and result of investigating postnuclear reality via imagination, fantasy, myth, or comic reversal of everyday expectations. A snarl or skein of strings intricately and mysteriously made is seen in the narrative's structure. Even more fragmented than *The Martian Chronicles, Cat's Cradle* consists of 127 chapter pieces. Some only a few paragraphs long, all carry titles that often are more puzzling than explanatory. Internally, too, each chapter breaks into discrete miniscenes, broken dialogues, and pseudoclimaxes. The result, from one angle, is a string game; from another, it is a fissionable form, a verbal bomb containing finally the end of the world fomented in its narrator's overworked imagination.

The novel's apocalypse occurs, symbolically enough for 1963, on a Caribbean island not far from Cuba. In a microcosm of the post–World War II world, here lives a postcolonial black population sunk in desperate poverty and ruled by the despotic General "Papa" Monzano. What cushions, if not redeems, life on the bitter edge are two "dreams" these islanders cling to. One is Mona Monzano, the perfectly beautiful adopted daughter of the dictator. Every man who sees Mona falls in love with her, imagines her as muse, mistress, or madonna. What guides the dark beauty to reciprocate love is her devotion to the second dream. Bokononism is the pseudoreligion created by a cynical castaway who becomes the holy man in the jungle, San Lorenzo's fugitive saint. Officially banned by Papa Monzano, Bokononism is secretly believed by everyone, including Mona and, eventually, John/Jonah. It is, of course, another cat's cradle, a man-made game of images and ideas collected in *The Books of Bokonon*. Quotations from the *Books*, in the musical mode of calypso lyrics, dot the narrative, highlighting or undercutting the moral or metaphysical assertions of the characters, both indigenous and foreign (American).

Bokononism is, quite openly, a construct of lies or *foma* that provides believers with magical explanations of, and escape from, reality. By God's decree, each convert becomes a member of a secret *karass* or hidden network of people, events, and things. Centered in one or two foci or *wampeters*, each karass becomes the object of its members' lifelong search. Meanwhile, all Bokononists practice love by pressing the soles of their feet together; this is *boko-maru*. Complicating Bokononist belief and behavior is a false form of karass called a *granfalloon*. This is a temporary, rigid, unsatisfying pseudoconnection, examples of which are Hoosiers, the Communist party, General Electric, the Boy Scouts, and the United States of America. "Anyone unable to understand how a useful religion can be founded on lies will not understand this book either," the narrator warns at the outset (14).

Religion of the foma sort is harmless, while science, although another skein of lies people believe in and practice, is not harmless. As Papa remarks on his deathbed, "[S]cience is magic that *works*" (147). His dramatic death underscores his declaration. It is caused by another of Dr. Hoenikker's "inno-cent" inventions. *Ice-nine* (a name whose homonym is *asinine*) is a magical substance that proves to be the wampeter of the narrator's karass, as it is for others in the story. It was invented to meet the request of a Marine Corps general anxious to solve the leathernecks' perennial problem in the field—mud. Hoenikker creates a substance that causes mud and all other watery matter to freeze, instantly and at nearly normal temperatures. Taken internally, ice-nine freezes the ingestor at once. Brought in contact with a body of water like the Caribbean, ice-nine soon turns the world's oceans to ice. In effect, Vonnegut in 1963 imagined an ultimate form of instant and endless nuclear winter. For the earth's atmosphere is also affected in chain reaction, producing wholesale death more quickly than the slow-moving radioactive winds in Shute's *On the Beach*.

How Hoenikker's lethal invention has reached San Lorenzo and triggers its destruction is part of Vonnegut's cat's cradle plot. The scientist, before touching ice-nine to his own lips, bequeathes equal parts of the sovereign poison to his three children. Newton bargains his third for the love of a midget ballet dancer from the Ukraine who proves to be a Soviet spy. Angela shares hers with a midwestern manufacturer who deals with the Pentagon. Frank Hoenikker, schoolboy loner and self-styled X-9 spy, bargains his share to become Papa Monzano's righthand man. It is Frank's portion that freezes the ocean. Thus Vonnegut's black humor plot has a realpolitik base. He has ar-ranged for the United States, the Soviet Union, and a small Third World nation to possess an equivalent of *Dr. Strangelove*'s Doomsday Machine. And the Third World Caribbean country accomplishes what the Cuban Missile Crisis barely failed to do.

Still another string in the snarled symmetry of *Cat's Cradle* is its marked literariness—the story's artifice as verbal sleight-of-hand. In addition to the fictional features of chaptering, imagery, zany ideas, and representative charac-ter types, Vonnegut's book keeps literate readers aware of echoes of other, less madcap authors and their ostensibly more trustworthy classics. The string of allusions starts with the opening sentence, "Call me Jonah." Melville's narrator, Ishmael, and *Moby-Dick* (1851), American literature's archetypal tale of human obsession, are evoked in a post-Hiroshima cataclysm exponentially grander, but no less symbolic, than the sinking of the *Pequod*. In the same spirit, the destruction of Papa's castle, which begins with a crack in the wall and ends with the edifice sliding into the sea, is a modern repetition of Poe's "Fall of the House of Usher" (1839). This literary joke is, in fact, doubled. For the castle climax also echoes Ray Bradbury's chapter "April 2005: Usher II" in *The Martian Chronicles*. Other literary allusions extend to American poets, including, most obviously, Frost's "Fire and Ice" (1923) but also Edgar Lee Masters's graveyard satire on war and religion in the *Spoon River Anthology* (1916).[26] Vonnegut so clearly shares with all these writers a fascination with apocalypse and death as imaginative and moral terrain that his remark to an interviewer, "I feel I have techniques enough to do what I want without ransacking the past," must be another piece of characteristic foma.[27] One of this satirist's battery of techniques is patently quoting from venerated voices of past American literature. Besides being the funniest novel or story treated in this chapter, *Cat's Cradle* is arguably the most literary. Its deadly seriocomic send-up of death and devastation in the Age of Anxiety also summons the comic/tragic/satiric/romantic visions of a number of revered mainstream ancestors. Whether younger colleagues—writing in the late 1970s and 1980s and also dealing with the legacy of Hiroshima and the anxieties of the Cuban Missile Crisis—look to Vonnegut for inspiration as he looks to his own chosen ancestral figures, is a question for the next chapter.

In all likelihood, however, Vonnegut's comic and satiric moral vision of nuclear disaster will prove sui generis. Though often linked to the black humor classics of the decade—particularly Joseph Heller's *Catch-22* (1961) and Stanley Kubrick's *Dr. Strangelove*—*Cat's Cradle* did not fit the more serious mood of the Reagan era. Certainly, the conclusions of Tim O'Brien's *The Nuclear Age* (1985) or Carolyn See's *Golden Days* (1987) (both of which are survival stories, which Vonnegut's, technically speaking, is not) are both soberer and more optimistic in tone and content than this stoical comedy. Vonnegut's story, for one thing, has a double ending. The first is simply ironic, for it mocks all survival stories of the atomic age. After ice-nine has turned the sea and island to deadly blue ice, the black population assembles in a valley where, upon the advice of Bokonon, they all ingest some of the poison. Even the beauteous goddess Mona touches her lips to the ice and dies with her people. As this mass suicide takes place, the small group of American characters remains, and for a time, they even thrive on frozen food. The narrator is one of their number. Another is the empty-headed Hoosier wife of a businessman. She knows John/Jonah has been writing a book on Hiroshima and holocaust. "How's the writing going?" she inquires breezily in the midst of death. "Fine, Mom, just fine," he replies. "Is it a funny book?" "I hope so, Mom." To which she remarks, "I like a good laugh" (185).

Bokonon, who has survived the mass suicide of his followers, speaks a farewell to his fellow writer in a different voice from Mom's.

> "I am thinking, young man, about the final sentence for *The Books of Bokonon*. The time for the final sentence has come."
> "Any luck? "
> He shrugged and handed me a piece of paper.
> This is what I read:
> "If I were a younger man I would write a history of human stupidity; and I would climb to the top of Mount McCabe and lie down on my back with my history for a pillow; and I would take from the ground some of the blue-white poison that makes statues of men; and I would make a statue of myself, lying on my back, grinning horribly, and thumbing my nose at You Know Who." (191)

Though neither John/Jonah nor Bokonon follows this advice, the image of statue-making man as artist and historian addressing his God is an appropriate apocalyptic gesture, though it marks no real ending to this story, the successor to the one Vonnegut's mouthpiece originally intended to write. That was to be called *The Day the World Ended,* and it was to be about 6 August 1945. This narrator, as Daniel Zins points out, is Vonnegut's 1960s notion of an archetypal post-Hiroshima artist—a "drug salesman" and maker of better foma.[28]

3

Fictions and America's Reawakening, 1979–1992

IN *NUCLEAR FEAR*, SPENCER WEART, LOOKING BACK FROM 1988, nicely summarizes the cultural and psychic history of the era of "enchanted peace," as he terms the years 1964–79, and the decade of renewed alarm and activity that followed. He highlights the ironic contrast (and indirect interconnections) between persistent private indifference and avoidance and equally persistent pursuit of the arms race and MAD by government, industry, and the military. Beneath the public's apparent acquiescence, he argues, still ran strong undercurrents of dread at continuing possibilities of nuclear warfare and devastation. These fears, fanned once by the Cuban Missile Crisis, were calmed for some but exacerbated for others by U.S. inaction on the SALT treaties (strategic arms limitations talks) and, more dramatically, by President Reagan's famous March 1983 speech urging a new nuclear defense policy that was immediately dubbed "Star Wars." Anxiety also simmered or boiled in response to new information from unofficial records. By 1977 the United States possessed some 7,000 nuclear bombs on intercontinental missiles and some 2,000 more on aircraft. By the mid-1980s the Reagan administration's emphasis on closing so-called windows of vulnerability had produced what some saw as even grimmer figures (though others may have found them reassuring): 37,000 warheads were now said to be in American arsenals, and only some 17,000 were thought to be deployed by the Soviets (Weart, 376–77).

During these tense years a new danger surfaced, or at least dramatically increased. Nuclear reactors in power plants across the country had for some years been the target of protest groups. But in the wake of three historic toxic accidents—Three Mile Island (1979), Bhopal (1984), and Chernobyl (1986)—national and international attention fixed on radioactive emissions by other sources besides MIRV missiles or thermonuclear bombs. These widely publicized disasters and near-disasters rearoused the activist cadre of the American populace, including new and older members of SANE, Friends of the Earth, the Union of Concerned Scientists, and Physicians for Social Responsibility, among others. Although Helen Caldicott was probably right to assert that "when compared to the threat of nuclear war, the nuclear power controversy shrinks to paltry dimensions" (Weart, 376), it remained true that the general hypertrophy of nuclear power, worldwide as weaponry and locally as nuclear power plants often sited perilously near major population centers, dismayed many and galvanized others to join the nuclear freeze movement. One notable event was the New York City peace march of 1983, said to be the largest such demonstration to date in our history. Americans of different generations, classes, races, and regions joined to question and contest the direction and force of nuclear policies.

As earlier, there would be ups and downs in such barometers of public attention and engagement. Yet the events of these six or eight years coincided with a remarkably steady outpouring of new works of imagination and analysis by younger writers and artists. These books, movies, magazine stories, newspaper articles, television documentaries, as well as paintings, poems, plays, and musical compositions, record as they simultaneously interpret and criticize the historical developments of the later nuclear age. Furthermore, these years saw the publication of a significant body of criticism dealing with the past decades' nuclear literature and culture. Of course, it cannot be definitively shown that either artistic or critical representations caused or directly influenced public policy. In some instances, though, historical and social circumstances did affect the writing and reception of specific texts. Furthermore, focusing on literary history may do more than help detect changes in artistic subject matter and stylistic innovations. These also carry forward (as well as alter or reinforce) shared attitudes and imagery from previous nuclear works. Thus a short story published in 1982, "The Brahms Lullaby" by Nicholas von Hoffman, recapitulates and updates Merril's *Shadow on the Hearth* of 1950.[1] At the same time, it interacts with a readership narrower, more sophisticated, and, of course, younger than Merril's, a readership with a new set of social expectations.

More broadly, the survivalist adventure story as variously exemplified by Frank's *Alas Babylon* and Miller's *A Canticle for Leibowitz* was repeatedly rewritten for new 1980s readers who possessed perhaps little or no memory of Hiroshima images and feelings. I shall here look at a representative example of such popular fiction, Kim Stanley Robinson's *The Wild Shore* (1984), in order to identify certain fresh and familiar features of a postholocaust adventure tale with a youthful protagonist. As in the previous chapters, I shall continue to speculate on the cultural work that narratives like Robinson's perform for which sorts of readers and critics—and, in some cases, still perform for 1990s audiences.

In this critique, the recent growth of science fiction as a distinct genre *and* an increasingly indistinguishable part of general American fiction comes prominently into play. New Wave fiction, combining probabilistic, science- and technology-oriented fables with more metaphoric, mythological, and psychological experiments, is again evident, especially in short stories. H. Bruce Franklin specifically cites stories as indices of this evolving pattern. "Neither the achievements at the negotiating tables nor the awesome new arsenals appear to have had a dramatic impact on American consciousness during the years from around 1965 to 1979," he declares. "After the post-Sputnik burst of fiction and film that climaxed in *Dr. Strangelove* and other works released in 1964, this period was marked by surprisingly little explicit cultural concern with nuclear weapons. As in the years before Sputnik, cultural activity overtly dealing with the nuclear threat receded into its original home in science fiction" (193). Franklin then identifies a new group of short-story writers—including Harlan Ellison, Kate Wilhelm, Philip K. Dick, Norman Spinrad, and Joe Haldeman—"for whom the bomb was a hideous totem in their bleak vision of America" (194). Though he mentions stories that originally appeared during the silent years and were reprinted in the 1980s, Franklin discusses none in detail. Several that deserve a closer look, both for their imaginative impact and wide availability, include Ellison's two tours de force, "I Have No Mouth, and I Must Scream" (1967) and "A Boy and His Dog" (1969), Spinrad's "Big Flash" (1969), and von Hoffman's "Brahms Lullaby."[2] These authors anticipate themes and techniques later employed in full-length fictions like Robinson's. As a group, these novelists, and others like Tim O'Brien, Don DeLillo, Denis Johnson, and Carolyn See, exemplify the crossover novel as a continuing option and opportunity.

"Science fiction has become our reality," Eric Rabkin observes of this situation. "Many things have made this so: our common fear of instant nuclear death, our common subjection to environmental hazard, our common participation in the communications revolution." Then the critic generalizes even more broadly. "The obvious problems of our world are consequences, at least in part, of science, and everyone now knows this; the solutions, if any there will be, will use science, and increasingly people know this too. The so-called mainstream of fiction has quite simply accepted writers of science fiction. . . . [T]he boundaries have become vague and the works mix."[3]

In these works, society's investment in science and technology as prime institutions and values becomes a loaded and debatable issue. As Weart, Franklin, and others emphasize, challenges to science—whether in the name of religion, art, nature, or environmentalism—proliferated and sharpened in the 1980s as at no time since the immediate post-Hiroshima years. One urgent question, therefore, recurs: if not rational science and practical technology, what alternative institutions and value systems ought to command American allegiances in the postnuclear, postmodern culture? In fiction, as in philosophy and politics, debates over reason versus intuition, nature versus society, fact versus image, domination versus rapprochement, are dramatized in both preholocaust and survivalist stories. As traditional science fiction contributed possible fantasies about men and their often magical machines, so mainstream or crossover fictions created other fables, more surreal than probabilistic, relying on figurative language and dream moods and inventing mythic actions and characters. This range of options grew even wider as *Dr. Strangelove* and *Cat's Cradle* showed more readers and younger writers the political values of black humor and fabulist satire. Distinct didactic patterns emerged. At one extreme lay the macho militarism and violence of Robert A. Heinlein; at the opposite pole were the futuristic nature tales of Ursula LeGuin and Vonda McIntyre. The latter led the way toward what Millicent Lenz in 1990 called a "biophile's vision of alternative *willed* futures."[4] Lenz argues that through humanistic and ecological commitments, "nuclear-catastrophe narratives have the emotive power to fill readers with the conviction that the irreplacable, beloved planet Earth and every cherished thing upon it must be spared destruction—not only spared destruction, but nurtured and reverenced" (261). This hopeful, humanistic environmentalism gathered literary supporters during the decade, though it was strenuously opposed in other narratives with sterner, more violent views of human nature and apparent penchants for domination and death. The ongoing tensions between biophilic and necrophilic visions are examined in the section that follows on stories by Ellison, Spinrad, von Hoffman, and others.

Where the very opposed visions of Vonda McIntyre of *Dreamsnake* (1978) and Robert A. Heinlein of *Expanded Universe* could conceivably meet is on the high ground that Frederik Pohl identifies in a 1984 remark. "Science fiction is the name given to a lot of old pulp magazines, some thousands of books, a handful of blockbuster movies and television programs and scores of trashy ones—and a way of life," he began. Then, dilating even more magisterially, he continued: "[W]hat science fiction is about is change, and change is the central fact of life for all of us inhabiting this planet now. The people who read science fiction are by and large the most alert and forethoughtful group of human beings in the world. There are clods among them, to be sure, and maybe one or two villains. But if there is hope for humanity, I think it lies among those who have contributed to or learned from science fiction."[5] Though flattering and perhaps self-serving, these words—especially *change, forethoughtful,* and *hope for humanity*—constitute a tripod of linked concepts and goals to be realized in the best work of Pohl's colleagues.

Two subliminal or nightmare impulses circulated in popular thought during these years. The first was the wish that thermonuclear weapons would just disappear. Joe Haldeman's "To Howard Hughes: A Modest Proposal" (1974) fulfills this irrational desire.[6] It is a James Bond–like story of a billionaire tycoon who commissions a secret group of scientists to assemble 28 nuclear bombs in an underground arsenal and then blackmails the world's nuclear powers into destroying their weapons. This serious satire on *Dr. Strangelove* and *Fail-Safe* first amused the readers of *Fantasy and Science Fiction* and continued to appear in antiwar anthologies. Its popularity derived, in part, from its simplistic appeal. But additional hopes were generated by political events. Beginning in 1963 and continuing through the late 1960s and 1970s, test ban treaties like SALT I, the multinational nonproliferation treaty of 1968, and the demilitarization of the ocean floor and the Caribbean, were, at least temporarily, hopeful signs.

To others, these hopes were as chimerical as Haldeman's simple melodrama. The other prevalent impulse, in some quarters, was a countermood of despair. In some minds, this state spawned—or reflected—nuclear death wishes, either covertly or openly acknowledged. Catering to this desperate and irrational response to cold war realities, Spinrad's "Big Flash" creates a 1960s death cult celebrating apocalyptic obliteration as mass psychosis. This tale thus epitomizes the dark underside of nuclear fear, later characterized by Weart as triggering "a corresponding all-destructive rage; homicidal and suicidal urges and the accompanying guilt" (424).

"The Big Flash" has as its active agent the Four Horsemen, a wildly hyperbolic 1960s rock band. Their multimedia performances invariably climax in visual reminders and musical imitations of a nuclear explosion. Their rise from obscurity in Los Angeles to national and international notoriety takes just 200 days. Spinrad's vivid account is divided into small vignettes dramatizing this wildfire phenomenon. Many topical features of American pop and military culture—Hell's Angels motorcycle gangs, Vietnam, desert nuclear tests—are incorporated into the Four Horsemen's thanatic performances. Driving the national mood toward a Dance of Death, the band's spectacles of heartbeat music, black robes, psychedelic colors, and chants of "The Big Flash" and "DO IT" are played out before a huge screen on which Hiroshima and Bikini images are flashed. Lyrics, sounds, and film clips all underscore the theme of American and global evil. Stony Clark, the leader, has demonic eyes that to a worshipful devotee "told me he knew where everything lousy and rotten was at" (Miller and Greenberg, 62). Burning Vietnamese villages, a Nuremberg rally, Auschwitz corpses, an automobile graveyard with Negro children: "*And we are all in here together*" (Miller and Greenberg, 60).

Spinrad's kaleidoscopic story structure and vivid evocations of rock music's power to excite and overwhelm all sorts of minds create a succinct and perhaps convincing dramatization of mass hysteria. The virus spreads from the band's manager, to soldiers and sailors manning missile silos and nuclear submarines, to Pentagon higher-ups. Everyone starts to wear "DO IT" buttons. The military seeks to capitalize on the frenzy by staging a nuclear performance of their own—a small nuclear test firing on the Yucca Flats. The only voice of reason is that of a lowly television executive who exclaims, " 'Those guys are . . . well perverts, B. D. . . they're in love with the atom bomb or something. Every number leads up to the same thing.'. . . 'I resign,' said Jake Pitkin, who had no reputation for courage" (Miller and Greenberg, 56–57). Caught between popular madness and commercial and political exploitation, Jake is the story's only sane character. Manic fascination overtakes everyone else. Awe, wonder, horror, dread, any rational determination to control or eliminate the Bomb, all go unmentioned in this story. Shock and surrender to suggestion are the psychic engines driving the frantic action, whose timed and dated sections ironically evoke the Doomsday Clock on the cover of the *Bulletin of Atomic Scientists*. Spinrad's prose deftly simulates the idiom and manic mood of the musicians' lyrics:

> Nothing but the blinding light now—
> "*. . . and zap! the world is done.*" . . .
> An utterly black screen for a beat that becomes black fading to blue at a horizon
> . . . "*but before we die let's dig that high that frees us from our binds . . . that blows all cool that ego-drool and burns us from our mind . . . the last big flash, mankind's last gas, the trip we can't take twice.*" . . .
> The fireball coalesces into a mushroom-pillar cloud as the roar goes on. . . . And the girl's face is faintly visible superimposed over the cloud. . . .
> A soft voice, amplified, over the roar, obscenely reverential now: "*Brighter . . . great God, it's brighter than a thousand suns.*" . . .
> And the screen went blank and the lights came on. (Miller and Greenberg, 55–56)

This frenetic theatrical performance is soon matched by the "real-life" reactions of soldiers and sailors, who finally vie with each other, on one submarine, to reach the firing button first.

As Thomas C. Bacig points out, Norman Spinrad was in the vanguard of short-story writers satirizing "the present and potential impacts of the communication revolution on American ways of living, loving, and dying."[7] Only the most perverse of American forms of loving are found in the story, underscoring the cultural connections between dying, the Bomb, and electronic media. "Spinrad is raising serious questions about the ethical vacuum that produces the wasteland we call the entertainment industry," Bacig concludes

(514). What needs also to be said is that the shock effect of science fiction *is* both form and message, for the literary form aims at entertaining and educating through the shock power of the unknown, even the outré. That Spinrad held a sensitive finger on the American pulse is borne out, at least in part, by the fact that after its original appearance in the science fiction magazine *Orbit-5*, "The Big Flash" was reprinted in at least five anthologies by 1985 (Brians [1987], 313–14).

Perhaps the only short-story writer in science fiction to top Spinrad in focusing postholocaust consciousness across a wide popular spectrum—in 1960s, 1970s, and 1980s audiences as well as in his fellow writers—was Harlan Ellison. From 1967 to 1969, Ellison published a handful of experimental stories, collected as *The Fantasies of Harlan Ellison* in 1979. In addition to a dozen works of speculative fiction, he also edited two influential collections whose titles afford a clue to his own work—*Dangerous Visions* and *Again, Dangerous Visions*.[8] "Speculative fiction" as "dangerous visions" aptly describes the two nuclear stories that subsequently entered the consciousness of possibly millions of American readers. Both "I Have No Mouth, and I Must Scream" and "A Boy and His Dog" throw a penetrating spotlight on American psychosocial thought and behavior in the aftermath of nuclear holocaust.

"This is one of the finest nuclear war stories ever written," Paul Brians flatly declared in 1987 of "I Have No Mouth" ([1987], 193). Because both setting and characters are so removed from conventional post-Hiroshima themes and tropes, readers must struggle to see the nuclear messages embedded in this disturbingly surreal narrative. Indeed, all normal distinctions between inner and outer reality disappear as the human narrator records his and four others' macabre imprisonment inside AM, a supercomputer that has gobbled up all Chinese, Soviet, and American computers in the wake of World War III. AM is a machine perfectionist. He strives to contain and control nothing less than all terrestrial consciousness. Only five humans have been preserved from global nuclear destruction. They exist, during this "one hundred and ninth year of the computer," on a diet of "thick ropey worms" that AM allows them as prisoners inside his mainframe (187). His aim, apparently, is to keep them alive forever, in torment leading to madness. For AM bears an almost human malice against his prisoners. "AM wasn't God, he was a machine. We had created him to think, but there was nothing he could do with that creativity. In rage, in frenzy, the machine had killed the human race, almost all of us, and still it was trapped. AM could not wonder. AM could not belong. He could merely be" ([1979], 195). As a multivalenced symbol of science, technology, the Bomb, and the Doomsday Machine, AM represents a vivid addition to the sum of imaginal memories through which readers now were able to think and feel about life and death in the nuclear era. Yet the distance between Hiroshima and the inside of a world-devouring computer is so great that, compared with previous nuclear stories—for example, Bradbury's "There Will Come Soft Rains"—"I

Have No Mouth" evokes and demands a whole new dimension in postholocaust communication.

In fact, Ellison's narrator endows AM with powers and feelings denied the machine's purely cognitive powers. To be sure, the narrator is creator as well as conduit of such articulateness. Thus what is inside AM as fictional plot is outside AM in imaginative imagery. "He would never let us go," the narrator explains. "We were his belly slaves. . . . He was Earth, and we were the fruit of that Earth, and though he had eaten us he would never digest us. We could not die" (1979, 196). Furthermore, the narrator's captive voice endows his fellow captives with their own imaginative activity. Norse and Dantean mythologies provide frantic yet traditionally structured actions inside the machine. Before killing each other or themselves in mad frenzy, the five go on a journey through a new Inferno. Harried by a hurricane bird and bewildered by a burning bush, the humans enter a "cavern of rats," follow a "path of boiling steam," through the "country of the blind" and across the "slough of despond" and a "vale of tears" into "ice caverns" ([1979], 198). This conventional landscape of spiritual experience is, however, more trite and less arresting than the language the narrator lends AM to describe his journey around the narrator's mind. "AM went into my mind," he reports. "He walked smoothly here and there, and looked with interest at all the pock marks he had created in one hundred and nine years. He looked at the cross-routed and reconnected synapses and all the tissue damage the gift of immortality had included" ([1979], 194).

Infuriated, however, that the other four humans have escaped into death (by murder or suicide), AM makes sure the narrator can never do the same. Leaving his mind intact, the machine changes the man's body into something else. Now he cannot dash his head against a computer wall or slit his throat or hold his breath until he faints. "I will describe myself as I see myself. I am a great soft jelly thing. I shamble about, a thing that never could be known as human, a thing whose shape is so alien a travesty that humanity becomes more obscene for the vague resemblance. . . . I have no mouth, and I must scream" ([1979], 201).

Ellison's satiric fable turns the tables on prenuclear ancestors like Mary Shelley's *Frankenstein* (1818) and Karel Čapek's *R.U.R.* (1920), just as it reverses the human-machine relationship in Bradbury's Allendale tale. Traditional relationships are reimagined in a postholocaust world wherein a thinking machine literally becomes the Earth, while a language-rich but tongueless man reverts to a sentient jellyfish. As a monstrous metaphor of the atomic age and its warrior-technicians, "I Have No Mouth" dramatizes the multiple forms of imprisonment conceivably awaiting the makers (and victims) of a Doomsday Machine. Ellison has arranged a fictional fate exquisitely endless as compared with the instantaneous finales of *Dr. Strangelove* and "The Big Flash."

Ellison's brilliant experiment in psychological surrealism was not, however, characteristic. More in line with his reputation as a science fiction innovator in emphasizing sex, violence, and obscenity is his second great tale, "A Boy and His Dog." The author stoutly defended the brutal directness of this 1969 story, whose success with readers and critics earned it both Nebula and Hugo awards, as well as many anthology reprints over the years. Only by using graphic language for street speech and thought, he argued, could the possible nature of postholocaust life in a bombed-out American city be adequately imagined. Vic, the narrator and human protagonist, is a "solo" who, with his telepathic dog Blood, roams the ruined buildings and movie theaters of an L.A.-type metropolis. Roverpacks, a paucity of surviving women, and radiation on the surrounding hills condition a precarious existence for the well-armed and sexually aggressive boy and his dog. Beneath the bomb craters and empty buildings, however, lies another postholocaust community. "Downunder" is "Topeka," the polar opposite of the blighted metropolis and a spotless new town "that looked for all the world like a photo out of one of the water-logged books in the library on the surface. . . . Neat little houses, and curvy little streets, and trimmed lawns, and a business section and everything else a Topeka would have" (Miller and Greenberg, 362). What is missing downunder, of course, is dirt, animals running wild, excitement, X-rated movies, and individual freedom—all found in the blackened city above. The Topeka half of Ellison's story is strikingly similar to Bradbury's "April 2000: The Third Expedition" of *The Martian Chronicles*, set in a Martian replica of an Illinois town that proves a trap for earthlings (Bradbury, 32–48).

The echo of Bradbury emphasizes Ellison's even more bitterly serious satire. For instance, his version of the rubble town of "Allendale," California, is filled with desperate people struggling to survive by exploiting each other. In this brutal battle, no vision of Martian grace exists to contrast with human aggression. Here, too, the telepathic powers are held by Blood, not Vic. The dog easily outdistances the master not only as deadly streetfighter and tracker of vulnerable females but as the unlikely custodian of literary and historical consciousness. Together, the pair make an effective street team, adept at raping women and killing rival roverpack gunmen. The contrast here with a later survival story, Whitley Strieber's *Wolf of Shadows* (1985) (discussed in the next chapter) could scarcely be stronger. Ellison's humans exhibit a misogyny and violence that confirm many readers' prejudices about 1960s and 1970s inner-city youths, whereas Strieber's sympathetic picture of a cross-species friendship is much gentler, though tinged, as we shall see, with sexist overtones of its own.

Pulp magazine conventions are exploited by Ellison only to transcend them in the interest of social satire. For example, Quilla Jean voraciously enjoys sex after her rape by Vic. Then the adventure turns out to be a deception game. Quilla Jean is a decoy, enticing Vic to follow her back downunder to serve as stud in a puritanical community in which all the males are now sterile. Her punishment is gruesomely severe. After a melodramatic fight with the burgers of Topeka, the boy and girl escape to the surface. Blood faithfully awaits them, wounded, starving, and bitterly jealous of the humans' attraction to each other. Vic must choose between girl and dog.

> She got a pouty look on her face. "If you love me, you'll come on."
>   I couldn't make it alone out there without him. I knew it. If I loved her. She asked me in the boiler, do you know what love is?
>   . . . And after Blood had eaten his fill, I carried him to the air-duct a mile away, and we spent the night inside on a little ledge. I held him all night. He slept good. In the morning, I fixed him up pretty good. He'd make it. . . .
>   I didn't eat. I wasn't hungry.
>   . . . It took a long time before I stopped hearing her calling in my head. Asking me: *do you know what love is?*
>   Sure I know.
>   A boy loves his dog. (Miller and Greenberg, 373)

Cannibalism, as Ellison's critics have observed, provides the necessary shock to his social parable on survivalism. Survivors of a holocaust could kill, rape, and devour. Violence, obscenity, and prurient sexuality are present-day and future realities. In both time frames, Ellison's prophetic fiction does what all prophecy does: addresses present conditions under cover of future time. Thereby the author attacks comfortable American hopes of a "winnable war" and returns to "normalcy" for "righteous" survivors. Indicating its broad appeal, "this striking example of the grotesque in contemporary science fiction was made quite faithfully into a film in 1975" (Brians [1987], 193).

Despite such signs of popular success for the innovative short stories of Spinrad and Ellison, their exploitation of the 1960s youth and antiwar cultures did not fit the tastes of all American magazine audiences. A safer fiction, tailored to middlebrow and female readers of, for example, *Harper's*, is exemplified in von Hoffman's "The Brahms Lullaby." The title of this preholocaust vignette signals its cultural and sociological niche. The 1982 readers of *Harper's* probably were closer to the *New Yorker* readership beginning to be profoundly disturbed by Schell's *Fate of the Earth*. Indeed, "The Brahms Lullaby" seems to be a quiet little alarm clock ringing in 1980s suburban, middle-class ears, readying them for the more exigent messages and metaphors of Schell's sterner best-seller.

These 1980s connections or reverberations were probably stronger—given the context of Star Wars rhetoric from the White House, nuclear winter disclosures, and Schell shock—than backward contrasts with Judith Merril's by now almost forgotten *Shadow on the Hearth*. Awareness of both sets of comparisons helps to identify some new preoccupations of literate Americans in the early Reagan years. Both the 1982 story and the 1950s novel, instead of dramatizing male encounters with apocalypse (by far the commonest theme in adult nuclear fiction during the nuclear age), focus sharply on domestic suburban settings and female protagonists. Both protagonists have sent commuting husbands off to meet the Bomb in Manhattan. In both cases, direct immersion of readers in the shocks of catastrophe is avoided—as, in fact, is the case with Spinrad, Haldeman, and Ellison.

Here, though, most parallels between 1982 and 1950 cease. Von Hoffman's yuppie housewife is only temporarily domestically anchored. Though alone with baby and cat when the siren sounds, she is actually a Wall Street lawyer taking maternity leave and so trying on an unfamiliar role. Her daily routine mirrors (without satirizing) contemporary suburban stereotypes. She jogs, takes beta-blockers and endorphins, watches daytime TV, admires Walter Cronkite, and glories in her serene baby. When danger arrives over the radio, she rushes to the supermarket and the gun shop. The latter impulse to acquire a pistol is triggered by fellow villagers who, even when facing threats of nuclear destruction, are more worried about an influx of "jigaboos" from the South Bronx. She also worries about radioactivity from a nearby nuclear power plant. But whereas Merril makes certain that 1950s gender lines are respected by the last-minute return of the husband, von Hoffman's modern mother enjoys no such reprieve. The 1980s story closes on an ominous note. When anxious mother and gurgling baby repair to the train station to meet their man, she stumbles down to the Hudson River bank. There, in a vivid, enigmatic epiphany, she hears (or hallucinates) a scream coming from the south off the waters. It is vastly different from but oddly reminiscent of Ellison's story of a silent scream. "A crying out, a lamentation, a rising scream carried along the water, up the river, between the palisades, from the city. 'Bruce!' Ellen said aloud. 'Bruce,' she shouted, one voice against eight million in the city, with their radiation burns, in their intact city. Manhattan still stands, their tomb" (59). The actual nature and outcome of this reenactment—if it is one—is immediate but uncertain: no train, no husband, no escape, but also no palpable flash or mushroom cloud. Whether the grim final words are Ellen's imagination or the narrator's knowledge, Hiroshima is never mentioned.

In this slender suburban sketch, von Hoffman illustrates the tendency of middle-class magazines to take safer looks at nuclear fear than many science fiction magazines do. This author's fearful protagonist raises no larger questions about causes or consequences of nuclear warfare. Indeed, the wife/mother/lawyer is left no time to speculate on the moral implications of the scream off the waters. In this respect, she differs also from the protagonist of Kate Wilhelm's analogous tale. "Countdown" (1968) is about a postnuclear family in a riskier locale—Cape Canaveral, where the husband is a satellite engineer. Coming home from a space launch, he suddenly sees the situation from his wife's viewpoint: "One day, he knew . . . her eyes would slide past him to fasten on the baby and she would also ask, 'What have we done?' "[9] Instead of such responsible awareness, von Hoffman's housewife dramatizes the wishful dream of *not thinking* about bigger issues while helplessly *feeling* their consequences.

As 1980s debates and discussions increased for real-life relatives of this subur-ban woman, such readers might well find it harder and harder to follow, or condone, her ostrich living and thinking on the brink of nuclear disaster. As we shall see, Carolyn See is another source of similar responses by virtue of the controversial conclusion of *Golden Days*.

In the brief compass of "The Big Flash" and "A Boy and His Dog," even responsible and talented writers can only announce themes they think preoc-cupy potential readers and develop them only in dramatic synecdoche. To describe and probe the long shadows cast before and behind the specter of thermonuclear devastation, the novel form continues to be essential and excit-ing. This is as true of the adventure-survivalist tale written for a popular audience as for more intricate experimental fictions aimed at elite, often older readerships. In the 1980s, the legacy of science fiction was at work in both popular and "serious" modes. Yet Terry Carr, in his introduction to Kim Stanley Robinson's *The Wild Shore*, draws a clear line between well-known forms of SF fiction—which he characterizes as "mostly of the traditional sort, often hackneyed and familiar stories that relied on fast action and obvious ideas"—and Robinson's New Wave book. The latter breaks fresh ground, he writes, by "a depth of characterization and background . . . rarely approached in science fiction before now."[10] Comparing it favorably with recent works by Ursula LeGuin (*The Left Hand of Darkness* [1983]) and Joanna Russ (*Picnic on Paradise* [1968]),[11] Carr, the energetic editor of Ace Science Fiction Special editions, promises readers a thoughtful narrative "of life in the United States as it might be after a nuclear strike that destroys our cities and reduces the nation to isolated enclaves of people living in the ruins and working their way back to civilization." It is "the story of a boy growing up rapidly in dangerous circumstances" (Robinson, viii).

These are indeed new and dangerous circumstances for Henry Fletcher in his particular place (San Onofre) and time (2047 A.D.). There he and fellow *hibakusha* of nuclear decimation actually experience what some Japanese went through a century before. This imaginative reversal is underlined by the fact that the California coast now lies under a United Nations quarantine, with the Japanese navy as watchdogs based at Catalina. Japanese thrill-seeking tourists also sneak ashore at San Clemente to buy souvenirs from Americans. To the south lies what is left of San Diego. Its warlike mayor, Timothy Danforth, yearns to restore American power by retaliating for the country's defeat in World War III. Henry and his aging mentor, Tom Barnard, are brought to San Diego to be recruited for the mayor's military dream. The ensuing confrontation between Danforth and Barnard symbolizes the choices Henry must make in becoming an adult.

Barnard is a relic, vigorous and thoughtful, of the old days. He remembers America before devastation, in a single hour, by 2,000 nuclear bombs earlier in the century. "America was great like a whale," he tells the young folk in the fishing and farming village, "but it stank and was a killer. . . . Lots of fish died to make it so big" (198). After listening calmly to the mayor's plan of attack and his version of recent history, Barnard observes, "'Interesting. . . . Seems to me we're like the Japanese themselves were after Hiroshima. They didn't even know what hit them, did you know that?'. . . 'What's Hiroshima?' the Mayor asked" (102).

Historical awareness or ignorance are actual options in Henry's initiation. The mayor and his guerrillas prove this when they mount a nighttime attack on Japanese and American smugglers at San Clemente. The raid backfires; a youth from Henry's town is needlessly killed. America's rebirth by force of arms—"a tiger from the depths of the pit" (105)—proves a fiasco. For his part, Barnard preaches peace, literacy, love of nature, historical memory, and deliberate myth-making. Reduced to tears at seeing the ruins of the LaJolla campus where he once studied, Barnard cannot understand Henry's resentment of these symbolic buildings, which the youth considers "the signs of a giant past that was now shattered bits of rock covered by weeds. . . . Ruins like these told us how little our lives were, and I hated them" (121). When the old man falls ill and seems near death, he confesses to his young protégé that some of his stories of the past were made up—were, in fact, lies. Disillusioned, Henry blurts out: "I know you survived. Now we're past that and that's all I need to know. I don't want to know any more" (294). Henry also listens impatiently to the father of a friend who shares, even more passionately, Barnard's love of peace through isolation from the warlike ferment of the postholocaust world. "America's gone," the fisherman exclaims. "It's dead. There's us in this valley, and there's others in San Diego, Orange, behind Pendleton, over on Catalina. But they're not us. This valley is the biggest country we're going to have in our lives" (188).

Young Henry, then, is a representative postholocaust American. With one nationalistic breath, he echoes Danforth and his fiery friend Steve: "I wanted those Japanese out of our ocean" (266). But in another breath he is pulled toward Barnard and the old fisherman's obdurate localism. An unusual sensitivity to nature—the ocean, beach, trees, and weather—strengthens the lad's allegiance to place. But to cement trust in this outlook means shedding his distrust of storytelling as lies. Old Tom, when he thinks he is about to die, pleads: "[O]h, Henry, can you see why I did it, why I lied to you, it was to keep you knowing it, to keep you from the nothing, to make us Greek ghosts on the land and defying what fell to us and make that something pure and simple so we can say we are still people, Henry, *Henry*—" (294).

What eventually teaches Henry the truth underlying such lies is turning his back on senseless nighttime raids that kill ignorant youths. Instead, he makes another, apparently simple choice. It comes to him in the form of an empty notebook given him and Barnard on their return trip from San Diego. Along with the notebook came a copy of *An American around the World* by one Glen Baum. Though the author's name is a covert reference to *The Wizard of Oz*, only later do the San Onofreans learn that Baum's "whole book is made up." They are indignant to learn it is neither history nor journalism nor autobiography, but an adventure story. What does not suffer from being deceptively "made up" is the empty notebook. " 'Write your own story in it,' the old man declares. . . . 'But I don't have a story,' Henry replies. 'Just do it. Write the way you talk. Tell the truth.' 'What truth?' After a long pause, he said, 'You'll figure that out. That's what the book is for' " (246). After hesitations, Henry begins writing his story. To do so, though, he must come to terms with "the God damned Past" (71). One view of history's power is held by old Tom: it's "about how we were all wedges stuck in cracks." Henry sees the inadequacy of that bleak historicism. "But it wasn't like that, I saw; we weren't that tightly bound. It was more like being on trails . . . like the one crossing the bog beside the river here" (262). A natural trope from the boy's immediate experience not only illuminates his own memories but frees the neophyte writer to link his young past to other older ones. As he struggles to put the immediate past on those empty pages, another metaphor occurs to Henry. Watching a friend weave a basket of pine needles gives him the clue: "Such patience, arranging all the needles! Such skill, whipping them all into place! . . . Watching Rebel coax the line between two needles and through a complicated little loop of line waiting for it, it occurred to me I had a task somewhat like hers. When I penciled in my book, I tied together words like she tied together pine needles, hoping to make a certain shape with them. Briefly I wished I could make a book as neat and solid and beautiful as the basket Rebel wove" (352). Other natural images are remembered as ways to make sense of the personal past. "I didn't lie—not much," Tom tells him, " . . . not about important things. Just once in a while to give you an idea what it was really like, what it felt like" (354). For one thing, remembering the past or predicting the future are never fully possible. They must, in part, be reimagined. Yet the youth still feels frustrated. "Here all these things had *happened*, they had changed us for life, and yet the miserable string of words sitting on the table didn't hold the half of it—the way it had looked, the thoughts it had engendered, the way I *felt* about it all. It was like pissing to show what a storm is like" (364).

Despite a plausible adventure plot, convincing details of character, and a sensitive narrator who realizes the connection between experience, writing, and understanding, *The Wild Shore* comes perilously close to a sentimental ending. Yet given its publication history and niche as an Ace Science Fiction Special, Robinson's achievement earns a place in popular culture closer to many major crossover narratives, like several to be discussed below, than to mere topical successes like Roger Zelazny's *Damnation Alley* (1969). Robinson created no formulaic plot of violent sensationalism. His hero is a convincingly rounded individual coping with personal and cultural issues that honestly worry all 1980s audiences, especially its younger members. Would there be an "America" after a nuclear holocaust? If so, would it be democratic or autocratic, peace-loving or still warlike? Should survivors, if any, bear a burden of guilt for past events and choices that brought destruction? How necessary are traditional Euro-American myths and legends, or verifiable stories of the American past, to the task of postholocaust thinking and acting? Can popular novels aimed at the general reader provide memorable images and symbolic actions that make sense of nuclear history along the three traditional time lines of past, present, and future? Will such stories actually clarify Americans' confused thinking about a scientific society? Would a postholocaust America still relying on science and technology inevitably restore warfare and the exploitation of nature for narrowly nationalistic ends? Is the only conceivable alternative to nationalism the parochial outlook voiced by the old fisherman on the wild shore of California? These are surely significant social issues dealt with, albeit simplistically at times, in *The Wild Shore*. Carr's claim for the freshness and permanent value of this unassuming New Wave novel seems, from a 1990s perspective, more than commercial puffery. It recognizes a modest but genuine triumph of imagination over commercialized sensationalism.

Turning from one adolescent's experiences in a future America to another's, from *The Wild Shore* and Ace Science Fiction Specials to Denis Johnson's novel of the next year, *Fiskadoro* (1985), one is at once struck by similarities suggesting how thin are the lines now separating SF from so-called main-stream fiction. The crossover novel of the 1980s has become, it seems, almost the norm. Few works, however, in either category, or any other category or convention, achieved the critical acclaim of Johnson's novel. Like Robinson's, his story has as protagonist a teenager undergoing initiation into adult realities under the bizarre and brutal circumstances of a postholocaust time and place. Both books are set in coastal territory, by now almost a trite nuclear literary convention. Their fictional futures are but 13 years apart; *Fiskadoro* takes place in 2060 A.D., six decades after a world nuclear conflict and nine decades after the fall of Saigon in the Vietnam War. Yet Johnson follows neither the adventure tale format nor traditional science fiction patterns. His narrative creates no series of fast-paced, violent actions, implausible escapes, and happy outcomes. *Fiskadoro* contains no nuclear explosions, Martian aliens, or spaceship expeditions, no supercomputers or augments. Almost exactly the same length as its English counterpart, Russell Hoban's *Riddley Walker* (1980), and hailed by many as the outstanding nuclear novel of the decade, *Fiskadoro* resembles its 1980 predecessor in its language's densely symbolic texture woven about the thoughts, dreams, and actions of a number of characters, adult and youthful. The kaleidoscope of voices and perspectives Johnson thus orchestrates makes his a more unusual survival story than either *The Wild Shore* or another 1980s favorite, David Brin's *The Postman* (1985). His richness of imagination and verbal artistry goes far toward confirming contemporary claims and suggest that *Fiskadoro* may be the most original American nuclear novel of its time.

Documenting this high claim might begin by noting Johnson's opening credits and acknowledgments. These signal the role popular culture plays in *Fiskadoro*. Among its many historical sources, allusions, and quotations appear the names of Mick Jagger and the Rolling Stones, Jimmy Cliff and Bob Marley, Linda Ronstadt, Sidney Bechet and Jimi Hendrix, Cassius Clay, Sugar Ray Robinson, and Bob Dylan, "the great poet of the times of hard rain."[12] These authorial favorites indicate a desire to attract younger and young middle-aged readers. They also confirm the permanence of electronic culture for this twenty-first–century society, where books and classical music are rare items but culture is built around listening to the radio's ancient recordings of the above popular idols. More privately important are three historical sources Johnson has used: a children's or general reader's story by Roy Chapman Andrews, *All about Dinosaurs*; an obscure 1969 nuclear book, Frank W. Chinnock's *Nagasaki: The Forgotten Bomb*; and the Koran. Such an odd set of sources warns readers to expect a strange set of social practices and pyschic states in the narrative.

The geographical setting, though, is strangely familiar. The Bomb has isolated the little strip of the Florida Keys where Fiskadoro lives amid several disorganized communities. His world is bound on the north by the dead city of Miami; on the south beyond the horizon lies Cuba, still a Communist state supporting *Cubaradio*. At the region's center is Twicetown. Formerly Key West, Twicetown got its name when two nuclear bombs, both duds, landed in its streets during the holocaust. This historical event affords residents and readers their first memorable nuclear image. At the city's center, an atomic bomb lies on its side. The spot is now "a gathering place for political and religious functions. When a great man died he was brought here. The missile itself was almost as big around as a house. . . . Its skin was scorched and welted, in some spots still olive drab, in others stripped of all paint and shiny as glass. . . . People said it was an American bomb that had gone off course" (158).

If this description obliquely reminds some readers of Moby-Dick, the possible irony may be intentional. At this small world's center lies a huge, enigmatic power marking its past, present, and future with potential destruction. The Bomb explains the Quarantine (shades of *The Wild Shore*), which for 60 years has cordoned off the coast. Within the Contaminated Zone are wrecked towns and beaches behind which, in the swampy interior, is Quraysh, a primitive society of African or African-American Muslims. When Fiskadoro follows a young black girl there (another echo—perhaps of Harlan Ellison's Vic?), he discovers a prehistoric community whose members "thought they had everything they needed—some plants, some huts, some ceremonies. They never appealed for help to the ghosts of their friends and neighbors" (169). Fiskadoro himself feels the ghost-filled air, though. Ghosts and dreams are by no means confined to the Quraysh or the boy's imagination. On a trip north with a drug dealer, Fiskadoro encounters an actualized dream peopled by disturbing ghosts. "Ahead, on the road alongside the channel, tangled black autocars made a breakwater of wreckage, behind which, as far as Fiskadoro could see down the diminishing road, stretched a motorcade of burned-black cars and trucks, every size and shape, with their tires melted into the road's ash." This happens as their raft approaches a cloudy vision of big houses, which proves to be Miami. "Every car . . . was being driven by a person made of brown bones who didn't shift or flicker or turn his head, but Fiskadoro knew they were all aware of him. There were riders in every car, big and little, twisted into different shapes, all made of brown bones. Now he understood that his purpose in this dream was to die" (187).

Because a young boy is remembering a "real" scene—a strikingly similar one occurs in Strieber's *Wolf of Shadows*—its freshness contrasts with other dreams and visions held or described by the adults of his contaminated coastal world. Older persons recall, now hazily but occasionally with anguished clarity, the dreamworld of the preholocaust past, "when the entire world had been paved" (42). These ghosts of truth about "the other age" occur in the consciousness of A. T. Cheung, the chief adult in *Fiskadoro* and Fiskadoro's sometime mentor and music teacher. Along with his 100-year-old grandmother, another refugee from that former world, Mr. Cheung clings to the past and spends much of his time keeping it alive for himself and others. His self-appointed title is manager of the Miami Symphony Orchestra (*oxra*, in the corrupted English-Spanish lingo of the Contaminated Zone). The group of motley musicians who practice together are a laughable travesty of a symphony orchestra. Like the members of the Twicetown Society for Science, one of whom cannot read, these survivors go through the motions of the practices of a long-lost institution. Mr. Cheung tries to regenerate such symbols and practices—in particular, historical consciousness. "He wanted to bring back the other age—just to get a look at it, the great civilization of helicopters and speedboats and dance parties atop buildings five hundred meters tall," but all he can actually do is "sit here with his clarinet in his lap, smoking marijuana in a cool Meeschaum pipe until the sun fell and sadness overcame him" (52–53).

The book's major climax—if there is one in a story that stresses surreal experience in a disordered society given over to dreams and drugs, religious ecstasy and rice brandy—comes when the Twicetown Society is invited up to Marathon to meet with its Society for Knowledge in a public reading of a newly acquired book. Among the episode's other wry ironies is the fact that the Marathoners have exchanged a functioning motorboat for a single book that once belonged to the Marathon Public Library. It is *Nagasaki: The Forgotten Bomb*. The reading is accompanied, outside, by a fierce tropical storm that causes some listeners superstitiously to fear that "merely by reading about this bomb they might wipe themselves off the earth tonight" (150). Supercharging such fear is the eerie fact that passages in the Nagasaki account anticipate or duplicate comments by the apprehensive listeners. Mr. Cheung, for one, "believed he was dreaming of a previous birth-and-death existence. . . .'Which one was I?' he asked himself."

"All Nagasaki surely had been destroyed. And he was about to fly into that ominous cloud. Cold perspiration . . .

I was there. My eyes burned up. It was the only thing I felt. I remember.

"I can't stand it!" someone shouted suddenly. . . .

"That's just what it says in the book!" Roderick Chambers said. "Look here—you read it: *'I can't stand it,' someone shouted suddenly, and when Lieutenant Komatsu turned he saw Chief Petty Officer Umeda vomiting."* . . .

[Mr. Cheung's] seasickness seemed to be coming back. He had a terrible headache and he felt nauseous. . . .

". . . *either the fumes or the heat,"* Roderick Chambers read above the protest of the hysterical listeners, *"had given him a terrible headache and he felt nauseous."* (152–53)

While no character is actually writing this story in a story, as is the case in *The Wild Shore* (and in Hoban's *Riddley Walker* and Vonnegut's *Cat's Cradle*), Johnson, too, playfully connects literature and history, memory and dream, past and present. His moment of hysterical comedy at this point recalls Vonnegut, as do elsewhere his clever uses of single lines or exclamations. When Fiskadoro, for instance, visits the Quraysh, he thinks to himself, "It was the first dream he'd ever peed in" (174). More poignantly, when Fiskadoro's fisherman father is drowned, his large dark mother (herself soon to die of cancer) greets her son with a big hug: " 'Real life now!' she cries" (58). Indeed, the whole spectrum of responses Mr. Cheung feels on a given occasion— insinuation, hysteria, denial, laughter, sobbing—are echoes of various literary modes and postholocaust moods of the narrative.

Johnson's humor seldom extends, however, to his second and older survivor from the old time. Grandmother Wright's actual voice is never heard in *Fiskadoro*, but the discreet narrator is privy to her barrage of memories extending over 90 years. As a young girl, she had escaped from Saigon in 1975 and, after her helicopter fell into the South China Sea, was rescued— "saved not because her hands reached out; saved because other hands than hers reached down and saved her" (218). At times, Grandmother Wright's vivid but senile reminiscences of Vietnam appear to take over the narrative of life in the Contaminated Zone. Death, though, is clearly the common thread of everyone's past and present realities, whether in dreams or from bombs or drownings. All such memories and experiences, like the sight of the black cars and brown bones, come together in the finale of *Fiskadoro*. Respecting a 30-year-old convention of nuclear fiction, the author places this ominous scene on a beach. Fiskadoro, Mr. Cheung, Grandmother Wright in an arm chair, and a group of "Israelite" survivors from the swamp who await the coming of a Messiah are all assembled, with a curious flock of seagulls in attendance.

From out of the haze-wreathed waves came

> sounds . . . that made no sense—a talking of horns, a shifting song of voices, and something too low and too deep to hear which was still much more definite than the other sounds. Everyone on the beach was silent. Mr. Cheung was frightened.
>   . . . Ship or shape, it came in slowly as the tide.
>   One day they would all be dead. If today was that day, then everything was clear. Now the sounds and visions and ideas coming at them from beyond the end of all thought were real. Now the white boat, or was it a cloud, came for the Israelites out of the fog of their belief. In all likelihood it was a ghost-ship, and the Israelites were ghosts, and the man standing at the bow was a ghost who had come for them. (219–20)

The narrator here moves from mind to mind, sampling characters' apprehensions of the approaching mystery. Many possible explanations are hinted at: the Cuban fleet come to lift or reinforce the Quarantine, Columbus, Christ, Moby-Dick, an atomic cloud about to carry true believers up in a Rapture. For Grandmother Wright, these are infused with memories of Saigon and Hiroshima. In young Fiskadoro's imagination, the memory of Miami's black cars and brown bones mixes with his initiation ceremony among the swamp people. He is confused by having once died and then returned. "How many worlds [were] there?" he wonders, then says aloud:

> ". . . I saw those skeletons in the cars that won't go."
>   "You'll be a great leader," Mr. Cheung said.
>   Fiskadoro didn't know what his teacher was talking about, as he hardly ever knew what anybody was talking about.
>   "I'm not like other men," he reminded Mr. Cheung.
>   "No, I know that. You've been to their world and now you're in this world, but you don't have the memories to make you crazy. It isn't sleeping under the moon that makes a crazy person. It's waking up and remembering the past and thinking it's real."
>   "I saw the ashes driving the cars forever," Fiskadoro said. (217)

Three generations of *hibakusha*, then, are living in, as they nervously await, the end of the world. Johnson's postholocaust vision is a complex vicarious experience of living *in* death. Nagasaki begets Saigon, which begets Miami. Ashes drive automobiles forever. As Mr. Cheung realizes, it has taken three persons and perspectives on time to dramatize this profoundly disturbing postholocaust historicism. "The Cubans will come, the Manager recited to himself, the Quarantine won't last forever. Everything we have, all we are, will meet its end, will be overcome, taken up, washed away. But everything came to an end before. Now it will happen again. Many times. Again and again.

Something is coming and something is going—but that isn't the issue. The issue is that I failed to recognize myself in these seagulls" (219).

Commonplace as are these meditations on history as endless repetition, and acknowledging the fact that neither the boy nor the middle-aged music teacher has the final word in *Fiskadoro*, still, the reader's attention is arrested by Mr. Cheung's humanistic lament, "I failed to recognize myself in these seagulls." Johnson's seagulls are the spectators watching apocalypse (if that is what happens on the beach) "through eyes too tiny to hold any questions" (219). They are naturalistic, ironic, perhaps nihilistic figures. They remind percipient readers of the shark at the end of *A Canticle for Leibowitz*, as Mr. Cheung's cyclical beliefs also recall the abbot's. If so, this 1985 story concludes far more bleakly—despite its youthful protagonist who is destined for leadership, despite its continual flickers of humor and its comforting echoes of 1960s music—than the more traditionally civilized, Eurocentric, and Christian views dramatized in Miller's fable 30 years before.

The year 1985 was indeed a great year for American nuclear fiction, as well as nonfiction. Besides *Fiskadoro*, a surreal tour de force, that year also saw the appearance of at least one other major work, this one in the real-time, social history tradition of Merril, Wylie, and Helen Clarkson. Tim O'Brien's *The Nuclear Age* is fictional autobiography. Its narrator-protagonist begins with a claim merging self and story. "I'm a man of my age, and it's an age of extraordinary jeopardy. So who's crazy? Me? Or is it you? You poor, pitiful sheep. Listen, Kansas is on fire."[13] As spokesman for the entire atomic age—he was born in 1946 and writes as a 49-year-old survivor in 1995—William Cowling is either its sanest or maddest member.

Wearing two faces, therefore, he feels confident of his representativeness. Like many others, he approaches the past in "terror mixed with fascination: I craved bloodshed, yet I craved the miracle of a happy ending" (11). Indeed, without actually dramatizing it, *The Nuclear Age* describes much bloodshed in 312 pages. It likewise manages something of a miraculous—and dubious—happy ending. Cowling incarnates and lives out the ambiguous commitments and fearfulness of a man who literally grew up with the Bomb. He first felt its oppressive weight as a schoolboy, was radicalized (almost against his will) in college, went underground with the Weathermen in the 1960s, married a poetry-writing stewardess, and settled down, in the Reagan years, to a prosperous life in his native Montana, rich at last from a uranium mine. Throughout this ironic narrative, Cowling maintains his persona as inveterate fence-sitter, a reluctant revolutionary who ends up selling ore to the Pentagon. Explaining a lifetime of trying to have it both ways, he says, "It wasn't heroism or cowardice. Just non-involvement" (219). Such deep ambivalence suggests a key fact about O'Brien's novel-as-autobiography. By virtue of its depiction of apparently verifiable times, places, events, and attitudes, *The Nuclear Age* imitates social history, while as subjective personal history it infuses all public "facts" with the emotions of a sane madman scarred from childhood with nuclear fear.

Two events and imaginal memories, one from William Cowling's schooldays, the other a running feature of the adult autobiographer's life, set him off from others even as they symbolize shared feelings of many in the nuclear age. The first and final image of Cowling and the Bomb is the hole the mature survivor is digging in the backyard of his redwood home in the Sweetheart Mountains. His compulsive, overdetermined Christmastime activity is to dig a bombproof hole in which he and his family will be safe. "I'm a father, a husband, I have solemn responsibilities. It isn't as if I enjoy any of this. I hate it and fear it. I would prefer the glory of God and peace everlasting. . . . It just isn't possible" (7). Yet before he can justify the ever-deeper excavation or the ever-growing mystification of his blonde wife and precocious daughter, Cowling must first relate his initial outbreak of "nuke fever" (15). Even as a 12-year-old schoolboy, William "understood there was nothing make-believe about doomsday. . . . It was real, like physics, like the laws of combustion and gravity. I could truly see it: a sleek nose cone, the wiring and dials and tangled circuitry. . . . I was normal, yes, stable and levelheaded, but I was willing to face the truth" (11–12). His concerns were those of his fellows in 1958: "all that CONALRAD stuff on the radio, tests of the Emergency Broadcast System, pictures of H-bombs in *Life* magazine, strontium 90 in the milk, the times in school when we'd crawl under our desks and cover our heads in practice for the real thing" (9). William's response at the time, however, is different from that of his classmates. In the family basement, he constructs his own nuclear cave, tree house, snow fort, den, bomb shelter. From school he steals enough No. 2 soft lead pencils to fill up a bookbag and lines them up on top of the ping-pong table. "Pencils contain lead; lead acts as an effective barrier against radiation. It made perfect sense. Logical, scientific, practical" (16).

The outcome of young William's reasoned response to real nuclear threat turns out, however, very differently from a similar action by the pair of children in Judith Vigna's *Nobody Wants a Nuclear War*, as we shall see in the next chapter. Instead of a mother's protective arms leading them to safety and a serious talk about Hiroshima, this duck-and-cover refugee is humiliated by his father's ridiculing laughter. "'Hey, dumbo,' they'd say, 'didn't you know that lead pencils are made out of graphite?' It was cruel and senseless. Why not come straight out with things? Bombs, for instance. Were they dangerous or not? Was the planet in jeopardy? Could the atom be split? Why wasn't anyone afraid? Why not clue me in? The truth, that's all I wanted. The blunt facts" (29).

Demonstrating William's eccentric rationality in an adult world of putatively sane ostriches, O'Brien has his protagonist taken to Helena to see a psychiatrist. Chuck Adamson, though, proves to be as candid as the boy (though not his parents) could wish. "I thought you and I were on the same wavelength about this," Adamson remarks.

> "About *what?*"
> "All of it. Civilization. I mean, yes, we all die. But we have these . . . these ways of coping. Our children. The genetic pool. The things we've made, books and buildings and inventions. Doesn't Edison still live in his light bulb? . . . That's what civilization is: life after death. But if you wipe out civilization—"
> ". . . See the sticker?" he said. "Nothing lasts. Doom. It means no children. No genetic pool. No memory. When the lights go out, Edison goes out. And what significance did his life have? Erased. Shakespeare and Einstein. You and me." (53–54)

Here, in very similar language, speak Robert Jay Lifton and Jonathan Schell, prophetically in a fictional 1958 but topically to 1985 ears. "Imagination," Adamson said gently, "that's what you and I have in common" (54). From a boy with far too much imagination, William becomes a college student aware that his awareness is barely adequate to comprehend actual nuclear dangers. Majoring in geology, he caresses a chunk of uranium dioxide; "rocks could be trusted," he observes naively (68). At Peverson State, he has found "a student body without student brains." Rejecting the comprehensive mindlessness of his fellows, he becomes radicalized, realizing that "we were at peace in time of war" (67, 66). Thus rocks lead to rockets, which lead to revolution.

A crucial moment in this 1960s education occurs at night on the eastern Montana campus, which is located between the famous battlefield and a SAC missile base. "I watched a missile rising from the plateau beyond the Little Bighorn. Yes, a rocket bright white with blue markings and a silver nose cone. . . . It passed across the face of the moon. For a moment I feared the flashes might come, but there was just the missile climbing against gravity, beyond the football stadium, toward Canada and the Arctic Ocean, a smooth, graceful parabola that was not without mystique and beauty" (70–71). Almost like an outtake from *Dr. Strangelove*, a film of the year before, the scene visually symbolizes cold war America just before the tumults of the late 1960s. When "the times of the hard rain" arrive, William, filled with conviction and misgivings, is recruited into the Weathermen. Again, he has too much imagination to make either a cold- or hot-blooded guerrilla. "I see Robert Kennedy's wide-open eyes, a twitch, a flash, Sarah oiling an automatic rifle, sharpshooters and a burning safe house and the grotesque inexpungible reality of the human carcass. Odd how the mind works. It goes in cycles. The year is 1968, and 1958, and 1995, and I'm here digging, I'm sane, I'm trying to save my life" (121).

The motif of these cycles is *fission, fusion, critical mass, quantum leaps*; the nuclear vocabulary provides the narrative its key sections and chapter titles. Unable to commit himself to radical politics, William falls willfully in love with Bobbi, a beautifully fickle airline stewardess, later his wife and the mother of his daughter, whom he seeks to save in the hole in the garden. Cowling's excavation gradually takes over the story as the ex-rebel becomes a 1980s engineer and uranium entrepreneur. But at story's end, the hole in Montana takes on more meanings than the missile or the nuclear submarine that surfaces one night in the Gulf Stream next to his motorboat. As the ground of human life, the earth—not air or water—symbolizes safety but surrenders precious and lethal ores, the very opposite of safety. Indeed, the dynamite bought to deepen the hole recalls a variety of past (and perhaps future) explosions. These sticks, too, may kill the ones he loves. Meanwhile, the hole in the ground signifies absence as well as presence. The Christmas tree lights he strings to illuminate his midnight digging highlight the absence of religious certainty in Cowling's world. Another domestic absence is Bobbi's diaphragm, suddenly *not there* in the medicine cabinet when she leaves for an unexplained vacation by herself. Still another resonance of a round hole in the earth is the Kansas missile silo, a reassuring hole when filled with a rocket but prophetic of disaster when empty. Thus implications of Cowling's crazy obsession keep alternating between public and private life in the nuclear age, as the dangers and dimensions of both realms proliferate, like the growing hole, beyond William's imagination.

What lies outside personal experience but well within the reach of imagination is the backyard hole as the image of death. In fact, a series of deaths—his father's, Sarah's (his college sweetheart and fierce fellow Weatherman)—reinforce the digger's own death wish. Readers of *The Nuclear Age*'s last pages cannot be sure whether Cowling is or is not wiring his hole for dynamite to blow himself, wife, and daughter to oblivion. It would, of course, be the perfect gesture for an archetypal American of the atomic age. But murder and/or suicide do not conclude this account of a man who has spent his whole life with the Bomb. He early learned to scream "nuclear war!" at the world and quote Oppenheimer. But he cannot kill. Instead, with fingers crossed, he promises himself and his readers a satisfying finale.

> I know the ending.
>   One day it will happen.
>   One day we will see flashes, all of us. . . .
>   I know this but I believe otherwise.
>   Because there is also this day, which will be hot and bright.
>   . . . I will dream the dreams that suppose awakening. . . . I will find forgetfulness. Happily, without hesitation, I will take my place in the procession from church to grave, believing what cannot be believed. . . . I will live my life in the conviction that when it finally happens—when we hear that midnight whine, when Kansas burns, when what is done is undone, when fail-safe fails, when deterrence no longer deters, when

the jig is at last up—yes, even then I will hold to a steadfast orthodoxy, confident to the end that E will somehow not quite equal mc^2, that it's a cunning metaphor, that the terminal equation will somehow not quite balance. (312)

Knowledge, imagination, hope, belief however ill founded—these are ingredients and lessons of William Cowling's survival manual for life in the nuclear age. O'Brien's fictional autobiography, especially its crucial period 1958–85, is by turns bleak and bright, wrily ironic and weakly sentimental at the close. Grace Paley is probably right to praise this brilliantly disturbing narrative while condemning its failure to engage *real* 1980s political complexities. "I wish the novel could have been either more surreal or less," she observes. Her implicit assessment is also one of the age that produced it. *The Nuclear Age* is most representative, that is, for both satirizing and accepting implicitly the general trend of a public "stuck (even against our will) in a trough of private, individualistic complaint."[14]

How to create a convincing ending to a nuclear novel is, as we have seen, a persistent problem, not wholly satisfactorily solved by Robinson or O'Brien. As book critic for the *Los Angeles Times*, Carolyn See had perhaps read these fellow authors and noted their several struggles to represent and refract nuclear reality. If so, the problem of an ending constrained her imagination in writing *Golden Days* less than did other issues and literary strategies. Everything in her novel reflects a still more basic challenge than closure. Post-Hiroshima America, not just in political, military, and scientific affairs but in literary practice as well, is a culture dominated by men. What these four decades can be reimagined to look and feel like to a woman writer, one aware of female readers as well as male, is the defining issue confronted in her 1987 novel.

For Edith Langley, the witty, resilient storyteller of *Golden Days*, gender is inseparable from the nuclear referent, as from everything else in American history and society. "There was a basic inequality in the country I grew up in and lived in" (4). In imaginative response, she turns inequality on its head: if male bias makes "one man, one story" the norm, she will explode the convention by consigning two or even three women to share a story, demonstrating that two or more women can between them make a richer, funnier, truer tale than any single man can create or be the subject of. "This is partly the story of Lorna Villanelle and me; two ladies absolutely crazed with the secret thought that they were something special. But if you think you aren't going to care about this story, hold on. It's the most important story in the Western world! Believe me" (4).

Some male readers may indeed be won to See's side when they discover that a real nuclear holocaust strikes California and the rest of the country two-thirds of the way through the two women's narrative. The time is 1986, when the beginning of the end of the world starts with a military caper in Central

America involving a tactical nuclear device. At this point, Edith stops momentarily. "Sometimes I wonder why, in the stories I tell now, I deal with men so unfairly. It's all how *women* felt, never how men felt, and the implication is, of course, they don't feel. Which may be absolutely right.... We talked about men all the time, but they didn't figure in our stories. But they have to go into the story, because aren't they the ones who did it? Didn't they make the world we were living in? Weren't they the ones driving the train?" (139, 142). Readers of nuclear fiction, whatever their gender, will remember that, from *On the Beach* to *Fiskadoro*, most novels in this realm have been by and about men more than women. "How come *you* get to tell stories?" Edith imagines her listeners saying. "In answer I say first, if a Caspar can destroy a world, why is it so strange that an Edith should preserve it?" (213).

Nonetheless, for many readers, both men and women, Edith's message from the rubble of postholocaust Los Angeles strains belief to the breaking point. "This fire! This blessed fire! Some say it was a bad thing, but I say it was a good thing! I waved my arms, and I could see radiant arcs in the sky, sparks from the jewels in my fingers flashing out into the night air. I caught the sharp smell of ozone" (210). As Edith addresses a huddled group of survivors on a California beach where the sand has been turned to glass by thermonuclear explosion, the scene and her words seem incredibly inconsistent. How can a culture's end, or at best a new Dark Age, be seen as a beginning of the Age of Light? Though a few survival stories have implied that nuclear devastation could be a beneficial fate, none exceeds *Golden Days* in proclaiming that a post-Bomb beach walk out on the glass could provide a joyful epiphany.

What makes See's confident conclusion especially problematic is the apparently satiric dystopia distilled from actual California society and 1980s cold war policies that precedes the final chapters. Edith's incurable faith in herself and others is one factor bridging two apparently disparate sections of the story. To be sure, her rosy outlook does not prevent her from seeing the truly self-deceiving avoidance behavior of her fellow Californians just before the holocaust. "By early summer," she recalls, "sometimes I thought that it was all delusion. I thought we were safe. I *knew* we were safe.... Didn't we, all of us, more or less, believe in God? Hadn't everything we'd learned told us that if we worked hard and headed west, that we'd be safe?" (136). Later, nuclear fear drowns out ignorance and denial. At a posh producer's party in 1987, Edith has an apprehensive exchange with a beautiful lady. "Listen," Edith said, "I'm scared."

> "I'm scared of a war." ... I know that my fears were no different from the fears of all my friends. The war. First our sons, then our cities. Then ourselves.
>
> Her eyes were wide. She gazed at me with terrific concentration. "Yes," she said. "I understand what you're saying.... But isn't it true—

that your fear of nuclear war is a metaphor for all the *other* fears that plague us today?"

My mind has never been exactly fine. But sometimes it has been good. "*No*," I said. I may have shouted it out through the beautiful sheltered room. "It's *my* view that the other fears, all those of which we have spoken, are a metaphor for my fear of nuclear war!" (137–38)

Driving both women's fears are personal memories carried into and beyond the catastrophe that does follow this conversation. For Edith and her friend Lorna, these are similar: growing up in poverty, coming west into an adulthood marked by shoddy education, multiple marriages, infidelities and divorces, motherhood, coming from nothing into some prominence and wealth by exploiting the dreams of Californians. Virtually every traditional institution—Christianity, marriage, public and private education, community life and politics, philanthropy—has betrayed these women. Caspar Weinberger and Ronald Reagan have been leading cold warriors. Thus California itself is See's, if not Edith's, prime metaphor of pre- and postholocaust America. When warning signals of the creeping nuclear threat—coming up from the south here, not down from the temperate zones as in *On the Beach*—can no longer be ignored, L.A. restaurants and boutiques and plant-watering services put up counter signs: "Open till the very end!" (123).

When it comes, Angelenos react much like other stricken victims. Edith's account of the Bomb's effect on the metropolis is vivid, sardonic, and a woman's:

> People fell where they were in the streets. They prayed on their knees, they wept. (On the other hand, some didn't.) In the last minutes, women turned on their husbands: "*You, you did this!*" speaking in tones, the tones they had used before only when giving birth, so that some men, even in the midst of their great fear were blown off the planet looking sheepish. . . . For a while a few women went to the few intact male corpses they could find, castrated them, pinned the bloody, dried penises to walls and tree trunks, with the scrawled word *peacekeeper*, but soon it didn't seem worth the trouble. Blacks halfheartedly offed whites; and whites settled scores, but it wasn't worth the trouble; panic prevailed. (172)

When, however, nuclear explosions, fires, and billows of radioactive dust sweep and swirl across the city, a quick miracle is arranged for Topanga Canyon. "The fire roared down on us like a train. And it passed us by. Our house survived. The rest of the world was ashes" (185). Though the ensuing pages describe a gruesome ordeal of survival for Edith and her family, lover, and friends, it is difficult to forget this original authorial feat of convenient salvation. (A hint of its psychic source comes from learning that Carolyn See herself lives in Topanga Canyon.) Indeed, devastation increases, it seems, in direct ratio to the distance from Edith's hilltop house: the holocaust hits the center of Los Angeles, east into the desert, in fact, all the way East. "But things worked out for us more exquisitely than we ever planned! Because when most people were dying, the weather was very dry. Because in our canyon we already knew how to fight the fire. Because whatever had happened all over the world, the snails loved it where we were, and we loved those snails!" (191).

Coincidence and magical thinking, to be fair to See, already marked Edith's career before the advent of the Bomb. Though satire and humor control or soften some of these previous operations of wish fulfillment, both she and Lorna have lived, loved, and prospered by projecting their dreams upon social reality and relationships. In a hilarious send-up of California cultism, for instance, the blond, white-suited guru of a positive thinking seminar in San Francisco gets everyone to sing his theme song: "Abundance Is My Natural State." In the name of abundance, all sorts of feats of mind over matter take place. After the Bomb, though, abundance carries an irony not felt before. "Was it the miracle of the loaves and fishes—one of Lorna's very favorite stories—that two thirty-pound sacks of brown rice lasted us till the first rains came? . . . Sometimes one of us might stand up and move over to the glass . . . [and] look at the swirling ash that had persisted for weeks . . . and croak out, in the choked voices we spoke with then, 'OOOO-eee! I see abundance *everywhere!*'" (187–88). Here as elsewhere, the candor and specificity of some horrors are inseparable from the crazy dreaming of their survivors. "To me the thing that seemed most clear and came in clearer every day was that—well, you know! This story proves it. We were *alive*, and going to be alive" (192).

Being alive necessarily means repossessing a voice with which to refashion memory and the past. Language and remembrance combine with magical effectiveness to start restoration and recovery. Edith and her lover recall one of the abundance seminar's most popular strategems: writing one's sadnesses on pieces of paper, wadding them up, and literally batting them away—a metaphor, on one level, for this narrative. With losses dismissed, memory is free to dwell on what was desired. This dream of rethinking the past (including the recent holocaust, almost) seems complete when Edith concludes, "[W]hat if we only remember *California*? What if we . . . wait, wait, what if we took the cash and let the credit go?" (198). Taking the cash of California seems at the end to boil down to repairing to one of California's archetypal dream spots, the beach. The surf, tanned lifeguards, even the "smooth jagged sheets of glittering colored glass that took the sun like rock candy," are reassuring features of a survivor community that swaps stories and thereby learns "to talk and sing. To make jokes" (208). Edith's speech to the beachgoing listeners, like much of the rest of the novel's narrative tone and tenor, is either a satiric tour de force on televangelists and self-help gurus or a touching revelation of an incorrigible optimist. "I had never been much for talking," she begins in laughable understatement. "At least not in the past few years. But I had a vision of all I had to say to these people. How they must remember how to *cook*, how it had been so blindingly beautiful in those last weeks at Michael's. How they must never turn down love, because, outside of a wonderful meal, it was the BEST. How they should practice kindness. How they could move mountains! How beautiful they were now, how perfect in their competence" (209). Isolated from the rest of this tongue-in-cheek survival story, such purple passages read like pure magazine romance. Yet it remains unclear—as it never is, for instance, with Vonnegut—how seriously See's readers are being tempted to take magical thinking as nuclear survival strategy. What, for instance, is the tenor of the following? "As I say, the ones who decided to come *west* instead of heading east, were by and large the ones who made it. And the wackos, the ones who used their belief systems, were the ones who got control over the radiation. Control is a silly word. It was surrender, really. The ones who *relinquished* control, who took it as it came, who seem—out here at least—to have lived" (212–13). Edith's grasp on a reality outside her own mind tightens and lets go (relinquishes?) with sometimes astonishing rapidity and disregard for conventional connections. Much of such insouciance or inconsistency is posited on the postholocaust world being radically different—it is, again, a better world. "I should say some girls have had some babies. Some babies are born angry or sad or marked, but mostly they're mellow. When I say I tell stories, I mean, of course, I tell what it was like before, how there were maniacs abroad, and how heartbreak hurt the world, and some things were lost. But mostly I tell about *affirming*" (214). See's narrator *affirms*, first of all, by denying the horror stories of previous nuclear literature, written mostly by men. Only afterwards can she offer her countervision, one hovering always on the edge of stereotype, sentimentality, or a child's sense of "telling a story" as lying. Hers is a story of "a race of hardy laughers, mystics, crazies, who knew their real homes, or who had been drawn to this gold coast for years, and they lived through the destroying light, and on, into Light ages" (215).

Despite a predilection for mixing—some would say diluting—social satire and popular romance, Carolyn See authenticates many features of 1980s thinking and feeling as expressed in novels, stories, and critical studies. Nuclear fear is inextricably linked in *Golden Days* to other drives and fears that women in particular experience—poverty, lovelessness, loss of loved ones, existential despair, the culture of war, misogyny, and sexism. See likewise paints a scathing picture of Western Americans of the middle and upper classes sedulously avoiding nuclear reality until, and beyond, the last second. What is conspicuously lacking, however, is a sense of a whole society, state, or region caught collectively in catastrophe. The novel's canvas grows, in fact, progressively narrower as military and political realities explode the coast of dreams. See's treatment of public events, personages, and issues is at best sketchy: Jane Fonda is mentioned, for instance, but never Helen Caldicott. Milton, Marvell, and Scriabin are names invoked to suggest cultural resonance, but relevant texts of popular culture are less present in this L.A. than on the surreal Florida beaches of *Fiskadoro*.

All of the stories and novels treated in this chapter participate, to some degree, in the interchange between science fiction and mainstream fiction writing and fiction reading. On the other hand, Carolyn See, no doubt unintentionally, opens doors in a very different literary-cultural direction—toward children's literature. For as will be seen in the following chapter, certain works of juvenile fiction in the 1970s and 1980s confront nuclear issues directly and responsibly; others contrive narratives built more dubiously on myth, magical thinking, romance, wish fulfillment. See may never have read books like Louise Lawrence's *Children of the Dust* (1985) or Pamela Service's *Winter of Magic's Return* (1985). Though quite different in important respects, all three entertain the premise that nuclear attack and devastation can not only be survived but will prove beneficial. See does not go as far toward literary or religious fable as Lawrence and Service do. See's California, by contrast, is never just dreamland, though its denizens often act as though it were. But, like O'Brien's *Nuclear Age*, her satire skirts many fundamental realities of nuclear fear. When the Bomb falls on Los Angeles, it raises problems for everyone that cannot be circumvented—to the moral satisfaction of many readers, at least—by authorial declarations that female (or male) fantasies can be declared exempt from the effects of radiation.

4

Children, Literature, and the Bomb

If we cannot agree on ethical principles, and if we cannot remember the horrors of history, perhaps we can at least take note of the children.
Marvin Bell ("Because Writers Are Scared")

Seeing comes before words. The child looks and recognizes before it can speak. But there is another sense in which seeing comes before words. It is seeing which establishes our place in the surrounding world.
John Berger (*Ways of Seeing*)[1]

IF HIROSHIMA AS FACT AND METAPHOR MARKS A TURNING point of modern secular and spiritual history, what has this fact meant to American children and youth? The thinkable event with the unthinkable implications has, for four decades and more, offered unique challenges and opportunities to all sorts of writers working, as we have seen, in popular and esoteric forms with adult audiences. One of the least esoteric but most neglected of these literary forms is children's books, written and illustrated for the very young and for adolescents. As with works for adults, writings for children are rich sources of cultural information on and attitudes about the nuclear age. They create, vicariously and movingly, informative and imaginative encounters with earthshaking events and their aftershocks long antedating young consciousnesses but present in children's lives as adult conversations, media messages, and significant silences. Such books often build early imaginal memories on which adult thoughts and feelings about the Bomb are deeply based.

To be sure, photography and electronic media contribute heavily to these formative impressions. For instance, Eric Barnouw and Paul Ronder's documentary of 1970, *Hiroshima-Nagasaki*, has given American viewers (and others worldwide) one of the most eloquent sequences of visual impressions of the mushroom cloud, the flattened city, and the burnt survivors' bodies.[2] One cannot ascertain, however, how many children have been permitted to share such confrontations, in this case one long kept secret by the U.S. government. Even the 1983 television film *The Day After*, though widely advertised as a family event, did not in fact reach all the young American eyes for which its fictional midwestern reenactment of a nuclear attack was in part intended. Nevertheless, both of these arresting visual messages—like certain fiction films of the 1980s, including *War Games* with its teenage protagonists—are important markers on the culture's road away from silence and secrecy about the matter of Hiroshima.

Yet movies and television documentaries may not in the long run outweigh the less dramatic but more cumulative effects of literature for children, a corpus embracing read-to books for the very young; elementary school books with pictures, adventure stories, and photographs for six- to eleven-year-olds; and secondary school books, biographies, and teen fiction. This literature is, to be sure, chiefly consumed by literate children, usually successful in school, and growing up mainly in middle-class households that regularly patronize the public library. In schools, libraries, Sunday schools, and other public institutions, certain books about the Bomb are now widely available, given sanction by parents, teachers, librarians, clergy, and youth workers and their various professional associations. These individuals and groups are supervisors of official and domestic indoctrination. As a result, a potentially influential and active segment of the population is learning about Hiroshima. Nuclear destruction and nuclear power have become potent psychosocial realities in certain children's minds, where new and frightening worlds of meaning, ideas, and emotions are reexperienced. This historical phenomenon has thus become part of the cultural legacy that must be passed on to the young, the initiates and future rememberers and actors of our society.

Indeed, as Frances FitzGerald, Gordon Kelly, and Jack Zipes have all argued, a key site for understanding a culture's shared and conflicted value systems is where social occasions, communication networks, and audiences of young and old converge to discuss the common past.[3] The nuclear era since 1945, in all its problematic dimensions, is a striking instance and fiercely contested battleground of such socialization. Such influential Americans as Benjamin Spock, Robert Jay and Betty Jean Lifton, Theodor Geisel (Dr. Seuss), Helen Caldicott, Stanley Kubrick, Jane Fonda, and Samantha Smith have contended that this educational enterprise is of ultimate importance. The future of immortality, in Lifton's apt phrase, may hang on its success. "I have been worrying about Russia and the United States getting into a nuclear war," young Samantha Smith, a Maine schoolgirl, wrote Soviet General Secretary Yuri Andropov in 1982. "Are you going to vote to have a war or not? If you aren't, please tell me how you are going to help to not have a war." Later she added, "[N]othing could be more important than NOT having a war if a war could kill everything."[4]

Whether addressing private fears of catastrophe, as Samantha Smith did, or seeking literary fame and commercial success, contemporary authors have notably enlarged the horizon of attention encompassing Hiroshima, Bikini, and future nuclear holocausts. Their targets are American children situated in homes, at school, or in the public library, before the TV set, or opening a birthday or Christmas present. Like other superintendents of cultural communication, these writers and illustrators are, of course, adults. As FitzGerald reminds us, both authors and their allies are influential because they are so strategically located. Zipes sharpens this insight when he observes, "[L]iterature for children is not children's literature by and for children in their behalf. It never was and never will be. Literature for children is script coded by adults for the information and internalization of children which must meet the approbation of adults. . . . It is the adult author's symbolically social act intended to influence and perhaps control the future of culture" (19).

This potentially powerful instrument in the hands of writers can be broadly categorized as either imaginative (that is, metaphoric) fiction or representational nonfiction, utilizing either fanciful illustrations or sharply focused photographs. In psychological terms, these writings provide free-floating pleasure but may also specify dutiful and even guilt-ridden responses. Hence they exploit both primary-process and secondary-process thinking. Socially speaking, children's nuclear literature is purchased, stored, and used in both public and private places. Indirectly or openly, such artifacts encourage or perhaps subvert the norms and goals of specific social groups and polities. Thus they fit most of the functions that cultural critics like Jane Tompkins, Gordon Kelly, Philip Fisher, and Barbara Herrnstein Smith assert are the cultural work that literature performs in literate societies.[5]

"Until fairly recently," Paul Brians writes of this literature, "little fiction about nuclear war had been written for young readers. Critics and scholars paid the subject almost no attention. Adults find it difficult to confront the danger of atomic warfare for themselves; explaining the unthinkable to children is a daunting task. Yet more and more authors are trying. Interest in the subject was no doubt sparked by the intense public controversy surrounding ABC-TV's movie, *The Day After*. The broadcast was a breakthrough. Previously it may have been assumed that nuclear war was an unsuitable subject for young people's fiction. Now more nuclear war fiction for young readers is being published each year."[6]

Some breakthrough novels widely cited by Brians and other pioneers in the field are Whitley Strieber's *Wolf of Shadows*, Louise Lawrence's *Children of the Dust*, Gloria D. Miklowitz's series *After the Bomb* (1984) and *After the Bomb—Week One* (1987), and Gudrun Pausewang's *The Last Children of Schevenborn* (1983).[7] But Brians reports that by 1988 he had read some 1,000 books on the nuclear theme, many available to the young. Among these, as the above short list suggests, are books popular with younger American readers but written by international authors—Lawrence of England and Pausewang of Germany, for example. Given the global dimensions of the nuclear predicament as progressively revealed to all Americans, cross-cultural authorship and readerships are not only understandable but essential. Indeed, for an ethically oriented critic like Millicent Lenz, a primary aim of all nuclear writing for youth should be, as mentioned in the previous chapter, to "show a planetary vision of unity and wholeness, the interconnectedness of all beings," as "a more powerful and seductive idea than any vision of war or fragmentation" (248).

As we shall see, equally noteworthy books in other genres address much younger readers and are likewise written by non-Americans. Of these, the pioneer work is doubtless Toshi Maruki's *Hiroshima No Pika* (The Hiroshima Flash) of 1980.[8] Maruki demonstrates to American writers, as do Maxine Kumin and Lifton, the worldwide impact of the Japanese novelist Masuji Ibuse's *Black Rain*—particularly, perhaps, on adolescent readers. A similar cross-generational as well as international influence earlier characterized the Australian Nevil Shute (*On the Beach*) and two later British novelists, Raymond Briggs (*When the Wind Blows* [1982]) and Russell Hoban (*Riddley Walker*).

Whether American adolescents are targeted readers of age-specific works or covert consumers of "adult" novels, they were probably at one time childish readers or listeners. Hence it is appropriate to begin examination of this literary-social phenomenon with illustrated books (accompanied, in nearly every case, by written texts). The 1980s saw publication of several outstanding illustrated books. As we have already noted in reference to more than one area of adult literature, this timing was no accident, since that was the decade when significant numbers of Americans learned enough about the Bomb to begin to overcome their ignorance and avoidance and became activists. Such renewed concern was triggered by events children could not help but learn from and experience along with adults: Reagan's warlike rhetoric and policies; Schell's book and Carl Sagan's "Nova" television series on nuclear winter; other television hits and successful films, including *The Day After*, *The Day after Trinity: J. Robert Oppenheimer and the Bomb* (1980), *The China Syndrome* (1979),

Testament (1983), *War Games* (1983), and *Miracle Mile* (1989), not to mention oldies often seen as reruns, such as *On the Beach* and *Dr. Strangelove.* If the 1980s were broadly experienced as a watershed in nuclear history and politics, it is peculiarly appropriate to focus on the nuclear literature offered in these years to American younger readers as both present and future participants in cultural dialogues.

In retrospect, two illustrated books stand out from others issued in the past decade or so: Maruki's *Hiroshima No Pika* and an American reply (by implication at least), Judith Vigna's *Nobody Wants a Nuclear War.*[9] The latter has apparently become a favorite of children's literature professionals, many of whom previously objected to any exposure of preschool children to nuclear reality. Both books, I will argue, are ideologically and culturally more explicit than many others of their kind that appeared in the same period, including favorites like Dr. Seuss's *The Butter Battle Book* (1984), David Macauley's *Baaa* (1985), and Umberto Eco and Eugenio Carmi's *The Bomb and the General* (1989).[10]

A recent commentary on this trend—and on nuclear literature for all young readers—came during the Persian Gulf War. In February 1991, a front-page story in the *Iowa City Press-Citizen* was headlined, "War Talk Can Overwhelm Children." The reporter observed that "some local day-care workers and pre-school and elementary school teachers are seeing the effects of war in children's play, language, emotions, and questions. Younger children may not understand war," she added, "but they sense that their parents are upset. They hear snippets of war talk on television and [in] adult conversations. They have questions and some have fears, but they can't talk about them as older children can."[11] What followed was a suggested list of books (including nuclear ones with illustrations) for use in helping children cope with "war talk."

As this topical item suggests, even preschool children who do not read yet can participate significantly in war hysteria and the nuclear fears that, off and on, have gripped American society for over half a century. The children's books cited in the *Press-Citizen* therefore constitute cultural communication at ground zero. *Nobody Wants a Nuclear War*, in particular, connects children's play, language acquisition, and emotional development to the matter of the atomic bomb and the dark cloud still hanging over American minds and households as well as other key locations like day-care centers and the Pentagon. To continue to dismiss child-adult transactions over a seemingly strictly adult issue is tacitly to perpetuate the ignorance/avoidance/repression syndrome so long characteristic of major sectors of the American populace. The sad history, a psychosocial as well as political reality, of "*lock the bomb in a burglar-proof safe and don't discuss it,*" precedes and postdates the 1950s, where the popular culture critic Michael Strada locates this common reaction (191). As initiation handbooks, works like *Hiroshima No Pika* and *Nobody Wants a Nuclear War* articulate, perhaps for the first time in some families, basic assumptions and values about war and violence, mass death and individual survival, passive avoidance and active (that is, suicidal) despair, curiosity and willful ignorance, rationalization and responsibility. "War is the culture of our age and the culture *is* war," we recall, was the judgment passed in 1950 by the Dun Commission; 40 years later, this generalization is no more easily kept from our children than on the day the H-bomb's birth was announced. "The mythology of war is alive and well in today's schools and in society at large," Millicent Lenz asserted as recently as 1990 (3).

If so, the first issue to raise about Maruki's and Vigna's books as bellwether texts of the 1980s is whether either writer for children dares to articulate such a blunt and sweeping diagnosis of American culture. Behind this issue, though, lies a more theoretical question: what model of cultural communication is most pertinent to child-adult transactions? In *Communication as Culture* (1989), James W. Carey argues persuasively against the conventional assumption that social communication is chiefly information transfer from one mind or entity to another. The implicit prototype for this oversimplification is the linear one of the railroad or interstate highway with its carriers of economic and cultural goods from one point to another. Carey posits an alternative model admirably applicable to children's reading formations. In his terms, reading *Nobody Wants a Nuclear War* is less information-sharing than community-building and communion. It is not simply data transfer but a social occasion that constitutes the culture of a household, school, or day-care center whose shared values are being *made* rather than simply *delivered*.[12]

Imagine, then, not just texts or pictures but the social interactions of one of these pioneer nuclear books. This might consist of a young child, old enough perhaps to pick out words or even read basic stories, either asking to be read to at home—snugly at the elbow of parent, older sibling, or babysitter—or willingly (or perhaps unwillingly) listening to an adult reader in a preschool or elementary school or at a public library's Saturday morning or summertime program. Remember, too, the child's mind, eyes, fingers, and tongue often participating in and precipitating new insights or questions in the older reader's mind as they together reactivate the story and discuss the illustrations. In such circumstances—doubtless no longer an everyday occurrence in many middle-class homes—the force of the psychological truism is felt: "While the family is bringing up the baby, the baby is bringing up the family." Seeing pictures, as the epigraph quote by John Berger declares, is central to socialization.

To connect such theoretical and practical considerations to these two picture books about the Bomb one must keep in mind that, although *Hiroshima No Pika* is set in Japan and was written by a Japanese woman, it was simultaneously published in Tokyo and New York. Yet no American soldier, B-29, or "Little Boy" bomb is actually depicted. Vigna's later book, on the other hand, has struck many readers as a thoroughly American story. Even though thematically similar and aimed at roughly the same age group of reader-listeners, it has an American suburban or rural setting and a cast of white middle-class characters. It, too, fails to show or mention a single engine or engineer of nuclear destruction. Though each book tells young readers that an American plane delivered the Bomb, both make sure that children do not see the aerial act actually performed.

As the earlier and trailblazing book, *Hiroshima No Pika* should be examined first, for it may have encouraged American authors like Judith Vigna to open up this touchy topic and treat it with untraditional directness. The linkage has not, to my knowledge, been made, but in general, nuclear literature, film, and art have often originated abroad and found American audiences before encouraging American creative imaginations. Americans perfected and dropped the first bombs, tested them at the Bikini Atoll, and developed an arsenal of ever more lethal weaponry in the years after 1950. But as creators and critics of nuclear cultural artifacts, we have often lagged behind European and Japanese artists. Such diffidence helps to explain the fact that, since 1980, *Hiroshima No Pika* has received considerably more critical attention than it has enjoyed bookstore sales. Maruki's humanitarian motives for telling the survival story of little Mii are welcomed, however, by peace activists, many librarians, and by biophilic critics like Lenz. "As an anti-war and anti-nuclear weapons statement," Lenz has written, "the book has few equals" (49). Yet even today, concerned citizens who are parents of five- or six-year-olds may hesitate to buy this book. The author confronts such fears boldly. "I am now past seventy years old," Maruki writes in an afterword. "I have neither children nor grandchildren. But I have written this book for grandchildren everywhere. It took me a very long time to complete it. It is very difficult to tell young people about something very bad that happened, in the hope that their knowing will help keep it from happening again."

Over several decades after Hiroshima's flash, Maruki collected stories from *hibakusha*. One interviewee became the prototype of Mii's mother. Then the author-artist thought about different strategies for simultaneously communicating, criticizing, and containing the horrors she had heard. One decision was to depict the postexplosion sufferings of Mii's family in graphic but at the same time artistic, even at times lyric, detail. Another was to surround images of death and destruction in a narrative envelope of comforting pictures of everyday events. Therefore, in the opening, three double-page spreads show "normal" wartime routine disrupted in the doomed city by the fateful flash (see Figure 4.1). Then, in the holocaust's aftermath, a final spread shows the anniversary lanterns set afloat on the rivers of Hiroshima each year thereafter, "in memory of those who died." Mii's father is one victim thus remembered, but Mii's mother is the survivor from the beginning to the end of the family's ordeal. On 6 August she serves sweet potatoes—not rice, which is severely rationed—at the family's breakfast. By story's end, her "hair . . . now turned white," she "watches sorrowfully as her daughter sets the lanterns afloat." Then she remarks with guarded hope: "[I]t can't happen again . . . if no one drops the bomb" (opposite last illustration).

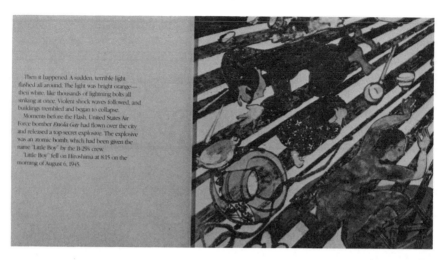

Then it happened. A sudden, terrible light flashed all around. The light was bright orange—then white, like thousands of lightning bolts all striking at once. Violent shock waves followed, and buildings trembled and began to collapse.

Moments before the Flash, United States Air Force bomber *Enola Gay* had flown over the city and released a top-secret explosive. The explosive was an atomic bomb, which had been given the name "Little Boy" by the B-29's crew.

"Little Boy" fell on Hiroshima at 8:15 on the morning of August 6, 1945.

Figure 4.1

In between these reassuring bookends is a remarkably graphic children's tale. A score of violently beautiful colored drawings depict Hiroshima's leveling, the firestorm, black rain, and piles of corpses. Yet all the while the two are confronting these horrors, little Mii clutches a pair of red chopsticks in her fist. Even as flames and flood threaten to engulf them, the mother's strong arm is raised and the chopsticks are clutched. They are signs of the pair's eventual preservation from the rain of death.

Nature, too, is both ravished and then redeemed—or at least partially preserved—in *Hiroshima No Pika*. In a central spread Mii, her mother, and her wounded father collapse on a riverbank (see Figure 4.2).

> Mii felt something moving past her feet. Hop . . . hop. . . . It was a swallow. Its wings were burned, and it couldn't fly. Hop . . . hop. . . . She saw a man floating slowly down the river. Floating behind him was the body of a cat. (opposite ninth illustration)

As elsewhere in this double-barreled message, death is represented as candidly and as peacefully as Maruki's honesty and discretion can permit. The cat seems almost tranquilized in contrast to the hopping swallows, which are dripping blood. Similarly, a grisly scene of black rain falling on a heap of dead bodies is overarched, at upper right, by a beautiful rainbow.

Another strategy for communicating a "very bad" message in untraumatizing words and images is Maruki's careful separation of Mii's individual escape from the fate of less fortunate victims. The latters' sufferings are drawn as stylized dances of death. Even thus depicted, they are usually further removed to different pages from Mii and her mother. One key moment when this does

Mii and her mother and father continued their escape and crossed another river. When they reached the far bank, Mii's mother put her husband down and collapsed on the ground beside him.

Figure 4.2

not happen, when the living and dying come together, is at the point when the narrator says: "Mii started to cry softly. An old woman who was lying nearby sat up and took a rice ball out of her bag and gave it to Mii. When Mii took it from her, the woman fell down again. This time she didn't move" (Maruki, opposite sixteenth illustration). On the opposing page, the artist depicts the girl dancing toward the life-giving rice ball, which is gracefully proffered by the half-naked, white-haired benefactress. In the foreground lie two women and two children, dead though visually asleep (see Figure 4.3).

"Life in death," then, is Maruki's bittersweet message to her fictional grandchildren, none of whom has actually survived nuclear bombing. This in effect reverses the title and message of Lifton's *Death in Life*. The hopeful reversal is visually reinforced as Mii and her mother return to the ravaged city. The artist separates the two figures from Hiroshima's lethal rubble by using white paint to create a magical aura around them. A similar safety zone, on the opposite page, preserves Mii's rice bowl. "Bent and broken, it still contained

Figure 4.3

some sweet potatoes." By this point in the story, Mii's mother has pried the chopsticks from her daughter's fist: "Four days after the bomb, Mii let go of her chopsticks." A final signal of escape is portrayed on the back cover, where Mii (now older but permanently stunted in her growth) holds the memorial lantern in the same little hands. But her once-abundant black hair is now stringy and thin and the adult reader must decide whether to skip the sentences about radiation sickness and the father's "purple spots" before he died. Mii's own chances of survival are unmentioned.

In 1980 Toshi Maruki opened a crucial decade in nuclear history by striking a new note in children's literature and minds. As the world's grandmother addressing all children (but especially Japanese and American ones), she paints and writes in wavy lines, using vivid (or soft) colors to allay brutal reality by reassuring signs of survival and hope. She leads children and their older coreaders and interpreters through an encounter with actual holocaust. She thereby reenacts for fearful, immature minds who identify with Mii and her mother a symbolic death and rebirth. Using traditional Eastern symbols like chopsticks and rice balls, she makes the frighteningly foreign understandable to American readers under the familiar rubrics of maternal love, food, birds, rainbows, hope. She thus contributes to the crucial but still widely uncompleted task of helping young American children begin the dual process of engagement and reconciliation that John Hersey started with adults in 1946.

Culturally and aesthetically, Judith Vigna's *Nobody Wants a Nuclear War* operates on a very different plane. It not only sends a simpler message than Maruki's but aims that message at American children only (so far as text and pictures suggest). Her audience appears to be six-, seven-, or eight-year-olds. If the *Press-Citizen* story is indicative, her book has probably sold many more copies to this audience than has *Hiroshima No Pika*, by comparison with which its consoling assumptions are more readily perceived—and welcomed—by key superintendents like librarians, teachers, and parents. The most obvious difference and asset is Vigna's imaginative distancing of the historical realities whose repercussions still give children nightmares or at least excite their anxieties. Vigna's distance from Maruki's direct treatment is as much emotional and geographical as cultural. She creates a conventional American household in which, as in Maruki's case, the central figures are children and their mother. The father is a shadowy presence in both stories, and one effect of contrasting the two books is to emphasize that the father's death in *Hiroshima No Pika* is treated with surprisingly little pathos. In Vigna's American suburban situation, the father comes home only at the end to serve simply as the cameraman who photographs the peace banner his children have made with their mother's encouragement.

Like Maruki, Vigna stresses children's fears and struggles to deal with a vague but threatening reality. A brother and sister, on the opening page, are running for shelter under a lowering sky. They worry not about a summer storm but whether

> "[t]he whole world will blow up.
>   There'll be no more houses or trees or animals or parents.
>   Only a dark smoky desert
>   like we saw on television."
>   (opposite second illustration)

Perhaps the last line indicates that these children have recently seen *The Day After*, which premiered three years before. But there were certainly other 1980s television shows that could have scared sensitive seven-year-olds and triggered their chief concern: "Will I ever live to grow up?" Vigna writes to assuage such fears. Though not those of a *hibakusha* or even an American adult, these anxieties are treated as eminently reasonable. Her protagonists seek to get away from the clouds of Hiroshima and Chernobyl by building a hideaway in a nearby cave. The hideout is secretly stocked with cans of meatballs and soup,

But it was only Mommy.
"We were making a hideaway
in case there's a nuclear war," I explained.

Figure 4.4

healthy American equivalents of rice balls and sweet potatoes. But the cave's chief feature is a "big snuggly picnic blanket" on which the girl and boy fall asleep, feeling safe. But suddenly a loud crash and bright light awaken them. Has a nightmare come true? "I thought the nuclear war had started," the girl narrator exclaims. "But it was only Mommy"—and the family dog (see Figure 4.4). The children are doubly relieved when

> Mommy, surprised, hugged us. "I know how scared you must feel," she said. "Lots of children worry about nuclear war. . . . Daddy and I will always try to be with you, no matter what. We care about you more than anything else in the world." (opposite eighth illustration)

Mommy carries reassurance a step further when, safely home, she gives her children a brief history lesson at the luncheon table. Whether her presentation is adequate to the needs of contemporary seven-year-olds or sidesteps fundamental facts and issues is a question that readers may disagree about, especially in the aftermath of *The Day After*. Vigna seeks to balance the choices by careful wording:

> "In 1945 . . . there was a kind of nuclear war. . . . The United States dropped an atomic bomb on the city of Hiroshima in Japan. The bomb brought an end to the war, but the destruction it caused was more terrible than anyone could have ever imagined." (opposite ninth illustration)

Whatever its simplifications, this explanation emerges from Mommy's own fears and reservations. One little girl, she explains, was once so frightened by duck-and-cover civil defense drills at school that she thought she would never live to grow up. But "that little girl *did* grow up. In fact, she now has children of her own. I know because that scared little girl was me" (opposite eleventh illustration).

Next, the pair learn from Mommy about active antinuclear involvement. Mr. Green, the next-door neighbor, writes letters to the newspaper, and the mother herself belongs "to a group which sometimes has rallies." For their part, the sister and brother decide to turn their snuggly picnic blanket into a peace banner. "Grown-Ups for a Safer World to Grow Up In" is their slogan. This childish act, however modest, gives Vigna's parable of fear, reassurance, and involvement an unusual outcome. Instead of explaining that the Bomb just happened, as most previous children's books even mentioning the subject had done—with no humans responsible and children (by implication at least) just waiting for it to happen again—specific ordinary adults are here shown taking responsibility and political action. Children, too, participate in these typical 1980s protests. The peace banner, like Mommy's semiactive group, are admittedly modest gestures. But at least no magical solution (including the promise of survival) is forthcoming. Hence nuclear critics like Paul Brians greeted *Nobody Wants a Nuclear War* with praise. "It is not enough, Vigna indicates, to reassure children (as does the mother in her book) that we have lived with nuclear weapons for a long time and that nobody wants to use them. They need the hope provided by adult action to prevent war" ([1988], 25). Brians, like Bruce Franklin and many other nuclear critics, is deeply disturbed by the wishful thinking and simplistic political answers young children and teenagers are still receiving in the late 1980s through illustrated books and even in most teen fiction. Vigna's timidly bold contribution at least underlines the dimensions of the problem.

These critiques, qualified by admittedly atypical illustrated books for children like Maruki's and Vigna's, underline the necessity (in cultural and political terms) of exposing American children, from an early age, to diverse cultural approaches to their world, which they already know is a nuclear one. Ideological conflicts or questions, even within a single cultural perspective, are inevitable outside of children's reading formations. Hence within the young readers' ken, the likelihood is high that readers or listeners of both Mii's story and Vigna's comfortable parable will note that emphasis falls upon maternal rather than paternal authority and support. Older, more critically sophisticated readers will also note that both books were written a whole generation or more after the nuclear age began, when the fears of children and grown-ups had become significant psychosocial data. Why did it take so long for reasonably honest stories to appear—first in the victimized nation, and only later in the (militarily speaking) instigator nation? Why, given the changing political climate around the globe, do Maruki and Vigna not take the next logical—and surely less threatening—step that their ideologies imply and openly invite their child readers to see that war itself, not the Bomb, is the root of their legitimate anxiety? Must not cultural critics conclude that *adult* fear, delay, silence, and evasion are still at play in these texts meant to allay childish emotions?

The gender issue is surely pertinent to these questions. Since women and children were prominently numbered among the first nuclear victims, it should surprise no one that, long before the activist 1980s, polls and interviews of Americans of different ages, genders, and classes indicated that, first, nuclear awareness and dread was more widespread among women than men, or at least more openly acknowledged; and second, that young persons were and still are particularly susceptible to the fact that "the bombs, like death itself [have] become part of the general background of living." As Weart points out above,

> [w]ell after the Cuban Missile Crisis, a poll found 40% of adolescents admitting a "great deal" of anxiety about war, more than twice the rate found in older groups. A survey that said nothing about bombs, but only asked school children to talk about the world ten years ahead, found that over two-thirds of the children mentioned war, often in terms of sombre helplessness. In 1965, a song lamenting that we were on the "Eve of Destruction" became the first song on a political issue to become a number one popular tune in the United States. (265)

If to such 1960s and 1970s evidence are added data from John E. Mack and William Beardslee, Robert Coles, the *Iowa City Press-Citizen*, and, most recently, a *New York Times* series, "After the Cold War," we can plausibly posit a long-range psychosocial pattern often ignored by sociologists and political commentators.[13] Children and adolescents are, in fundamental respects, *hibakusha*; even though most of them would not recognize the word, they have internalized the postnuclear condition. Thus the *Times* series opened on 1 February 1992 with personal memories of the cold war by the 42-year-old John Driscoll, particularly memories of "the fear that came with the air raid drills at school when he and other students crawled under their desks, practicing for the day the Soviet hydrogen bombs fell. 'It seems surreal now,' he recalled recently, a short time after the Soviet Union announced its demise. 'Every summer, when I heard heat lightning over the city and the sky would light up, I was convinced it was all over. My whole childhood was built on the notion that the Soviets were the real threat.' "[14]

From this ground of actual memories, as well as from popular or avant-garde reading formations, we may assemble a consensus agenda of questions on the minds of many youthful readers that stimulated socially conscious writers like Maruki, Vigna, and Whitley Strieber. After all, authors of all degrees of sophistication routinely imagine what readers want to know and how to feel about their worlds. Their stories are tailored, in part, to satisfy these overt or unconscious needs. Here is a synthesis of likely queries that juvenile (and even many adolescent) readers have about the swirling arguments and underground murmurs of their elders in the ongoing dialogue over the matter of Hiroshima.

1. What *is* an atomic bomb, anyway?
2. What actually happened at Hiroshima, Nagasaki, Bikini, Three Mile Island, and Chernobyl?
3. Were families and children really targeted by American nuclear bombs?
4. Could the same happen to me?
5. Is the nuclear threat still something to fear after 40-plus years?
6. What is radiation sickness? Can it kill me even if the Russians don't attack?
7. Why aren't these questions answered in this book I'm reading (or listening to)?
8. How necessary to our American way of life are atomic bombs?
9. Will plants, animals, and the world be destroyed in World War III?

We should not suppose that these are just adult concerns projected onto children as readers. Indeed, many or most are shared openly or covertly between the generations. For example, around 1980, one Newton, Massachusetts, high school student polled 550 of his schoolmates. "About one-third of these young men and women were fairly certain they would see a nuclear war take place," Robert Coles reports in *The Moral Life of Children* (1986). Three years later, a poll in Akron found that a "high percentage" of Ohio schoolchildren "associated the word nuclear with destructive imagery as opposed to peacetime use" (Coles, 245)—this, in the face of the decades-long effort of the government and the nuclear power industry to make post-Bikini Americans happy and hopeful about nuclear energy.

To be more precise about other psychosocial drives impelling designated socializers of troubled American youth, an adult agenda of nuclear questions is also desirable. Here are some repeated issues and concerns of grown-ups emerging out of the dialogue's records:

1. How much information do young people of various ages need to know about nuclear war and weaponry?
2. How may stories and pictures be combined to calm even very young children's fears of mass destruction?
3. Can we pretend or actually believe that large-scale nuclear attacks are survivable?
4. If as adults we are not sure what to think or feel about Nagasaki and its legacy, how can we answer children's or teenagers' questions about, say, *The Day After*?
5. Why do we hide or mask information and moral attitudes about the Bomb when we no longer do so with other key issues—death, divorce, drugs, racism?

    6. Who is chiefly responsible for dealing directly with these touchy topics—
       parents, teachers, Dr. Spock, librarians, the clergy, kids' peers, television,
       books?

Though very different age groups and social classes are mixed together in this reconstruction, I think some such formulation helps the cultural historian thicken what anthropologists call "-etic" analysis—that is, the natives' own discourse as the basis of analysis—of the nuclear phenomenon. From many different and widespread sources like John Driscoll's testimony in the *Times* article emerge data suggesting that adult Americans share with children the practice of magical thinking and fantasizing about nuclear matters so as to calm their own as well as others' anxiety and dread. Thus Stephanie Tolan, author of *The Pride of the Peacock* (1986), a popular teenager's story, probably speaks for many when she declares, "I would not speak against anything that offers children an alternative to despair, no matter how unlikely a scientist might find the idea."[15] If widely shared, this strain of anti-intellectualism represents a sharp reversal of our society's onetime admiration for scientists and their standards of public knowledge and freedom from censorship. (However, we have already seen the fate, during World War II, of Niels Bohr's passionate argument for sharing nuclear secrets, thus honoring science's ideals and working principles.) Though the heroine in *The Pride of the Peacock* decides to join the nuclear freeze movement, Tolan usually favors dreams, romance, beauty, fantastic plots, and miraculous solutions to the nuclear threat. There are many such stories for the young. In Pamela Service's *Winter of Magic's Return* (1985), for instance, an atomic bomb blows a Welsh mountaintop away, liberating Merlin from its depths to wave his magic wand again over the threatened world.[16] This truly unscientific solution is complete with unicorns as an answer to post-Hiroshima realities. "Do we really want to encourage children to think of nuclear war as a gateway to a more exciting, adventuresome future?" asks Paul Brians ([1988], 25).

His question and Tolan's reply should also be applied to texts written for teenagers—and addressed to their authors—as well as the texts written and illustrated for younger readers. Doing so involves entering a twilight zone between adolescent and adult fiction, a market and taste community of indeterminate but probably large size. Beginning with Hersey's *Hiroshima* and later embracing coterie classics like Shute's *On the Beach*, Golding's *Lord of the Flies*, Roshwald's *Level 7*, Bradbury's *Martian Chronicles*, and Robinson's *The Wild Shore*, precocious youths and even average adolescents have often shared imaginative experiences and picked up similar value statements with and from grown-ups. To be sure, each group filters a given book through different screens of knowledge, emotion, and ethical awareness.

One critic raising some grim questions about the consequences of such cross-generational book-sharing is Hamida Bosmajian, who writes:

> We express our fears and anxieties about nuclear war through images, plot patterns, and narrative modes shaped by the conventions of apocalyptic writings and science fictions. . . . Those conventions hold for nuclear fictions intended for adult readers and even more in narratives for adolescents. . . . Nuclear narratives for the young are at best pseudo-critiques of nuclear arms and war, for none of them probe the political, military and economic forces that maintain power through the arms race. . . . In spite of occasionally gruesome details, these narratives *entertain* not only in the sense of "amuse," but also in the archaic sense of the word—"to continue with," "to maintain."[17]

Teenage novels, Bosmajian claims, comfort, reassure, and evade at least as blatantly as do illustrated books for the very young. Their chief mode is the survivor adventure tale, a formulaic narrative that begins after the (future) Bomb has exploded. All too frequently, its action unfolds in a historical and ethical void, without any realistic depiction of what, how, or why nuclear catastrophe has happened.

As Millicent Lenz argues, there are in print many teenage fictions—as well as nonfiction and quasi-fictional accounts—by which to test Bosmajian's contention. In terms of popularity, fictions probably outnumber, and are more influential than, "scientific" or factually responsible narratives. A popularity advantage is all the more likely with a fiction series that, as in other sorts of adolescent literature, traces successive adventures of a teenage hero or heroine. One example is Barbara and Scott Siegel's *Firebrats* series, which, as Lenz points out, is closely modeled on the more sensationalistic adult *Survivalist* series by Jerry Ahern.[18] Less romantic, more responsible, and more culturally revealing of basic values and attitudes are two novels by Gloria D. Miklowitz, *After the Bomb* (1985) and *After the Bomb—Week One* (1987). The author's intent in these paperback stories is directly to pass on to young readers the findings and viewpoints of prominent adult nuclear writers. "The events in this book, while fictitious, are based on what might well happen in the event of a single one-megaton bomb falling on any large city in the world," her preface to *After the Bomb* declares. The following fiction is openly indebted to Hersey, Schell, and *The Final Epidemic: Physicians and Scientists on Nuclear War* (1981). But she also pays tribute to Maruki's *Hiroshima No Pika*. In addition, this conscientious author has interviewed a dozen or so California scientists, doctors, nurses, firefighters, police officers, and military experts on disaster control. Therefore information-hungry adolescents are likely to grant Miklowitz considerable authority, despite her being a fictionist.

Strengthening emotional as well as cognitive ties is a reader's easy identification with her 15-year-old protagonist, Philip Singer. As the urban community of Los Angeles struggles to survive an accidental Soviet nuclear attack, Philip struggles with his own identity as younger brother in a representative American family. Naturally, the younger not only triumphs over the condescending older brother, Matt, but wins the fight with his self-doubts and immaturity. In the process, Philip, Matt, and their girlfriend Cara turn the tables on other, younger nuclear age fictional characters. Instead of relying upon a strong maternal guide—the father *is* absent from much of the action in both novels—the boys must carry their badly burned mother to a hospital. There they encounter enough "gruesome details" of nuclear violence to please Bosmajian. In this representative moment, Philip enacts an all but explicit parallel to *Hiroshima No Pika*.

> The hand pulled [Philip] firmly toward a woman holding a baby. The woman's mouth was open in a silent scream. Most of her clothes had been burned off. The skin on her face and arms hung loose. . . .
> The woman didn't seem to hear or understand, and clasped her dead baby in a vise-like grip. The lifeless form resembled something overcooked. Philip turned away and began to heave.
> "Stop that," the nurse said quietly. "Now help me. I'll hold her arms and you pry the baby free."
> He couldn't bear to touch the charred body, afraid it might disintegrate within his fingers. The smell of burned flesh was overpowering. He continued to gag. He looked away but willed his arms to reach for the baby. He held it at arm's length while the nurse lowered the mother to a mat. She then took the infant from him, wrapped the small form in a towel, and took it away. Philip bent over and threw up. ([1984], 89–90)

Although Miklowitz never dwells on such moments, her stories are sufficiently explicit about nuclear bomb realities to justify amply her young characters'—especially Philip's—sober recognition of their own responsibilities in such a crisis and their previous ignorance of nuclear politics. Philip reflects on these bitter lessons: "A sickening anguish filled his stomach. Until yesterday he'd tuned out everything except what happened in his own small world of school, music, running, his family and friends. Now he realized he'd been stupid, that he should have paid attention to what was happening elsewhere. If grown-ups were so dumb as to keep building bombs and threatening each other like kids with snowballs, then maybe grown-ups weren't any smarter than kids" ([1984], 138).

Part of this ironic awakening is the fact that Philip's father is a scientist at Cal Tech, and it is indicative of Miklowitz's reticence about which grown-ups are culpable that Allen Singer plays an offstage role in *After the Bomb*. He emerges only near the end of its sequel. His belated appearance results from Philip's resolute return from the California evacuation center in the desert to Pasadena and the Cal Tech campus. The 15-year-old son, in a sense, "rescues" the father just as he has carried his wounded and helpless mother to the hospital. Indeed, Philip's exemplary character as competent survivor and caregiver derives from his very American qualities of self-reliance, will power, and resourcefulness. "There were always ways to solve a problem, if you tried hard enough" ([1987], 101) is his working motto. An ancillary quality is Philip's sudden religious realization, amid the holocaust: "Strange how often he called upon God these days when before he hadn't believed" ([1987], 117).

What Philip Singer believes in most devoutly is individual effort—first, on his own behalf, then for family and neighbors. Aiding others more remote—like Soviet scientists and the Soviet people—comes later. As the refugees gather in the desert to listen to the president's explanation of the disaster, he realizes that something more than individual effort on behalf of one's own is required.

Miklowitz's adventure tales conclude, as Bosmajian predicts, on an upbeat, politically inconclusive note. One adolescent exemplar of native pluck, self-centeredness, and cooperation in a crisis survives the destruction of Los Angeles. Together with family and newfound girlfriend, he awaits radio assurance of presidential leadership in a message that, like much of this story's future, is not spelled out. Therefore Millicent Lenz, for one, is left dissatisfied. "Philip's adoption of the 'me and mine first' survival ethic is presented as admirable in the novel and all readers will rejoice that his mother has an edge in obtaining treatment. If one tries to translate this ethic from the personal realm and make it a universal principle, however, hard questions are raised. On reflection, one can recognize how it incorporates the myth of the chosen tribe (one's own) and falls dismally short of the ethic needed by a global, nuclear community" (151–52). Lenz proceeds to underscore an important shortcoming of the teenage survival story as here exemplified. "The effects of radioactive fallout are not dealt with, presumably because they would not surface until later," she observes, "but this is questionable, given the knowledge we have of actual *hibakusha* experience, and suggests authorial (or editorial?) timidity." Then she mentions "the far superior and more truthful narrative" by the German prizewinner Gudrun Pausewang, *The Last Children of Schevenborn.* "If it could be set side-by-side with [*After the Bomb—Week One,* it] would demonstrate the gulf between the wishful soft-pedaling of the consequences of nuclear destruction and the preferred fantasy mode of narration so characteristic of the American approach" (152). In light of the fact that Pausewang's 1983 novel did not appear in English until 1988 and even today is available to North American readers only from a Canadian publisher, Lenz's cross-cultural critique is apt and underlines further the need for American readers to become more familiar with foreign books for youth. Indeed, comparing the German book with Miklowitz's pair demonstrates not only the inevitable similarities of adolescent survival tales but also the range of insights and nuclear information that can be included in the formula.

Both Philip Singer and Roland Bennewitz are young teenagers suddenly catapulted into terrifying maturity by the Bomb. Both learn how to endure by working in a hospital, where providing water to the burned and dying is a vital and symbolic act. Both show greater will and energy than their parents, a moral lesson explicitly linked to adult irresponsibility toward prewar nuclear politics and the arms race. Sibling rivalry and nascent sexuality are still other realistic ingredients of these coming-of-age stories. Though shorter than its American counterpart, *The Last Children of Schevenborn* covers a longer time span during which the full game of nuclear truth-or-consequences can be played out. It is a grim game, marked successively by explosion and firestorm, black rain and radiation sickness, typhoid, dysentery and flu, and finally, mutation horrors among the survivors' children. Pausewang's title proves to be literally accurate. The 37 children who survive to attend school in Schevenborn Castle are a steadily shrinking group. "We'll be closing one of the classes soon," Roland, the narrator, observes at the end. "'You can take over the pupils who are left,' my father said to me yesterday. When I gave him a surprised look, he added, 'They won't call you a murderer.' Yes, I'll take over the class. I like teaching. Of course, I'm still too young to be a teacher and I've never really learned how. But the children will accept me because I wasn't a grown-up when the bomb was dropped." Then the teenage teacher draws some concluding lessons for his reader-pupils.

> There are so many things more important than reading, writing, and arithmetic that I absolutely have to teach them. They must want a life without looting, stealing, and killing. They must learn to respect each other again, and to give help where help is needed. They must learn to talk with each other and work together to find solutions to their problems, instead of immediately striking out at one another. They must feel responsible for each other. They must love each other. Their world must be a peaceful one—even though it will not last long. For these are the last children of Schevenborn. (116)

The 17-year-old voicing these ancient values echoes, at least superficially, Philip Singer's sentiments at the conclusion of his nuclear adventure. In the American story, though, the youthful refugees in the desert demonstrate their politics by singing "We Are the World" as "something hopeful" to face the future with. Even the youngest readers will, of course, identify the song with the Coca-Cola commercial, though Miklowitz seems oblivious to this irony.

Irony is, in fact, a major difference between the two stories. Unlike the American narrative, the German one is laced with ironic twists and terms. When Roland and his father, on a food-foraging trip, encounter an East German (who tells them the Bomb has erased the border between the two countries), the stranger bids them an ambiguous goodbye.

> "Everybody has the same slogan now. Survive however you can, even if it's at somebody else's expense."

"That's right," my father said. "We've forgotten all our good up-bringing. It's a case of only the strongest surviving."

"That's the way it is, all right," the man replied. He took off his knapsack, reached inside, and handed me a side of bacon.

"Here," he said. "You could use some fat. You look like the suffer-ing Jesus himself. By the way, if you're going along the border you can make the fastest time on our side; the road that the patrols used to drive along is still there. I see lots of people riding by on bikes. Well, happy survival!" (65–66)

The several changes rung on the idea of survival are indeed subtle here. That living in this postholocaust world means killing, exploiting, or at least witnessing deaths is a truth whose implications thicken as the East German undercuts his own ethic with the bacon. Then, in a story not notably religious in plot, tone, or reference, the image of the 13-year-old boy as "suffering Jesus" is juxtaposed against "happy survival" as a vain wish in one sense but true prophecy in another. Pausewang's young readers are meant to grasp the fact that in a radioactive world all children and adults could be doomed, so the brave acts of service Roland performs at the hospital and castle are at once realistic and worthy examples of "happy survival."

The richness of historical and ideological reference in this ostensible adventure tale is most comprehensively exemplified in the book's major meta-phor of postholocaust experience. Schevenborn Castle looms over the stricken town and world. Less damaged, it comes to house the orphaned, crippled, and abandoned children who are progressively neglected or abused by the adult survivors. The children band together to protect and feed their weaker mem-bers until, one by one, they die. Andreas, a legless refugee living in a baby carriage, expresses the children's disgust for adult life by painting "PARENTS BE DAMNED" on the castle wall. Later, when winter and the Bennewitz baby arrive, the castle becomes their only haven—an ironic Bethlehem stable. The irony is extreme at this point, for this "Christ child" born in the castle's dark and frigid depths is a pitiable nuclear victim huddling in her brother's arms. "My little sister Jessica Marta had no eyes. Where they would have been was skin, nothing but ordinary skin. . . . There she lay now, naked and bloody, and I saw she had only stumps for arms" (105). But this bitter birth is not the castle's final meaning. There the townspeople learn to cooperate enough to clear two rooms for a school. When the children, braving the castle's rats and their own fears and hunger, come to be taught, it is the one hopeful sign of human civilization restored. Their first teacher, however, Roland's father, is far from a culture hero. "Shortly after he opened the school, a boy with a scarred face threw a piece of chalk at him and screamed, 'You murderer!' Later the boy died a horrible death brought on by radiation sickness. . . . Once a girl in his class asked him, 'Did *you* do anything for peace?' He only shook his head. But at least I could respect his honesty" (115).

In the epilogue, Pausewang extends the political-moral discourse that links her to Maruki, David Macauley, and other 1980s authors. "There can be hardly any doubt that our very existence is being threatened by the steadily growing number of nuclear weapons. But many people put this threat out of their minds and refuse to think about it. . . . I have tried to make it imaginable through this story. . . . I have depicted the disaster and its consequences as less catastrophic than they presumably would be in reality, since I had to allow for a survivor who would later be in a position to talk about what had happened" (117). Such explicitness presumes that German adolescents deserve to learn the essential nuclear facts, whether through fictional or nonfictional discourse.

David Macauley's *Baaa* (1985) shows younger—and perhaps older—European readers the same issues and implications through another literary device, the illustrated parable. Before presenting readers with a disturbingly empty world inhabited only by sheep, the author justifies his conceit. "There is no record of when the last person disappeared. The only person who could have recorded when the last person disappeared was the last person to disappear. But no matter who left last, the place was deserted" (7). Then, in case literal-minded readers have missed the irony, Macauley concludes with this imagined vignette: "Much later, a fish cautiously swam toward the beach. It stared at the land for a long time and then turned and swam in the opposite direction" (63).

At this point, it may prove useful to cite the criteria Millicent Lenz employs for recognizing truth about nuclear consequences in catastrophe narratives. Several basic principles can be applied to distinguish stories containing "accurate, careful depiction of probable events and effects" from those that exhibit "wild and misleading wishful thinking." First, all nuclear stories for children must provide honest descriptions of radiation. "Factually based information is essential and can be conveyed through fiction as well as non-fiction. Accuracy entails critiquing the pseudomyth that radiation can somehow improve the species. A variety of non-fiction sources presenting the facts in clear terms is needed to keep the imaginary accounts in perspective." Moreover, Lenz advises both readers and critics that "a harsh view of the consequences of nuclear catastrophe has more survival value than mindless optimism." One should be especially wary of children's stories promoting the false myth of a "successful New Adam and Eve or some version of the Captain America complex." It follows from the first that stories for both adults and children should never promote "total despair and absolute nihilism." Even the most uncompromising of truthful narratives (that is, those depicting the direst consequences) should "convey the idea that *this does not have to happen*." Despair is both insufficient and inaccurate when expressed in stories "that portray nuclear devastation as caused by unknown or unbeatable forces against which there is no human defense" (161–62).

For Lenz, the logical next move for writers is to communicate clearly to young readers that scientific or technological solutions (that is, the "Star Wars" program or bigger bombs) will never solve nuclear dilemmas. Only new ways of thinking and acting toward disarmament and peace will work. Children are never too young, she maintains, to learn that politics, ethics, and the psychology of peaceful coexistence are essential interconnected means of survival in our post-Hiroshima world. This leads inexorably to her final criterion: fictional or nonfictional accounts of nuclear living that, based on whatever principles, condone the destruction of massive numbers of humans are themselves unmitigatedly antihuman disasters. Such realpolitik solutions are "anti-biophilic." Further, such denials of life must never extend to the plants and animals of the earth.

Lenz sometimes rides her biophilic ethic so hard that youthful readers—teenagers in particular—may rebel against the heavily didactic stories she endorses. Nonetheless, her ideology is widely shared across countries and cultures by 1980s writers for the young, particularly Whitley Strieber. Nowhere is Lenz's first principle—that accurate and detailed information should be conveyed to even the youngest of participants in a literate culture—better exemplified than in *Warday: And the Journey Onward*. Arguably intended for both adults and younger readers, this widely read book is also arguably the most successful combination of information and imagination directed at the nuclear dilemmas of the mid-1980s. Its pair of protagonists are adults—Strieber himself and his real-life friend and coauthor, James W. Kunetka. This choice appears to slant *Warday* toward nonfiction, if only because most adolescent stories have a youthful protagonist or two. Yet the book is clearly a hybrid, mixing journalism, imaginary scenes and characters, hypothetical conversations, and real graphs and statistics. It contains numerous affective scenes that Michael Perlman would hail as embodying imaginal memories worthy of incorporation into the psychic bank of Americans, young and old.

Such imagery proves, by the story's conclusion, more significant to the two narrators than the information-loaded messages contained in interviews, government documents, and maps. The plot takes the two men around the United States some years after a nuclear war that has destroyed New York City's eastern boroughs, Washington, D.C., San Antonio, and the silos of North and South Dakota. On the return train ride east, Strieber reflects, "In my mind I am trying to assemble the elements of my journey into some whole image: the people, their voices and faces and stories; the landscapes; the documents; my perceptions and what I feel about all of it. The vision that remains of the journey is complex. It is a great mass of haunting images, of suffering and work, of people who keep on even when they ought to be unable."[19] The cheering power of image and metaphor over "scientific" detail and description underscores the dust jacket's assertion that *Warday* is "a work of fiction that reads like fact." Strieber and Kunetka, like other authors discussed here, believe that "the survivor's tale is the essential document of our time" (3), and they demonstrate that "tale" and "document" can indeed reinforce each other for young readers as for adults. Both readerships, after all, belong to the same generation: they are survivors or the children of survivors and may both be readers of Hersey, Lifton, and Schell. "We are all *hibakusha*" is the common message taken over from *Death in Life* and *The Fate of the Earth*. Their contribution to an essentially nonfiction tradition is a mixed-media narrative that looks back as a way of looking forward. For the book's fictional present is 1993, five years after 28 October 1988, the "Warday" that, in 20 minutes, virtually destroyed the United States. "We are the first generation to see places instantly vaporized," they declare. "Hiroshima and Nagasaki were destroyed, but not so completely as this. In a vaporized place, not even rubble remains" (7).

California and large stretches of the Midwest and South have been spared vaporization in this fiction. Nonetheless, a 30 percent decline in population is one consequence of blast, fire, radiation, electromagnetic pulse, famine, the Cincinnati Flu, and Nonspecific Schlerosing Disease (NSD). Twenty-one million are dead from Cincinnati Flu alone; "the heart does not understand this sort of death, neither the suddenness nor the scale" (7). Strieber himself has sustained a lethal dose of radiation. This means the medical system has triaged him—no further hospital treatment allowed—since, as Kunetka observes, "his ten-year survival probability is zero" (31).

Not only this pathos but Strieber's special sympathy for young people make him an attractive figure for younger readers to identify with. A dying protagonist thus links *Warday* to *The Last Children of Schevenborn*. So, too, do powerful opening and closing scenes with Strieber's son. Elsewhere, children's experiences also carry an extra charge of affect. On the train back from the West, for instance, the adventuring journalists are caught in a terrible duststorm of radioactive particles. Herded off the train in almost pitch-darkness, they take refuge in a Kansas City elementary school. "They do not look like the kids Andrew went to school with," Strieber notes. "When I meet those eyes, they do not look away and they do not smile" (327–28). He offers samples of the personal writings of these post-Bomb children, in which they reveal what is behind their unsmiling faces.

SPRING RAIN INSTRUCTIONS

If it rains get inside right away. And if you get wet you have to go to the office for geiger, then showers and get rid of your clothes. If you don't have any more you have to be in your underpants. You have to be careful, but spring rain is also nice.

RAINBOW

Lord Jesus sent a rainbow to say its OK, folks. Dad and Mom went on the cleanup. I was scared, I was home alone all night. Then Miss Wilson came and said come to the cleanup. They taught me how to get the particles with the Dustbuster, and I got a lot. . . . The Dustbusters are heavy because they have lead on them. (329–30)

Similarly, when Strieber and Kunetka reach radiation-stricken Chicago, they notice at once how few black faces are now seen there. Rita Mack, a black singer and "professional rememberer" of the black American past, enlightens them. "I wouldn't say we were extinct," she remarks.

> "But you look around this town and you see the worst emptiness in the black neighborhoods. There was a whole world here that is gone now. . . . And violence, there was that too—kids running around with the guns and the knives and whatnot. But the drugs were made in white factories. . . . The black kid was the one they paid a dollar to let them mainline him out behind the school when he was fourteen years old. And why did they do this? They know that the black kid is strong, so the smack won't kill him before they get the profit, and the black kid is brave and smart, so he will be a good and cunning thief, and he is sad, wrapped up in that black skin of his, and he does not much like himself, so he will not be able to resist the smooth things the smack does to his body and mind." (370–71)

Such sober, backward-looking, and contextual reports from pre-1988 America inform young readers of much more than nuclear realities. Here, Rita Mack reinforces a central theme of the book—the touching mixture of vulnerability and toughness displayed by American children before, during, and since the 20-minute war. One such tough-minded survivor easy to identify with is a Pennsylvania fifth-grader. "When I got TB, they gave me pills at the hospital," he tells the narrators. "There are kids, like in Texas or somewhere like that, who probably die if they get sick. We pray in school that God will keep us" (410–11). Computers and a girlfriend make this schoolboy easily recognizable by present-day readers, some of whom might begin to wonder how any pre-Bomb children survived in "peacetime" America.

At *Warday*'s close, the most poignant post-Hiroshima image of all is created in an extended description of another train ride. In Philadelphia they encounter the Children's Train carrying 1,000 orphans southward to possible haven in Alabama. In Thirtieth Street Station are "quiet children sitting in rows on the floor. Here and there, one slept in another's lap. Older kids attended babies. The cries of babies echoed in the huge waiting room. . . . They were all dressed identically, in white T-shirts and jeans, girls and boys alike. On the back of their shirts were stencilled their names, years of birth, blood types, TB susceptibilities, and Pennsylvania ID numbers. . . . This scene was being repeated commonly all over the country. How many orphans are there? What are the support programs like? What are we doing to protect the future?" (486–87).

When the Children's Train reaches Georgia, it is stopped and the children are shunted off to a treeless stockade. "We can't handle 'em, T. K. We got to send them back," says a harried immigration officer. T. K., a kindhearted funeral director, expostulates, "Don't you dare say 'orphan' like it was a dirty word. Kids like these are the future and the honor of this country. There's no shame in being an orphan, Bob. Look at 'em. They ought to get medals, the way they behave." In the spirit of *Warday*'s hopeful turn toward its close, the orphans' fate in the Georgia field is left unsettled, since "one of the other Southern states would probably agree to take the children" (498–99, 500).

In the same spirit, Strieber, at home with wife and son, concludes his report of the continental journey with a qualified but consoling message to younger readers. "When I awake in sweat and dread, sensing that things are starting to grow in my body that shouldn't be there," he writes, "I get my heart to stop its thrashing by remembering that at least the war is over. . . . There is a sense of completion now. At least I am going to sleep. I lie down, drawing the sheet up around my chin. I sit with my pad on my knees. Music comes to me, an unknown melody, and an image of my son rises in my mind. I want to allow myself to have hope for him and his generation" (514–15).

Warday: And the Journey Onward—the full title aptly summarizes this book's messages to the young and old. Learn the facts, recognize the moral implications, for you are both victim and hope for the future of your culture. Hence Strieber and Kunetka conform as closely as any to Lenz's biophilic prescription: factual honesty, reassurance that "this does not have to happen," no quick fix via magical technology, assurance that mass death is possible but so are hopes of survival. Paul Brians concurs. Praising *Warday*, he writes, "[D]espite its unremarkable style, its rudimentary plot, its political improbabilities and its shallow characters," it remains "by far the most thoroughly researched of all the attempts to depict nuclear war realistically" (317). Susan Williamson goes further: it is a "must read for the human race, it is so powerful that the ruin it depicts may ultimately be our salvation" (Lenz, 153).

Nevertheless, Lenz herself resists calling *Warday* the ideal youth's book on nuclear matters. Her biophilic criterion—demanding that nuclear writings should dramatize threats to plants, animals, and ecosystems, even the globe itself—is not met by these authors. One of them, it seems, agrees. "After writing *Warday* with Jim Kunetka, I got a large number of letters, some expressing opinions or ideas for peace, some asking questions. Most of these letters were from young people . . . under the age of twenty five," Strieber explains in the afterword to his next book, *Wolf of Shadows*. "One letter in particular touched me deeply . . . [a young woman] asked the question, 'What about the animals?' So I tried to write a book that would express the plight of helpless life which, after the terrible war, also includes humanity. The wolves and their human companions can only struggle and hope" (104–5).

Strieber's ecological responsiveness indeed proved a speedy stimulus to *Wolf of Shadows*, an anthropomorphic romance of postdisaster survival. Set in a northern Minnesota wilderness, the protagonists are a pack of gray wolves and a mother and her two daughters. The humans arrive on the lake in a Cessna after a nuclear explosion over the Twin Cities, witnessed by Wolf of Shadows. A wise, black wolf whose consciousness centers the story, Wolf of Shadows has a ready premonition of disaster. "A boiling, flaring cloud was rising from the human territories. Its light fired the evening sky like dawn. . . . From his hilltop Wolf of Shadows could already see the glare of the fires that had started burning in the human lands. . . . His sensitive footpads knew the language of the ground, and it was beginning to speak in an unaccustomed way. Something was rushing up from the earth, a great disturbance" (10). Sooner than the other animals or the human hunters on the lake, Wolf of Shadows feels the man-made force unleashing fires, smells, winds, and ice. "It was hate unbound— not the struggling rage of an animal trapped by the human hunters' agony-jaws, nor the anguish of a mouse wriggling on a hungry tongue, but something else, a steaming clotted malevolence that killed all and killed indifferently, humbling everything from mayfly to man" (13).

The wolf pack and the humans soon make contact as Wolf of Shadows becomes the leader and teaches his fellows that the woman and her cubs are not dangerous like the male humans with their death-sticks. One child soon begins to smell of death, a state echoed by a flock of "ruined geese" crippled by flying through fallout. Though it is only June, all survivors are soon con- fronted by the arrival of nuclear winter. The hungry hunters shoot at the wolves, whereupon the woman attacks them verbally:

> "Why do you have to kill everything you see?"
> "Look, lady, those were wolves!"
> "They're no danger to us, they're scared to death of us. Not only that, they're a rare species, they—"
> "Lady, after what happened yesterday, I got a feeling we're rarer by far." (33)

A symbolic scene sets up a prophetic scenario here. Amid icy and wounded nature, animals and women defend themselves against the monstrous violence men have perpetrated far away from Minnesota and still live by there. By improbable yet comforting acts, the animals and women come to trust and help each other. As they struggle southward to find food and warmth, "they moved through a shadowy dream of the old human world" (54). The ruins of Minneapolis lie beneath an icy blanket, a tumbled maze. "Beyond the dens there were long lines of the round-pawed things, and frozen humans sitting in all of them. The lines stretched away over the rolling hills, on and on. The frozen human beings sat with their eyes open or closed, their faces in peace or agony, their hands around their bodies or clutching parts of the things they were in. 'My God, it's a traffic jam of the dead'" (56).

Compared with human society, before and after the disaster, the wolves and women behave and smell better—and their microsociety survives. Commu- nication across species is slowly established. Wolf of Shadows is both guru and leader. Even the forceful woman scientist, who knows when the group strays too close to ground zero, eventually succumbs to the male domination Wolf represents. In a crucial fight over a surviving cow in a barn, the woman tries to save the milk-giver from the ravenously hungry animals. Wolf of Shadows must subdue her, even though she wounds him in the fight.

> She lay helpless beneath him, groaning and sputtering as he licked her, smearing the blood of the cow on her furless skin. Her throat was pale in the dark. When he cocked his ears he could hear the blood hissing in her veins. . . .
>
> The mother's eyes opened, slowly refocused, and once again met the wolf's. She growled softly, and Wolf of Shadows responded to the tones, which were very strong, of sorrow and of loyalty. A shiver of joy went through him. Now that he had vanquished her rebelliousness, she would truly belong to the pack. . . . She lay before him, showing her belly. (78)

Hamida Bosmajian is surely correct to point out that Strieber romanticizes not only animals and Native Americans in *Wolf of Shadows* but women as well. He writes, "The central point of view—the wolf's—is male. It is the wolf that perceives and cares, rules the pack, and forces the mother into the posture of subordination. . . . In this way the concept of governance through male consciousness is maintained surreptitiously, the wolf simply exhibiting the kind of leadership qualities the author admires" (80). Since the choice of animal narrator makes it virtually impossible for Strieber to articulate more fully a critique of warlike men and nations, *Wolf of Shadows* delivers a mixed message to young readers. As wolf and woman grow closer in a relationship often bordering on the erotic, Strieber puts the story's moral in the woman's mouth. "'You know what the difference is between wolves and men? Each of you is all of you—pack and species,' she growls to her nuzzling companion. 'And you know it, and take your love of one another from it. Before the war people became so separate from one another we were like leaves in the sea. We were alone.'" In light of the male violence and brutality threading the narrative, it is significant that the wolf cannot understand her words. "He could not even whimper consolation to such a tone" (91).

The story's outcome nevertheless meets several of the criteria Lenz advances for responsible, hopeful, realistic fiction. In the nick of time, the emaciated band feel rain, not snow or sleet, on their faces. "Then the sky lifted from the land, revealing a long view down the mountains. In the southerly valleys here and there, were patches where the ice had melted. Wolf of Shadows got to his feet. . . . Was it warmer below? . . . Would there be a place for them in the valleys, where at last they might rest? Wolves and humans together, they set off to find out" (103).

In the afterword, Strieber promises that animals and humans "can only struggle and hope." Such guarded optimism is based upon Native American ways of thinking and acting toward all beings. Yet beyond this grounded hope lies "the true end of the story"—"when we decide, as a species, to dismantle the [nuclear death] machine and use our great intelligence on behalf of the earth that bears us, instead of against her" (105). To some, perhaps including Bosmajian, "species" is a conveniently loose word to leave intelligent readers with. Might not young readers of *Wolf of Shadows*, some of whom surely come to it out of admiration for *Warday*, expect a more forthright manifesto, one that at least mentions nations, classes, genders, professions, perhaps even specific nuclear policies, as causes—and possible consequences—of Minneapolis' "traffic jam of the dead"?

This selective survey of 1980s nuclear books for children and adolescents is meant to sugggest some plausible conclusions about the cultural work their adult authors performed—and may still perform—for young literate Americans. Though all points on the generic spectrum from very literal representation to pure fantasy or myth have not been touched on here, such a spectrum has been assumed, as in the previous chapters on adult fiction. Furthermore, the relative neglect of nonfiction writings—informative handbooks on the nuclear submarine, for example—may be defended by pointing out that few if any explicitly informational-ideological books for youth have so far come close to paralleling the popularity and influence of *Hiroshima* or *The Fate of the Earth*. It may be assumed, for at least part of the youth audience, that teenagers read up to (and perhaps beyond) Hersey and Bradley, if not Lifton and Schell. In any case, I have not been able to identify purely nonfiction works that capture young American imaginations as have *Warday*, *Baaa*, or *Wolf of Shadows*. To date, I would argue, Strieber and Kunetka's mixed-media success has proved far more factually informative than such 1980s histories for high schoolers as Carl Feldbaum and Ronald Bee's *Looking the Tiger in the Eye: Confronting the Nuclear Threat* (1988).[20]

Americans' preference for fiction, fable, and romance is most clearly reflected in and satisfied by the favorites discussed above, all of which I have found in children's libraries across the country. Such impressionistic opinion is strengthened, too, when children's stories written by non-American authors—*Hiroshima No Pika*, *When the Wind Blows*, *The Last Children of Schevenborn*—are counted as "American" as well as Japanese, British, or German. "The survivor's tale is the essential document of our time" stands up as a valid generalization in this field and serves as a measuring stick for critical arguments by Brians, Lenz, and Bosmajian. These texts and the critical arguments about them converge upon the following formulation of the social function of imaginative nuclear stories for children and adolescents. Traditional American values are stressed in most of these accounts: self-reliance, determination, hope, individual effort, and devotion to a possible future rather than a demonstrable (but potentially embarrassing) historical past. Although certain critically acclaimed texts by international writers are arguably more circumstantial, historical, and ironic about the future than most American stories in the same readers' age categories, it must be pointed out that few narratives (even those for teenagers) go as far as Bosmajian or Brians would wish toward informing and guiding young readers about the origins, course, and policy choices of the nuclear age. American militarism and imperialism are subjects still treated very gingerly by nearly all imaginative writers on the Bomb.

Imagery and metaphor, therefore, outstrip information as ideological instrumentalities. Although especially true of American authors and books, these features also characterize world literature in the wake of Hiroshima. This can be seen in texts as diverse in origin, style, and focus as *Hiroshima, Death in Life, Hiroshima No Pika*, and *Riddley Walker*. As social tools for introducing newcomers to a fearful postnuclear world, children's books are essentially transparent instances of cultural choices and communications conventions. "Imaging is the primary preconceptual and pre-analytical means by which socialization (both public and private) occurs," Bosmajian points out, "for images become significant for us long before we have understood their meaning." Three basic imagistic clusters, he continues, characterize children's nuclear literature, as they do most adult writing. "At the core of nuclear imaging is 'the flash,' the moment that once occurred in human time, but has been made into a metaphor of an instant of time that gives birth to the future. The 'flash' and its associative clusters of mushroom, wave, blinding light, fireball occur in almost all the works under discussion." Then, as happens in the imagined experiences of Mii, Roland Bennewitz, and Wolf of Shadows, the "wasteland" emerges, a second image cluster that knits together dust, radiation sickness, and nuclear winter. Finally, a third cluster defines postholocaust worlds in which an afterlife or survival stage may occur; "it may be a 'hell on earth' or an evolution towards a better world" (Bosmajian, 74–75), as contrastingly exemplified in *The Last Children of Schevenborn* and Louise Lawrence's *Children of the Dust*.

Conspicuously absent from this metaphor-based, essentially fictional formulation, however, are still other image clusters and mixtures of connotative-denotative language (including photography) treating the history of the Bomb's development, deployment, and global impact. Instead of natural imagery— clouds, rain, fire, ice, southerly valleys wth melting snow—this historical and often photographic literature dramatizes for young readers the age of Hiroshima via images of Einstein and Oppenheimer, Truman and the *Enola Gay*, the Bikini Atoll and Three Mile Island, a missile silo in Kansas wheatfields. Such real-life resources are exploited in photographic books like Betty Jean Lifton's *A Place Called Hiroshima* (1985), R. Conrad Stein's *World at War: Hiroshima* (1982), and Martin McPhillips's *Hiroshima: Turning Points in American History* (1985).[21] For older readers and students in high school history classes, these persons, events, and photographic images are represented in textbooks like the recent and exemplary *The American People: Creating a Nation and a Society*.[22] The work of Gary Nash and his fellow historians is "exemplary" because they combine succinct and balanced historical descriptions with striking uses of photographs and other pictorial resources.

On one page, for instance, teenagers can read the following description of America in the early post-Hiroshima years.

> Anxiety lurked beneath the exuberance, though it did not surface while the United States maintained a nuclear monopoly. Then, in September 1949, reporters were called to the White House and told: "We have evidence that within recent weeks an atomic explosion occurred in the USSR.". . .
>
> The American public was shocked. Suddenly the security of being the world's only atomic power vanished. People wondered whether the Soviet test foreshadowed a nuclear attack. At a meeting of the Joint Committee on Atomic Energy, legislators struggled to comprehend the implications of the news. When a thunderclap filled the air, someone in the room said, "My God, that must be Number Two," cutting the tension for the moment. (909)

On the same page appears a color photograph of a nuclear explosion with the low-key caption, "Frequent nuclear tests filled the atmosphere with fallout." Some pages before, a more emotional image accompanies the authors' explanation of how "The Atomic Age Begins." For American adolescents, this picture, showing a shockingly graphic department store window display in Osaka of Hiroshima victims, is as unfamiliar as it is disturbing. The juxtaposition of a Japanese child staggering through rubble, skin hanging loosely from arms and face, and the cool historical account of the bombing, is in itself an arresting exercise in 1990s historiography.

As I hope the preceding pages suggest, children's illlustrated stories also exploit similar educational uses of contrasting words and pictures. They do so sometimes even more effectively and affectively than the fictional stories of "successful" survival that are aimed at older, more sophisticated readers. The progression from one form of children's literature to the other is a social and psychological process going on in many literate American homes as well as in public places where literacy is inculcated and ideological messages about the Bomb and its ethos are passed to future American citizens. Marvin Bell is but one adult, as we shall see in the following chapter, who seeks to express and criticize the nuclear ethos through poetry. We shall also meet children as poets doing the same thing.

5

Anguished Poets on the Edge of Darkness

In our time, a political poetry untinged with anxiety, even when it evokes and salutes moments of hope, is unimaginable.

Denise Levertov (*Light up the Cave*)[1]

IN AMERICAN WRITERS' HALF-CENTURY STRUGGLE AGAINST the "End of the World," poets have commonly faced an additional uphill fight—to gain a hearing from fellow citizens comparable to the attention paid novelists, science fiction storytellers, and authors of nonfiction prose. Poetry and its traditional modes of expression, chiefly lyrical but also narrative, satiric, and didactic verse, is too little taught or practiced in schools as living art, too often relegated to the specialized attention of *Poetry* magazine, *American Poetry Review*, or other little magazines. When included in the table of contents of the *New Yorker* or *Harper's* (not to mention more highbrow magazines like the *American Scholar* or *Commentary*), poets' work is commonly scattered in single pieces among the essays, stories, editorials, and advertisements. When poets publish their verse in either slim volumes or fatter anthologies, sales are likely to be modest, reviews and advertisements likewise. There seems, therefore, a certain historical-social plausibility to treating poets' engagement with Hiroshima and the nuclear age in a later chapter of this cultural history.

Before reinforcing such marginalizing, however, a closer look is in order. This has not occurred often or in much detail in recent discussions of nuclear literature. A notable exception is Rob Wilson's "Towards the Nuclear Sublime: Representations of Technological Vastness in Postmodern American Poetry" (1989), and it is a significant fact that Wilson is not only a critic but a poet and passionately committed citizen as well.[2] As we shall see, many of the most searching critiques of this literary-cultural topic come from practicing poets who are, not surprisingly, politically active.

In historical terms, however, poetry and politics (whether nuclear or otherwise oriented) have only spasmodically come together in the postwar era. Few have followed the example of Walt Whitman, America's politically conscious poet par excellence—Allen Ginsberg being the notable exception. Far more influential, over the past 40 years, has been Wallace Stevens, elite literary culture's poet par excellence. The public's and the scholar's image of the poet seems to be of a sensitive private self creating "supreme fictions" within and about an apolitical realm of the imagination. This is the dominant legacy of modernist poetry. "Since World War II, the consensus of writers and critics has been that poetry and politics, acknowledged or unacknowledged, simply don't mix," Richard Jones observed in 1985. "The political role of the poet in society has dwindled, reduced now to that of the occasional spokesperson for this or that issue—civil rights, women's rights, the Viet Nam War. . . . What is truly curious, however, is that poets have been largely silent on a crucial issue of the second half of the twentieth century: the bomb. The bomb has made its way into a few poems, but it has only recently been openly discussed by poets."[3]

One poet awake to and alarmed for some time by this silence is Hayden Carruth. Nearly two decades before Jones wrote, Carruth published a scathing commentary on the, to him, sorry situation. In "Poets without Prophesy" (1963), he deplored his generation's failure to follow in the footsteps of committed artists like Archibald MacLeish, Muriel Ruykeyser, Richard Eberhart, and Randall Jarrell. These 1930s and 1940s poets wrote about war and destruction, fascism and communism, and militarism. Their example, Carruth averred, is even more pertinent in the aftermath of Hiroshima. "The supreme political fact of our lives is the atomic bomb. Am I wrong? " he wrote. "It is not only what it is but also the concentrated symbol of all hatred and injustice in every social and economic sphere. . . . I believe there are actually some Americans who never think about the bomb. But poets? That would be incredible. No matter how hard they try they cannot escape being included among society's most percipient members. Yet if one were to judge by their output one would have to believe that poets are the least concerned people in the world."[4]

Backing up his grim arraignment, Carruth cites an informal survey he conducted about the time of the Cuban Missile Crisis. Taking *Poetry* as the representative site and 1961 as a conveniently recent date, he discovered that 335 poems were published there by 139 different poets. "In the whole year I found two explicit references to the bomb, one a passing seriocomic remark, and ten poems on the general theme of suffering in war, two of which were translations from foreign poets of an earlier time." His conclusion remained harsh. "Not spokesmen then. But hermits, lone wolves, acolytes—building poems in the wilderness for their own salvation" (Jones, 286). Indeed, the contrast between poets and journalists as barometers of political reality was even starker. "But when the correlation between the output of *Poetry* magazine and the leading headlines of, for example, the *New York Times* is as disparate as my little tabulation for 1961 indicates, then the [political] context has receded so far that it no longer furnishes a useful field of reference to most of the people who read the poetry." Hence the lesson learned: "[T]he larger vision has been turned over to the newspapers, to the so-called industry of so-called mass communication. . . . We poets have gone straight through fifteen years without seeing them" (Jones, 287–88).

Carruth's jeremiad, as he admits, is subjective and time-bound. It should not be read backward from 1961 to Hiroshima's immediate aftermath. But if one casts a wider net than the pages of *Poetry* over these earlier years and then moves beyond the 1960s to the early and mid-1980s to try to fix continuities and changes, then evidence will appear to qualify Carruth's diagnosis. The search for fresher data and new images might begin by noting that Carruth's 1960s essay was reprinted in Richard Jones's 1985 collection of essays, *Poetry and Politics*. This anthology, which tracks views from T. S. Eliot to June Jordan, concludes with a remarkable outpouring of recent testimony to a changed situation among American poets. This emerges from a historic event. On 27 May 1982 there took place at Town Hall in New York City a public reading by Poets against the End of the World. Organized by Galway Kinnell, a dozen other prominent poets joined him onstage to declare and discuss their nuclear politics.[5] To list their names is not only to stress a central theme of this chapter and book—the awakened voices and involvement of writers over the past decade and a half—but to highlight as well the social, regional, racial, and gender backgrounds from which these 13 addressed their fellow Americans. Besides Kinnell the group included Amiri Baraka, Robert Bly, Jane Cooper, David Ignatow, June Jordan, Etheridge Knight, Stanley Kunitz, Denise Levertov, Philip Levine, W. S. Merwin, Josephine Miles, and Simon J. Ortiz. Represented here were men and women, including gays and lesbians; Jewish, African, Hispanic, and Native Americans; and, through the agency of Etheridge Knight, penitentiary prisoners as amateur poets. Each of the 13 published political verse; several brought public (some would say, notorious) reputations as political activists. If Carruth's 1960s diagnosis, however partial, is one relevant datum of that era's literary somnolence, the presence and testimony of the Poets against the End of the World are additional clues to a possibly different level of consciousness in 1980s America.

Supporting this hypothesis is the presence of no less than five other anthologies or collections of American poetry that, in addition to Jones's *Poetry and Politics*, were published during the early 1980s. Their social and geographical diversity significantly expands that of the Town Hall meeting. From the *New England Review and Breadloaf Quarterly* came, in 1984, the first collection, *Writing in a Nuclear Age*, edited by Jim Schley. From the opposite end of the country, *Warnings: An Anthology on the Nuclear Peril* (1984) was assembled, like Schley's, from a thematic issue of a periodical, in this case *Northwest Review*. Out of the heartland (Iowa City) in the same year appeared Morty Sklar's *Nuke-Rebuke: Writers and Artists against Nuclear Energy and Weapons*. Further proof of 1980s involvement is provided by two lesser-known anthologies. One is Joseph Kruchac's *Breaking Silence: An Anthology of Contemporary Asian American Poets* (1983), likewise a reprint from a little magazine, the *Greenfield Review* of upstate New York. Still more unusual is *A Chance to Live: Children's Poems for Peace in a Nuclear Age*. This collection of verse and drawings was put together by Gayle Peterson, Ying Kelley, and Patricia Carvin in 1983. "The children who composed these poems and artwork for peace," wrote the school principal, "are all students at the Berkeley Arts Magnet School . . . a public school in Berkeley, California, consisting of kindergarten-8th grades. Their families reflect the wide range of racial, ethnic, educational and economic diversity of our city. They are both very special and very ordinary children. Although I have known some of these children for many years, I was stunned by their passion for peace."[6]

None of these volumes, to be sure, became best-sellers. They represent something less than a groundswell of public enthusiasm for nuclear poetry and politics. Nevertheless, these collective voices and verses did contribute to a reawakened discussion of cold war realities and nuclear dangers, triggered at the same time by other literary-cultural events like Schell's *Fate of the Earth* in the *New Yorker*, television programs like *The Day After*, as well as the appearance of novels and movies like those mentioned earlier in this study. Though neglected or cited only summarily by most nuclear age commentators, these anthologized poets added to the broadening body of nuclear literature of which 1990s readers are now aware. The political points and ethical energy expressed in many of these verses qualify Carruth's gloom while at the same time confirming his claim that poets, regardless of numbers, are indeed among our society's most percipient observers and prophets.

To get the most from this promising but not abundant resource, one must pay attention both to individual poems of marked cognitive, affective, and moral insight and to patterns of content, language usage, and perspective. In each case, we shall confront a common situation: a group of diverse artists forging a body of writing, and specific readerships as well, that buck the fashionable tide of private aestheticism and psychological introspection. Instead, they insist on speaking out on public issues defined, by them and others, as matters of life and death. Robert Lowell and Allen Ginsberg; Carolyn Forché and Denise Levertov; Maxine Kumin, Alan Dugan, and William Stafford; Minnie Bruce Pratt and Honor Moore; Horace Mungin and June Jordan; Joseph Landauer and Jude Hall of the Berkeley elementary school; Joy Kogawa and David Mura—this is but a partial enumeration of the contemporary poets around the country with nuclear imaginations and distinctive voices. They have furnished the six 1980s anthologies, and other books and magazines as well, with a common content and many different inflections of a common moral and emotional urgency. Some of their shared outlook is articulated well by another of their number, Marvin Bell. "I have written and published poems about World Wars I, II, and III, about Viet Nam, about other assorted political and military matters, and about ethics," he writes. "If it were not the Nuclear Age (and I have known no other), I would still have written them. Because people are scared. The privileged of society, which includes most writers, no longer feel safe from the daily carnage faced by others. The Bomb can reach them . . . ; there being no rear echelons in nuclear warfare, the issue is becoming immediate and emotional" (Schley, 188–89).

Immediate events and emotional experiences are traditional and overlapping provinces of all lyrical poets. Hiroshima and its worldwide aftermaths of awe and horror at the prospect of absurd deaths in the foreseeable future are among our age's defining experiences and affects. As we have seen, they have been variously and repeatedly imagined in fiction and nonfiction narratives. Their descriptions and tropes of fire and cloud, whirlwind and black rain, leveled cities and charred corpses, shadow-impregnated stone and cement, radioactive dust, missile silos amid the wheatfields, nuclear holocaust—these compose a unique vocabulary of human destruction and victimization. In its explosive splendor and sunlike power, the Bomb excites sentiments of a sublime subject outstripping in mystery and majesty the natural images American poets have in the past employed: Niagara Falls, the prairies of the West, Grand Canyon, El Capitan, the Pacific (Wilson, 410–13). In their stead has now appeared a new geography of sublime landscapes: Alamogordo and Yucca Flats, Hiroshima and the Bikini Atoll, perhaps even Chernobyl, Bhopal, and Three Mile Island. Instigated by these twentieth-century images of human/ demonic/divine puissance is the current of dread and horror that is the psychic bass-note of the present age. How this sublime anguish has been felt, understood, and communicated in poetic images and symbolic clusters over the past four decades is the concern of this chapter. The mushroom cloud and its trail of associated features, its fear-filled permutations as charted in successive literary forms and expressions, and the cultural significance of individual and collective interventions by writers in the death-in-life discussions periodically occupying our public and private consciousness—these are the vital social issues already treated in terms of fictional and nonfictional discourse. Now I wish to ask, how does the accumulated imaginal memory of Hiroshima (writ large) play itself out when articulated through what devotees and defenders claim is the matchless medium of poetry?

"The poet is a local animal," Bell asserts in the 1983 declaration cited above. "He must be satisfied to score small observations and reports, building his authority by the force of his mind and his allegiance to truth and clarity." Then Bell makes a crucial point. "Poetry does not consist of exercises in style and theme. It has content, and its form must be wrung from that content, not the other way around" (Schley, 189).

As content, Americans' first encounters with nuclear mystery and power in the explosions at Alamogordo, Hiroshima, and Nagasaki are initiating events of the new age. To focus first on this actual history and imaginative responses thereto is to reawaken the psychic shocks and excitement of 1945 and their recurrences in the years following. Yet the most truthful, clarifying responses to the news and first photographs were not on-the-spot lyrics and verse narratives. Poetry is not journalism, even when published in daily newspapers. Often a longer perspective produces deeper insights, even as it continues to pay obeisance to topical news and actual data.

This said, immediate poetry can be immediately revealing. Cultural historians are often more attuned than literary critics to topical or ephemeral expressions. Paul Boyer is an apt example. In *By the Bomb's Early Light* he reports several early pieces of what highbrow critics would term semidoggerel. One is by America's favorite poetaster of the early twentieth century, Edgar A. Guest. His "Atomic Bomb" was published in the *Detroit Free Press* on 17 September 1945, informing readers of the historic event's meaning:

> The power to blow all things to dust
> Was kept for people God could trust,
> And granted unto them alone,
> That evil might be overthrown. . . .
> It was the 6th of August, that much we knew,
> When the boys took off in the morning dew,
> Feeling nervous, sick, and ill at ease
> They flew at the heart of the Japanese,
> With a thunderous blast, a blinding light,
> And the 509th's atomic might. (Boyer, 244, 211, 399)

Guest's pedestrian couplets neither seek nor attain a sublime vision. That would come later. Yet the poet's ready-made patriotism doubtless reflected many of his audience's immediate rationalizations of the Bomb's advent and military deployment. If so, these feelings were shared by President Harry Truman (*Warnings*, 3).

The following year, a lesser-known poet, Herman Hagedorn, carried the news of Hiroshima to further lengths, if not greater heights. "The Bomb That Fell on America" (1946) was, as its title suggests, a soberer message, whose kernel of prophetic truth Boyer identifies in these lines:

> The heart and the soul must be as great as the brain if the work of the
>   brain is not to wreck the world.
> We are one hundred and thirty-five million people, and we must grow
>   up, overnight, or make the world one
> final Hiroshima. (Boyer, 245)

Most academic critics, scornful of these dogtrot rhymes, would be dismayed to hear Robert Penn Warren's name mentioned alongside Guest's and Hagedorn's. Yet in "New Dawn," Warren, a temperamentally historical poet as well as historical novelist, also records the onset of the revolution delivered by the *Enola Gay* (Schley, 67). His much later evocation (1983) is briefer than Hagedorn's but still runs to some 200 lines. A combination of narrative, description, and meditation, "New Dawn" shows by its content, language, and form a willingness to meet the popular reader and share a more thoughtful vision of the now-distant event than the others once communicated. For one thing, narrative momentum is maintained through 15 clearly titled sections. These relate the events of 6 August from takeoff to late-night reflections on their deed by members of the returned crew. At several points in the versified story, Warren maintains a deliberately prosaic tone and vocabulary. Typically, though, even a description of the Bomb's mechanisms ends with enigmatic suggestiveness. As the plutonium is detonated, the crew will "wake it from its timeless drowse. And that / Will be that. Whatever / *That* may be."[7] Though brute power and "triumphal beauty" are saluted in Warren's poem, his narrator is finally arrested by mystery and the dilemma it poses for the individual. In section 7 ("Self and Non-Self"), for instance, narrator, reader, and Colonel Tibbets are united in an intimate moment in the Pacific skies:

> Tibbets looks down, sees
> The slow, gray coiling of clouds, which are,
> Beyond words. The image
> Of sleep just as consciousness goes. He looks up, sees
> Stars still glaring white down into
> All the purity of emptiness. For an instant,
> He shuts his eyes.
>
> Shut your own
> Eyes, and in timelessness you are
> Alone with yourself. You are
> Not certain of identity.
> Has the non-self lived forever?

> Tibbets jerks his eyes open. There
> is the world . . . (Schley, 68–69)

Although Tibbets and his crew are awestruck by the Bomb's immense cloud mounting to the heights in "triumphal beauty," that fearful memory does not dominate their nighttime thoughts upon the return to Tinian, even after the celebrations and decorations. Instead, the final section of "New Dawn" holds the image of a single American staring or closing his eyes in somber reflection. Alone in the barracks,

> Some men, no doubt, will, before sleep, consider
> One thought: I am alone. But some,
> In the mercy of God, or booze, do not
> Long stare at the dark ceiling. (Schley, 71)

The poet's implications for the new dawn are plain—and, for some, politically disturbing. The flight's hidden meanings include recognition, not only of cataclysmic change but of the fact that man is ultimately alone in confronting this national responsibility for "Whatever / *That* may be." The historic deed is, in fact, both within and beyond time, and mankind's inability to discern the lineaments of both realms is figured in the pilot closing his eyes. We now realize that doing so signifies both blindness and spiritual premonition.

Hindsight, of course, affords Warren's contemporary readers with ironic resonances untapped in "New Dawn" itself. For one thing, Warren's poem is strangely silent about the flight's effect and outcome on the people below. "Coiling" clouds and a plume of "pure whiteness" prevent us from ever glimpsing ground zero. As was the case with virtually all of the first photographs of Hiroshima published in the United States, this aerial focus obscures the stricken city, the flash and fire, and all other lethal consequences that might have made the inner eyes of Tibbets or his crew stare even harder at the dark ceiling.[8] The mushroom cloud, not the actual devastation, was the initial image and official American message to come from Hiroshima. Warren's 1980s poem still echoes this policy and convention and encourages later readers to continue to identify the historic event through sanitized images of natural, abstract grandeur.

For younger poets, the tradition of Guest, Hagedorn, and even Warren has proved inaccurate, insufficient, irresponsible. Richard Oyama's 1980s voice in "The Day after Trinity" (1983), for example, takes American readers a step further into history and its problematic geography by reimagining the fall of "Little Boy" onto its target, "once a Buddhist castle town." Victims' suffering is not evoked in detail, as some others will do, yet after a brief résumé of the attacks, Oyama ends with banal economy: "This is the day after Trinity when / ten thousand suns explode" (Kruchac, 219).

Though only 37 lines long, this low-key lyric in Kruchac's 1983 collection marks the move toward the *hibakusha* consciousness that we have noted occurring in other 1980s literary minds. Empathy for the victims of the two cities goes hand in hand with proud consciousness of this loyal American's Japanese heritage. He and others likewise share a mounting recognition of the global repercussions of fallout and radiation sickness. David Mura's "The Hibakusha's Letter (1955)" (1955) and "The Survivor" (1984), as well as Joy Kogawa's "Hiroshima Exit" (1983), are even more strongly charged lyrics by Japanese-American poets, all part of a shift in consciousness that must have owed something to the powerful prose statements of Schell and Lifton.[9]

For Mura, a harsher, more ironic use of nature is the common ground on which public and private, emotional and cognitive responses can meet. In "The Hibakusha's Letter (1955)" an imaginary survivor traces her strong revulsion against fish and red meat to unforgettable memories of blood, corpses, and wholesale death on 6 August.[10]

> . . . This year I've changed my diet
> And eat only rice, utskemono, tofu.
> Sashimi sickens me, passion for raw meat.
> Sister, remember how mother strangled chickens?
> . . . .
> Like them, we had no warning. Flames filled kimonos
> With limbs of ash, and I wandered beneath
> Smouldering toriis away from the city.
> Of course, you're right. We can't even play beauty
> Or the taste of steel quickens our mouths. (Kruchac, 200)

More disturbing still is Mura's second linkage of animals, eating, and holocaust in "The Survivor." As before, time shifts back and forth between the poet's and reader's present and 1945. Parallels between the two lyrics are triggered, first, by the sight of a keloid-scarred fisherman scaling his day's catch:

> Sparks flying from his knife.
> He placed the bodies in
> Boxes: row on row of eyes
> Stared upwards, astonished
> At their first glimpse of sky.

This triggers a second memory from childhood: watching another fisherman slit open a fish, "revealing cat-whisker bones / And a small heart, still beating." The two images are then vividly combined in a historical picture of Hiroshima suffering:

> The river was leaking flames
> And skulls like lilies floated
> On the current, you passed a man

> Moaning at the roadside—He rose,
> Held out his eyeball in his hand.
> And everywhere you looked
> You saw his pain. (Sklar, 160)

Here, of course, the now world-famous image that Michael Perlman calls the Eyeball Man chillingly universalizes Mura's fish eyes and still-beating heart (Perlman, 115).

Effective as these second-generation poets are in reconstituting natural and human reminders of Hiroshima in personal (and American) terms, they do not engage the prehistory of Atomic America. Though the Japanese cities are properly the literal and symbolic centers of later imaginative and moral encounters, the historical fact remains that the nuclear age actually began at Alamogordo. In a real sense, the first atomic bomb test was the more decisive turning point; this generalization embraces not just the awe-inspiring explosion but the aftereffects of radiation in the Southwest. The enduring literary epitaph of Alamogordo—despite endless representations by later historians, novelists, and documentary cinemaphotographers—remains Robert Oppenheimer's murmured quotation from the *Bhagavad-Gita*: "Now I am become Death, destroyer of worlds."[11]

Nevertheless, another more modest memorial to the coming of the nuclear age exists within the circumscribed community of contemporary poets and their audiences. William Stafford's 12-line lyric of 1960, "At the Bomb Testing Site," is justly admired for its masterful economy and figurative suggestiveness in using animal imagery. Even more so than he does in "Indian Caves in the Dry Country," the poet turns a small spot of the American desert into a symbolic nuclear stage. His central figure is a desert lizard whose agon is so carefully constituted that a generation of readers and critics, like Leonard Nathan, remember and can quote the poem in toto:

> At noon in the desert a panting lizard
> waited for history, its elbows tense,
> watching the curve of a particular road
> as if something might happen.
>
> It was looking at something farther off
> than people could see, an important scene
> acted in stone for little selves
> at the flute end of consequences.
>
> There was just a continent without much on it
> under a sky that never cared less.
> Ready for a change, the elbows waited.
> The hands gripped hard on the desert.[12]

As Nathan (himself an activist poet) has noted, Stafford's "poem never alludes directly to its subject except in the title." The "important scene / acted in stone for little selves / at the flute end of consequences," indeed, seems obscure, inasmuch as "stone" is seldom associated with Los Alamos or the Bomb, except as a highly generalized image of rubble devastation. Nathan believes he knows why Stafford plays such an indirect game between title, voice, and content. "In a time when so much poetry contains, as a sort of authenticating credential, the personality of the poet, the treatment of really tremendous topics deserves something better than pathetic personal stance, more or less grandiose." In reaction, Stafford bends over backward to avoid such a voice and stance, "and this, I think, is why a poem like Stafford's seems memorable," Nathan concludes. "It is able to shift its subjectivity to another creature—a creature noted for its cold blood—and offer instinctual anticipation as a kind of measure for the unspeakable." Such indirection, he adds, is good politics. "I do not doubt . . . that effective poems can be written on the unspeakable. They may seem modest, perhaps innocuous, because they work through indirection, not startling us to mindless action like a siren charging through our sleep, but subtly shifting the way we see the reality, keeping our imaginations alive to possibilities."[13]

Nonetheless, Stafford and Nathan, like Bell, do not speak for all their fellow poets in advocating self-limitation to small insights and indirect reports. Far less discreet is Eleanor Wilner's "High Noon at Los Alamos" (1984). Like Stafford's much-reprinted lyric, this poem's explicit context and content is the New Mexican desert, our first atomic landscape. Wilner, too, deploys animals in place of people as symbolic counters in a political address. Her animals, however, differ greatly from the fish, chickens, or lizard of some of her contemporaries. Wilner evokes a real prehistoric age, "the dim time of dinosaurs" in the Southwest, when these monsters with pitifully small brains once turned upward to face "the white flash / in the sky the day the sun-flares / pared them down to relics in museums."[14] Humanity now seems bent on provoking its own "white flash" cataclysm in place of nature's sunspots or meteorites. Our scientific bent "to unearth again / white fire at the heart of matter—fire / we sought and fire we spoke," cannot save us, wise successors to the dinosaurs and apes. But because fire is a double-edged instrument, fire-seeking humans are not just scientists and warriors. Artists and orators, too, have repeatedly invoked fiery destruction as they light the way to oblivion in, for example, Greek myths and poetry:

> our thoughts, however elegant, were fire
> from first to last—like sentries set to watch
> at Argos for the signal fire
> passed peak to peak from Troy
> to Nagasaki . . .
> our eyes stared white from watching

for the signal that ends
the epic—a cursed line
with its caesura, a pause
to signal peace, or a rehearsal
for the silence. (*Warnings*, 47–48)

Through classic forms of poetic line and voice rest, poetic discourse here becomes a synecdoche of history and potential holocaust in the next—and final?—canto of the human epic. Wilner's verse leaves small space for hope, but much room for anguish. Her dinosaur, fire, and Greek images articulate a more direct human response to Nagasaki than Stafford's lizard.

In fact, all six of the 1980s anthologies I am using here preserve precious few hopeful poems, even fewer in the patriotic vein of Edgar Guest. Stafford, Mura, Wilner, and Kogawa typify the techniques and themes of the poetic majority in focusing narrowly upon specific facets of Alamogordo, Hiroshima, and Nagasaki to dramatize past history and future danger. Furthermore, those who manage to assert a personal voice in the act of empathizing with particular victims (human and animal) are likely to be women. As I hope to suggest in these discussions of poets of the nuclear age, women are better represented in this province of nuclear literature than in either fiction or nonfiction.

One representative woman's voice raised in empathic backward meditation is Maxine Kumin's. Although she was not invited to participate in the Town Hall event, Kumin was in 1982 already well known as a politically committed poet. Perhaps her most direct contribution in verse to the common cause is "How to Survive a Nuclear War" (1985). Here she activates her own engagement with the history of Hiroshima by sensitively and guiltily entering into the Japanese culture from which victims and *hibakusha* came. In the process, she manages to exploit the "local animal" imperative that Bell advocates, while at the same time reaching beyond her singular self and small observations.

In this lyric, Kumin's narrator is an American woman (apparently a Jew) who resembles the French heroine in the 1959 film *Hiroshima, Mon Amour*. She comes to postwar Japan, the site of World War II's most spectacular killing field, carrying a double burden of victimization and guilt from that war. The poem's actual setting is Kyoto. The speaker is caught in Japan's spiritual capital by an attack of the flu, which prevents her from taking the bullet train to Hiroshima. That city was her goal after reading and being powerfully moved by Masuji Ibuse's *Black Rain*. In sickness's twilight zone between dreaming and waking, she is jolted out of Japanese geography by a nightmare in which she is pursued by Nazis. Awakening in autumnal Kyoto, she observes from her hotel window preparations for a harvest festival. It is the Holy Radish Festival, containing also a ritual

> . . . for the souls
> of insects farmers may have trampled on
> while bringing in the harvest.
> Now shall I repent?
> I kill to keep whatever
> pleases me. Last summer
> to save the raspberries
> I immolated hundreds of coppery
> Japanese beetles.[15]

Catching the flu, killing an infestation of Japanese beetles—these are indeed minute acts of suffering and death. How to tie such domestic dramas to Hiroshima's monumental devastation? Ibuse's novel makes a segue possible. Radiation sickness, according to the novelist, is a far more fearsome reality, though sometimes "less terrible than cancer." Its memory surely trivializes her own illness.

> . . . the hair
> comes out in patches. Teeth
> break off like matchsticks
> at the gum line but the loss
> is painless. Burned skin itches,
> peels away in strips.
> Everywhere the black rain fell
> it stains the flesh like a tattoo
> but weeks later, when
> survivors must expel
> day by day in little pisses
> the membrane lining the bladder
> pain becomes an extreme grammar. (51–52)

In the final section, Kumin tries to bridge this enormous gap between actual and vicarious suffering, thereby confronting an American Jew's complex historical guilt as perpetrator and survivor. She does so by identifying with Japanese ritual as well as Japanese victimization. In a second dream, she invents a new postholocaust ceremony. Looking out the window at a row of old ginko trees, she imagines their ritual pruning. When the lopped branches are burned and the smoke ceremonially inhaled, each shoot, ascending as human exhalation, returns to earth in human form. These ghosts are "ancient, all-knowing / tattered like us."

> This means
> *we are all to be rescued.*
> Though we eat animals
> and wear their skins

> though we crack mountains
> and insert rockets in them
>
> this signifies
> *we will burn and go up*
> *we will be burned and come back.*
>
> I wake naked, parched,
> my skin striped by sunlight.
> Under my window
> a line of old ginkos hunkers down.
> The new sprouts that break from
> their armless shoulders are
> the enemies of despair. (53–54)

Despite, or perhaps because of, its modulations from the tiny to the sublime, Kumin's poem can evoke conflicting responses. The domestic trope of American raspberries and Japanese beetles may strike some as monumentally—indeed, insultingly—incommensurable with the poem's bitter Hiroshima details adapted from *Black Rain*. Still other 1980s readers, familiar with Grace Mojtabai's *Blessèd Assurance* (1986), might cavil at Kumin's narrator's dream of expiation and transcendence. Surely the hotel-room vision of burning, going up, and being rescued, curiously italicized in key lines, smacks uncomfortably of the Rapture eschatology believed by, for instance, the fundamentalists in Amarillo, Texas, who confidently and joyfully await Armageddon in the form of worldwide nuclear holocaust.

In striking contrast to Kumin's idiosyncratic imagery in a fantasized return to Hiroshima, Galway Kinnell's parallel lyric, "The Fundamental Project of Technology" (1984) displays a cooler, more ambitious version of an American poet's actual visit to the Bomb site. As is also true of Joy Kogawa's "Hiroshima Exit," Kinnell's formal meditation centers on the Atomic Bomb Memorial Building. But in place of Kumin's Kyoto dreamer or Kogawa's anguished narrator overhearing American tourists defending the Bomb's use—"Well, they started it . . . / They didn't think about us at Pearl Harbor" (Kruchac, 113)—Kinnell's spokesman never dramatizes or even identifies himself. Instead, the seven sections are organized, emotionally and intellectually, around a brief quote from another Japanese source, Tatsuichiro Akizuki's *Concentric Circles of Death* (1981): "A flash! A white flash sparkled!"[16] Each stanza works "a white flash" into its final line. These three words mark the end to each evocation of Hiroshima, past and present. Victims' touchingly personal belongings; an old dying veteran smoking a cigarette; black-uniformed schoolchildren in the park; old trees; crushed lunch boxes—all remind us of a previous life. Each image frames differently Kinnell's central stanza. Here, instead of another vignette of Japanese history, the poet offers a complex and paradoxical meditation on what it signifies:

> To de-animalize human mentality, to purge it of obsolete
> evolutionary characteristics, in particular death,
> which foreknowledge terrorizes the contents of skulls with,
> is the fundamental project of technology; however,
> the mechanisms of *pseudologia fantastica* require,
> to establish deathlessness it is necessary to eliminate
> those who die, a task attempted, when a white flash
> sparkled. (Schley, 41)

Though readers will have to struggle with unfamiliar terminology here—especially "de-animalize" and its synonym, *"pseudologia fantastica"*—the thrust of Kinnell's title, epigraph, and key stanza are unmistakable—especially to Vietnam-era survivors who can translate Kinnell's somewhat tortured diction as, "In order to save the village we had to destroy it." Long before My Lai, the Bomb already incarnated Western technology's implicit agenda: to replace human (that is, animal) fear of one's own death with a de-animalized, universal, and irreversible deathlessness. Such fantastic illogic is neatly symbolized in "a white flash" that reveals its raison d'être in the instant of obliterating the illuminated consciousness.

Kinnell's austere meditation lies on the far side of abstraction from Kumin's private dream. His is a territory unfamiliar or uncongenial to many lovers, and some writers, of verse. A single arresting phrase from a Japanese author does not sustain, it appears, a long or very individualized narrative. On the other hand, Kumin's more elaborate use of Japanese writing and religion does little better to humanize the other as well as the American self.

Another resource within the Hiroshima record did stimulate many to see the self and the other as imaginatively one. Widely fixed in the consciousness of both Western and Eastern adults and schoolchildren in the decades after Hiroshima and Nagasaki is the story of Sadako Sasaki's life and death. The Japanese schoolgirl, dying of Hiroshima-induced leukemia, became the heroine of many children's stories in Japanese, British, German, and American books. The youthful poets at the Berkeley Arts Magnet School were among those taken by the fable of the thousand cranes that Sadako attempted to fold in origami as a magical postponement of her death. Their poems offer some arresting, often eloquent, proof of the appeal of this tale of victimization and the awareness and empathy it awakens in younger postwar minds. Adults, too, respond to the myth of Sadako and the thousand cranes. For instance, just a year after *A Chance to Live* was published, Morty Sklar's *Nuke-Rebuke* volume carried on its opening page of epigraphs a poem on Sadako by Dennis Brutus, a South African political exile.

Given their common plot, set of images, and emotional cues, this adult lyric and one entitled "When the Cranes Fly" by Joseph Landauer, a fifth-grader at Berkeley, offer an instructive contrast in outlook and language. Here are key parallel passages from the pair's conclusions:

Dennis Brutus	*Joseph Landauer*
Sedako's [*sic*] cranes are crying	When the cranes fly
a thousand cranes are crying	The bombs die.
pleading:	A hare or a bear
"Keep the dream of peace	or any other creature
in your hearts."	will not have to sigh
	When they see paper cranes
This is our cry	hanging together in one
this is our prayer:	peace
peace to the world.[17]	They will know that
	their race
	Will not die.[18]

Both poets, the exiled man and the schoolboy, write conventional and general strophes carrying conventional and general, albeit heartfelt, messages. Landauer, though, shows surprising subtlety in turning a schoolroom full of hanging paper birds (each folded from a single sheet) into one "peace" uniting animals and humans, Japanese victims and American schoolchildren. Though not all Landauer's schoolmates wrote about Sadako, most wrote about peace. Mollie Price, Jude Hall, Daniel Su, and Eliel Johnson are among the more accomplished.[19] Collectively, their empathy and skill augment the insight and skill in their schoolmate's verse.

Indeed, Jude Hall transcends the somewhat conventional and sentimental story of Sadako. In "When Nature Is Dead," he displays a sophisticated awareness of the inner state of many post-Hiroshima Americans, young and old, during the cold war.

> They've come to mean nothing to me
> In this day of death and destruction
> I find myself unable to feel,
> Unable to think,
> Unable to care.
> Humanity was never meant to face
> such despair as impending death
> How can we accept such an
> unnatural destruction?
> How can we see that death
> is a part of nature
> When nature is dead? (Peterson, Kelley, and Carvin, 28)

Though the next four lines fail to conclude convincingly this train of feeling, Hall's eighth-grade grasp of the postnuclear implications of "humanity" and "nature" is sure. This and other schoolchildren's verses—segregated probably into "children's literature" library alcoves until they emerged, through the efforts of Mindbody Press of California, into the larger antinuclear and peace community—illustrate a growing shift in American consciousness elsewhere detectable in 1980s writing. By mid-decade, a fresher, wider nuclear geography replaced the Hiroshima-centered vision in contemporary poetry. No longer must the Bomb itself—or its historically linked imagery of desert, city, cloud, atoll, missile silo, and so forth—be directly mentioned. Total destruction can now be taken for granted in a way not even Stafford or Bell would have felt free to assume. Even entire post-Hiroshima narratives like Sadako's can be implied or indicated obliquely. (Jude Hall may be doing so in his opening line.) This opens the way for a new mixture of themes and tones. Philosophical and psychological reverberations can now be explored with historical referents or political causes touched on only occasionally, or at least less heavily. Though the earth's imminent end is, however, still linked backward in time to Alamogordo and Japan, radioactivity, nuclear power plants, and the cold war serve as intervening, often more pressing, concerns.

The *earth*, the *self*, and the *end* thus merge in multiple combinations as successor issues, after Hiroshima and *hibakusha* consciousness, in each of the bellwether anthologies of the 1980s, including, as we have just seen, those that collect children's writing. Yet collections, even as they revive old texts and introduce fresh ones, with new issues and preoccupations, are by their nature assemblages of diverse as well as congruent pieces. However well organized thematically or chronologically, anthologies call attention to their particularly arresting (that is, idiosyncratic) components. Upon certain key or specimen poems, it can be argued, an editor's agenda of themes, contrasts, patterns, and repetitions is basically built and communicated to readers, who may not read, nor could surely remember, each contribution. Two poems, each dealing with the new overriding postnuclear issue, the end of the world, exemplify the individual-as-representative voice that evokes nuclear holocaust in imagination as present fact. One is June Jordan's awkwardly titled but moving "Who Would Be Free, Themselves Must Strike the Blow" (1984). The other is William Pitt Root's "The Day the Sun Rises Twice" (1984).

Though it takes its title from Frederick Douglass—thus hinting at an explicitly political statement and, more covertly, at the poet's black identity—Jordan's lyric works more closely with natural imagery. It is a postnuclear pastoral—an oxymoronic category perhaps, but an instrument with a political target. Her poem has a neutral, deliberately low-key refrain, however—"It was pretty quiet"—a refrain that comments indirectly upon all three sections, each of which depicts an aftershock of a nuclear holocaust. With a bucolic setting, the poem's central character is a cow.

> The cow could not stand up. The deadly river
> washed the feet of children. Where the cows

> grazed the ground concealed invisible
> charged particles that did not glow or make
> a tiny sound.[20]

Death spreads abroad in the second section as humans enter the polluted pasture beside the polluted river.

> . . . the deadly clouds
> bemused the lovers lying on the deadly ground
> to watch the widening nuclear light
> commingle with the wind their bodies set
> to motion.

Finally arrives the fated outcome, in a series of abrupt declarative lines:

> The cow could not stand up.
> The milk should not be sold.
> The baby would not be born right.
> The mother could not do anything about the baby
> or the cow.

While Jordan, like others, never specifies what the "bemused" lovers or the concerned mother might do to prevent or counter radioactive death, another poet, dramatizing another nuclear holocaust, has at least one positive response to record. In "The Day the Sun Rises Twice," William Pitt Root compressed into 16 lines (two less than Jordan—neither is prolix) an inevitable, terrible, sudden catastrophe.

> The day the sun rises twice
> the primitive dream of fire comes true,
> fire that burns forever,
> fire no water on earth can quench,
> fire whose light pins shadows to the stones,
> fire whose killing edge turns flying birds to ash.[21]

Humans, even less in control here than on Jordan's pastoral killing ground, are present simply as shadowy, short-lived *hibakusha*, "one-eyed prophets" who, after the catastrophe, can only chant mankind into "permanent darkness." Then only "countless minute embers will linger among the omens." The poet alone remains to react or prophesy. In either stance, his is a futile irony:

> I make this black mark on the silence now
> because none shall write
> and none shall remain to read
> when the clouds rise in our eyes

> against those suns rising around us
> like the thousand trees of life all clad in flames.

Only in the last line is Root's biblical reference hinted at. Mankind's "primitive dream of fire" denotes not only civilization's beginning and its culmination in Hiroshima but also the Garden of Eden, where, in myth, that dream began. The Tree of Life has, over millenia, become "the thousand trees of life" set aflame in nuclear firestorms. Root's narrator, recording humanity's ultimate discovery upon eating the apple of knowledge, remains on the edge of darkness to make a last black mark on the preholocaust silence, "because none shall write / and none shall remain to read."

Each of these contemporary poets—Kumin, Jordan, Wilner, even young Jude Hall—has settled for making a relatively restricted statement. Rather than attempting a public sermon or jeremiad, an epic narrative of science and technology, or a transcendent vision that might try to comprehend the awe-inspiring power of the Bomb and its political significance, these writers feature fewer facts, familiar natural imagery, private voices balancing thought and emotion, and the more or less passive roles of witness and dreamer. Brevity is a formal characteristic of their verses, enforcing other poetic choices. Their titles sometimes sound more portentous or political than their contents. Like many of the other writers discussed earlier, they appear to have implicitly accepted the advice of Marvin Bell and Carolyn Forché. "The facts are too big and too many," Bell observes in "Because Writers Are Scared: This Writer in the Nuclear Age." "We must fight back with our emotions, our *common* emotions. Only local action will accumulate and connect" (Schley, 190). To which Forché later adds: "There is no metaphor for the end of the world and it is horrible to search for one."[22]

Though it is hard to fault the sincerity of such advice, or the achievements of poets working within its constraints, there remain a modest number of more ambitious lyrics that manage to articulate ampler visions—if not of the end of the world at least of nuclear realities, evoking a range of responses to the threat of wholesale destruction. Three longer poems that risk more—perhaps falling short more often but also achieving more satisfying successes for their anguished authors and readerships—are the subject of this final look at poetry, the Bomb, and the permutations of sublime anxiety.

Two of these ambitious antagonists of despair, neither as well known as the third, are women. Minnie Bruce Pratt in "Strange Flesh" (1983) and Honor Moore in "Spuyten Duyvil" (1982) are both included in Schley's *Writing in a Nuclear Age*; Allen Ginsberg's "Plutonian Ode" (1978), arguably the most famous nuclear poem so far composed by an American, stands outside all the 1980s anthologies. The "Ode," however, was widely reprinted in magazines and newspapers following its appearance in the summer of 1978. As might be expected, Ginsberg's poem represents the public poet striving for an ambitious statement ("epic" being too grandiose a genre claim) in order to move the nation. The women's poems, on the contrary, are more private reflections and dramatizations. All three focus upon the same historical content and repeat strategies of language and form used in other nuclear verses. They are, therefore, both unique and representative works of the poetic imagination, epitomizing thoughts and emotions of a significant cadre of concerned Americans in the third and fourth decades of the nuclear age.

"Strange Flesh," the shortest and angriest of the three, is likewise shorter—and a great deal angrier—than Robert Penn Warren's "New Dawn" of the same year. Nevertheless, Pratt's lyric, despite a central italicized section recounting the attack on Hiroshima, is as "feminine" a political poem as Warren's is "masculine." Beatrice, the poet's alter ego, travels from her home through a postwar city to a skyscraper university building where an antinuclear demonstration is taking place. A native setting thus distinguishes this second-generation lyric from Warren's Hiroshima and Tinian meditation. Beatrice's personal memories and thoughts about the Bomb combine to create a passionate counterstatement to the beliefs she attributes to the men busily teaching and learning in the university's sterile environment. Her outlook likewise differs from that of the women and men circling with placards in the building and falling down in a die-in. Hers is indeed a contrary vision and discordant voice. She feels out of place in both worlds as they face each other in the blue glass skyscraper of learning.

Defending the ground on which *she* stands entails, first, celebrating the reality and associations of the mushroom older than the more familiar one now being flashed, as reminder and inspiration, on the wall at the demonstration:

> *A bomb fell through air, the pilot veered*
> *up from incandescent light. A puffball*
> *of dust, the button of a mushroom emerged*
> *at ground level, swelled with its own heat,*
> *stalked and spread its cap, released spores*
> *of invisible poison. . . .*[23]

Her version of countless previous representations of this historic scene treats the Bomb as both monstrous and natural; it was an organism growing and scattering its spores of destruction. Beatrice's trip to the strife-torn campus begins in her own backyard, where real mushrooms, some blue, others brown, sprout and seed in the "elemental dirt that smelled cold and alive." Left alone to fertilize other plants, these mushrooms will eventually mature into sweet gum trees, "taller than twenty people."

> Standing on that ground, Beatrice couldn't tell beginning
> from end, what was dirt, what was blue, what was her.
> But inside the tinted glass she felt out of place,

dirty jeans, dirt blackening her fingernails.
She could see no leaves ever blew in on this floor. (198)

Beatrice's brown and blue world, then, is radically divided. It is at once stark and complicated. Inside the blue skyscraper, white plastic chairs sit around "like ideas." In cubicle classrooms, old men teach young men to use numbers "to abstract from the particular instant." Her own failed career as student suddenly returns as a bitter memory of her once-pregnant self out of place and ashamed of "her swollen stomach that grew / stripes of hair like an animal." In those days, she had "tried to be not herself." She had decided to model herself on Marie Curie, the Slav-Frenchwoman scientist who had literally poisoned herself extracting the lethal powder of pale blue radium from tons of boiling pitch.

> Was it suicide, Beatrice wondered, if you killed yourself
> trying to change from dirty cunt into pure mind?
> And who to blame: western civilization? . . .
> At twelve
> she'd known that breasts were the opposite of thinking,
> could have murdered hers for pulling her down. . . .
> Yet here
> she was, and here were her breasts, wary, but prancing slightly
> as she walked. (Schley, 199)

As a representative woman of the nuclear age (Beatrice was born the year the Bomb fell), she is horrified at the pictures shown at the demonstration. Women and children at Hiroshima, they attest, were special victims: "people of a different color dying in another country." So she hates even more her own race, skin, and flesh. Especially humiliating is recognizing also that

She was caught in the skin of the little white man
who was nodding through the crowd, head huge as a globe,
father of the bomb. But he wore his skin like a summer suit. (Schley, 200)

This Einstein-like figure reminds her—somewhat implausibly—of her own father, a southern racist, misogynist, and religious bigot whose Sunday morning Bible lectures fixed Beatrice in her inescapable pollution as a rebellious woman. *That* was what first made her flesh "strange." She cannot forget his words:

> . . . how those who know
> as beasts naturally, the followers after strange flesh,
> the filthy dreamers who despise dominion, would burn,

> ashes of Sodom and Gomorrah, wells without water,
> trees of withered fruit, twice dead. (Schley, 201)

What this paternal "voice of apocalypse" never told his terrified daughter was the truth she has discovered in the wake of Hiroshima, about Navajo women in the desert and black women along the Savannah River who became radiation's native victims.

Beatrice's legacy, then, as white woman of her generation is incurably complicated by physical, psychological, and family factors. With a mother dead of cancer and a puritanical father, she comes into political maturity carrying an overwhelming burden of shame, resentment, rage. Yet she never succumbs to her father's or others' xenophobia and despair:

> He would never tell her she was both
> us and them, that opposites did not have to kill
> each other off. . . .
> . . . In the hall a door shut
> behind the scientist. People dropped silent to the floor,
> a die-in, crumpled like any heap of defeated bodies.
>
> Beatrice looked at the predictable despair, and left.
> She wouldn't just lie down and die: she would act
> contrary somehow, like hair, or an angry wasp. (Schley, 201)

In this narrativized reflection on an American episode—of the 1970s or early 1980s, presumably—Minnie Bruce Pratt adapts to her special purpose many common tactics and tropes used by other writers: natural imagery, a private and thoughtful rather than public and oratorical voice, indifference to concrete data or rational antinuclear argument. What sets her apart from Kumin and Jordan, however, is a refusal to tolerate the role of mere witness or dreamer. In place of Marie Curie she has taken as model "an angry wasp." Her fiercely feminine vision merges images of Hiroshima with those of a woman's body, the earth, and a past polluted by patriarchal domination. An adult's experience with higher education confirms her distrust of Cartesian dualism, the split between abstract mind and dangerous, dirty body-matter. That division has served a man's mad world. Its products have been the Bomb, Hiroshima, the desert, and the Savannah River plant. Further, it has condemned her and other women to angry, isolated existences within their so-called strange flesh, a false and unacceptable status and self. The poem ends suddenly with this bitter vision articulated but no ready-made response formed, save undespairing angry withdrawal.

Though Beatrice can accept neither the cool world of science and technology nor a pallid, liberal peacenik protest, she no longer stands alone on the ground staked out at the poem's outset. Her vivid words and feelings—especially those associated with the female body—have become shared *political* statements. To her contemporaries in the women's, gay and lesbian, abortion, and other 1980s movements, Pratt bequeathes a renewed awareness of nuclear history and, indeed, of Western civilization itself, as essential factors in her/their/our bondage and hope of freedom. The definition of politics has changed.[24]

Honor Moore's "Spuyten Duyvil" is also a long soliloquy and a portrait of another woman's anxious existence in the age of the cold war. In fact, Moore and Pratt illustrate brilliantly but differently the political awareness that Galway Kinnell pleads for from his fellow poets. They must delve deeply into the self, he counsels, as a necessary step toward dramatizing the Bomb's shadow falling on the whole of modern experience. "In that sense solidarity occurs. The poem is no longer just personal" (Daniels, 296). Although, at least in some men's eyes, Pratt hesitates on the brink of political commitment, she actually has redefined feminist solidarity. Moore's narrator pursues a more conciliatory course. At the close of a 200-line, often-dramatic meditation on life under the cold war and the Bomb, she, too, addresses a solidarity plea to husband/friend/readers. She urges him/her/them to open up in imagination, to empathize with the desperately painful needs of *all* others:

> . . . If their anger frightens you,
> try to understand their grief. If you can't
>
> understand what they say, watch
> how they move. It's thunder. She
>
> is young. Tell her the truth. He is near
> ninety. Help him cross the street. It's
>
> thunder. Reach for my hand, I will
> let you go. It's raining. If you
>
> visit, we will walk down through the fields
> and I will show you the river.[25]

Though some readers might fault what they could call a stereotypically "feminine" tone and sentimental hopefulness, these elements are, if present, offset by the political and social cogency demonstrated in the body of the poem. Her narrator's imagination, for one thing, is especially sensitive to the ways in which contemporary television, film, radio, and other mass media condition nuclear thinking and feeling. For instance, an almost radio play–like scenario characterizes the poem's opening section:

> A computer chip malfunctions. A micro-
> scopic switch slips. You cut an apple into

quarters. East of the Urals, a technician
sweats into gray fatigues. In Nevada

a video screen registers activity.
The President carries a briefcase called

the football. His men sit at a small table
or cluster in easy chairs watching a screen

tick with revelation. You adjust your
blinds. I flip a cellar switch. A terrorist

monitors the football. A red light on a red
telephone flashes. The technician cues

his superior. Afternoon in the desert.
Dead of night in the Urals. Rockets

surge from concrete silos like lipsticks sprung
from gargantuan tubes. I have seen bridges

dynamited in 3-D color, mushroom clouds
engorge and shrivel in 4/4 time, faces

of children etched with acid to rippling
wound on screens the size of footballs.

So have you. . . . (Schley, 203)

In crisp couplets, the connecting links of popular, military, and governmental
cold war vocabularies are identified and, in the final phrase, brought home as
"natural" to readers' lives. Equally commonplace is the little plot that then
unfolds. The narrator drives across the Spuyten Duyvil bridge into Manhattan.
A summer thunderstorm threatens. (These are the thunder and rain references
in the last section.) Normal weather sounds trigger abnormal fears of nuclear
attack and universal obliteration. Her fevered mind reacts:

. . . I am blind and
I step from my car. My hair is

on fire. It could be an earring
or an orange pinwheel. My hand is

burning. My hair stinks when it
burns. Below this bridge at the tip of

the city is a white sand beach. Did you
know that? Tell me, why don't you

reach for my hand? . . . (Schley, 204–5)

Such private fears evoke collective memories—drawn from all sorts of sources—of Hiroshima and *hibakusha* suffering. Moreover, the incongruous white sandy beach at Manhattan's tip evokes other beaches in the nuclear archive—Bikini's from history, fictional strands from Nevil Shute, J. G. Ballard, and Jean Baudrillard's observation in "The Year 2000": "The end of this century is before us like an empty beach."[26] Moore's melding of geography, history, and literature helps underscore Manhattan as a symbolic as well as actual site. It finally stands for an entire cold war society poised on the brink of danger and destruction. When the narrator observes, "they say cities will melt / like fat," it applies to a whole society and way of life. Similarly, Moore's imagery of gardens, vegetables, and old trees reminds readers of poets like Maxine Kumin and Minnie Bruce Pratt. In addition, still other nuclear images—"hot oceans, thick soot, flat darkness," as well as desert, rocket, War Room, and red telephone—recall a host of popular stories and images from movies (*Fail-Safe* and *Dr. Strangelove*), television dramas (*The Day After*, *Threads*), and novels (*On the Beach*, *The Nuclear Age*). The poet's alter ego, reaching out to desperate or indifferent others, floats her anxious appeal upon a succession of images, ideas, and emotions that 1980s readers readily recognize and can endorse.

In the final section, Moore contributes a small new nuclear story to this cultural storehouse. Her narrator imagines a confused man caught like herself in preholocaust fear and indecision. She counsels the reader to share his condition and offer acts of solace and solidarity:

Because he is afraid and powerful
he lives encircled by water.

We hold her as she dies, turn the chairs
to face each other. We breathe with her

as her child is born, let him
cry in the dark as he mourns her death.

. . . One day he
swims the moat to explore the place
which confuses him. There is food
    when

he reaches the lit house, and stars
hang from the towering branches

>of ancient trees. We must learn to rest
>when we are tired. Every morning
>
>the sun rises. Every spring green
>returns to the cold climates. Bathe
>
>with her, stand with her in the house
>smiling as she shows you the
>
>new wood. . . . (Schley, 208–9)

In this final series of simple tropes and life-affirming acts, Moore offers neither political program, transcendent vision, nor stoic acceptance of death and the end of time. Without retreating from nuclear realities, she accepts wholeheartedly the advice of Kinnell, Bell, and others: to speak for life in whatever combination of old/new language may steer readers' consciousness toward recognition, resistance, and change. In "Spuyten Duyvil" the dangers of U.S.-Soviet nuclear destructiveness are squarely faced. The cold war and the fate of the earth provide a familiar context within and against which her sublimely anxious narrator tries to construct a microcosm of love and care. Moore's poem embodies as distinctively as any by Kumin, Jordan, or Pratt a woman's vision of past, present, and possible future. Her narrator inhabits intimately a historical moment, strategic place, and common psychological state. Her imagined world is created and dominated by men but can be redeemed by womanly—that is, truly human—actions: following the news intelligently, observing nature closely and the weather, digging a garden and driving a car *into* the vulnerable metropolis, counseling the young and consoling the old, assisting at childbirth, holding out her hand to husband or lover. Her modest contribution to the world's bank of post-Hiroshima imaginal memories is the "lit house" surrounded by trees and illuminated by stars—which might turn into rockets at any moment. Poetic setting thus serves as symbolic content. It bespeaks an old/new order that, momentarily at least, is sustainable though not necessarily survivable. The distinction is, I believe, major. Nevertheless, the imminent threat of nuclear destruction with which "Spuyten Duyvil" opens turns in the last section to summer certainty: ". . . It's thunder. . . . It's raining."

As compared to Moore, Pratt, Kumin, and the Berkeley schoolchildren, Allen Ginsberg inhabits a very different social space. He was and remains the archetypal public poet of his generation of American *hibakusha*. So it is hardly news that his "Plutonian Ode" and other nuclear verses like "Nagasaki Days" (1978) received immediate and wide attention.[27] Yet Ginsberg's standing with the general reading public remains distinctly problematic. The much-publicized details of his private life (endlessly repeated in his own verses, for he is the most autobiographical of contemporary poets), the spiritual-political roles he inhabits of guru, orator, and outlaw poet, constrain to alienate as well as attract audiences. These factors help explain the imputed "failure" of "Plutonian Ode." In the eyes of some academic critics and fellow poets, Ginsberg's nuclear verses during the late 1970s and early 1980s were misunderstood and rejected. By comparison with *Howl* (1956) and *Kaddish* (1961), it was averred, not to mention some poems by his contemporaries, including several cited here, the "Ode" was criticized for an obscurantism that called for no fewer than 23 footnotes in the *Collected Poems, 1947–1980* (1984) (795–97).

From today's perspective, however, these criticisms lose much of their punch. I would argue that no single nuclear poem is more deeply embedded in or more powerfully evokes its cultural context than the "Ode." It brilliantly exemplifies Wallace Stevens's famous dictum in "An Ordinary Evening in New Haven" (1950): "The poem is the cry of its occasion / Part of the res itself and not about it."[28]

To begin to justify this claim, the poem was, in a sense, unpremeditated, born in the heat of the moment. Its history is traced in Michael Schumacher's recent *Dharma Lion: A Critical Biography of Allen Ginsberg* (1992).[29] There we learn in detail about the middle-aged poet's life and art during a period of political, poetic, and spiritual turmoil. This occurred in 1978, especially in the summer, when the 65-line "Ode" was written. As Ginsberg claims, the poem was written over the space of six hours during the night of 12 June. The publication date of the version that appears in *Collected Poems* is 14 July of the same year. At that time, Ginsberg was living and teaching at Naropa, a school for poets in eastern Colorado. The poet was deeply into Buddhist mysticism (under the tutelage of Chogyam Trungpa, the Vajrayana Buddhist guru) and just as deeply involved in antinuclear demonstrations at nearby Rocky Flats, home of Rockwell's plutonium bomb manufacturing plant. That summer the poet, his pupils, and fellow demonstrators, stirred by the New York City peace march of 27 May, discussed at length the dangers of nuclear energy and weaponry. On 16 June Ginsberg was arrested and arraigned in a Colorado courtroom, charged with obstructing passage of a nuclear-materials train at Rocky Flats. In his defense, Ginsberg read aloud the entire "Plutonian Ode." Later, Ginsberg, Daniel Ellsberg, and others were again arrested for a demonstration marking the thirty-third anniversary of the bombing of Nagasaki. Lines in "Nagasaki Days" memorialize that confrontation:

> Middleaged Ginsberg & Ellsberg taken down the road
> to the grayhaired Sheriff's van—
> But what about Einstein? What about Einstein? Hey, Einstein come
> back! (699)

Subsequently, following publication of the "Plutonian Ode" in the underground press and elsewhere, Ginsberg again performed his poem at Saint Mark's in the Bowery Church in New York, at a memorial benefit in which over 100 poets, actors, dancers, and musicians participated. "I think he's changed the role of the poet in America," John Ashbery remarked of Ginsberg's long record of moving poetry from the page to the stage; "now everybody experiences poetry" (Schumacher, 635). Indeed, the poet had already succeeded in placing his protest performances in the widest possible perspective. In "Nagasaki Days," he included this paean to significant cosmic and terrestrial numbers:

> 200,000,000 years for the Galaxy to revolve on its core
> 24,000 the Babylonian Great Year
> 24,000 the half life of plutonium
> 2,000 the most I ever got for a poetry reading
> 80,000 dolphins killed in the dragnet
> 4,000,000,000 years earth been born. (701)

The "Plutonium Ode," too, embraces in its 65 long lines decades, centuries, millenia, aeons. It centers on the active hero-poet who addresses, enters in imagination, and challenges the plutonium bomb. "I dare your Reality, I challenge your very being! I publish your cause and effect!" (703). Speaking in the name and lineage of Whitman, Blake, Neruda, and other political poets, he hurls ancient and modern epithets at the nuclear force, boldly calling it "Lord of Hades," "Sire of avenging Furies," "billionaire Hell-King," "Radioactive Nemesis," "absolute Vanity," "Canker-hex," "Death-Scandal of Capital politics," and more. His own strength, on the contrary, is strictly spiritual and aesthetic:

> I turn the Wheel of Mind on your three hundred tons! Your
> name enters mankind's ear! I embody your ultimate powers!
> My oratory advances on your vaunted Mystery! This breath
> dispels your braggart fears! I sing your form at last. . . . (703)

As a puny human mind confronting matter's oldest and most powerful expression, the poet does not underestimate that enemy power:

> Father Whitman I celebrate a matter that renders Self oblivion!
> Grand Subject that annihilates inky hands & pages' prayers, old
> orators' inspired Immortalities, . . .
> I enter with spirit out loud into your fuel rod drums
> underground on soundless thrones and beds of lead
> O density! This weightless anthem trumpets transcendent through
>   hidden chambers and breaks through iron doors into the
>   Infernal Room!
> Over your dreadful vibration this measured harmony floats
> audible, these jubilant tones are honey and milk and wine-sweet
>   water. . . . (702–4)

Ginsberg's long lines and name lists, deliberately Whitmanian, evoke the Civil War odes of the Wound Dresser poet. In place of battlefields, he now chants a different American landscape:

> I begin your chant, openmouthed exhaling into spacious sky over
>   silent mills at Hanford, Savannah River, Rocky Flats, Pantex,
>   Burlington, Albuquerque
> I yell thru Washington, South Carolina, Colorado, Texas, Iowa, New
>   Mexico
> where nuclear reactors create a new Thing under the Sun, . . . (702–3)

Like Whitman, too, he celebrates and incorporates the American countryside
and the mountains visible from his Boulder balcony. Closely observed yet
grandly panoramic and traditionally romantic, Ginsberg's vision seeks to do-
mesticate the nuclear sublime—or, conversely, to politicize the romantic sublime—as few of his contemporaries have dared to do. His is at once old-
fashioned and space age verse. Galaxies, our solar system, and plutonian
history are all yoked to the year 1978. A transcendental ode of such scope and
chutzpah gives as much space to the sparrows on Marine Street, Boulder, as
to the Rocky Flats reactor and the Rocky Mountains. All time and space, in his
elevated, often awkward, Oriental-inspired discourse, are symbolically compressed into "this wheel of syllables . . . these vowels and consonants to
breath's end." The reader is invited to respond emotionally as if reading "When
Lilacs Last in the Dooryard Bloom'd" (1865) or "Passage to India" (1868).

> take this inhalation of black poison to your heart, breathe out this
>   blessing from your breast on our creation
> forests cities oceans deserts rocky flats and mountains in the
> Ten Directions pacify with this exhalation,
> enrich this Plutonian Ode to explode its empty thunder through
> earthen thought-worlds. . . .
> . . . destroy this mountain of Plutonium with ordinary
> mind and body speech,
> thus empower this Mind-guard spirit gone out, gone out, gone
> beyond, gone beyond me, Wake space, so Ah! (705)

Ginsberg's vatic strophes and grand climax were neither familiar nor
congenial to many of his contemporaries. Those accustomed to the taut econo-
mies of Stafford's "At the Bomb Testing Site" or Robert Lowell's "Fall 1961"
(1964), for example, could belittle this poet's Whitmanian language and expan-
sive spirit. Others would be mystified (in the wrong sense) by an Oriental
religious belief calling into question the very self, world, and reality of nuclear
rockets that the poet is urging his readers to get serious about. The paradox
seems inescapable and uncomfortable. Ginsberg's antideath and proenviron-
ment politics, widely known at the time, seem at odds with his Buddhist belief
in transcendent merger with the infinite.

   To this cosmic contradiction, Richard Eberhart's "Testimony" (1983) offers a typical counterstatement.

> Because praise of the highest visions
>
> Unattainable, glimpsed in a high moment
> Is altogther unattainable,
>
> We are here in a ground of earth structures,
> Every day bread, workmanship,
>
> We are beings who are held down to time,
> Amazed at a glimpse of immateriality, . . .
>
> When it comes, when it comes, the blast,
> Destruction of the best and worst,
>
> We wanted to look in the eye of God,
> We got six feet of radioactive sod.[30]

Though Ginsberg's and Eberhart's are not totally opposed viewpoints on the nuclear dilemma, the spiritual differences are inescapable. Eberhart's earthy humanism probably speaks to and for the mass of Americans. Nonetheless, Ginsberg has an articulate ally in Gary Snyder, another American Buddhist. In an interview, Snyder once observed:

> Nanao Sasaki once said, "No need to survive"—just as we were bundling our leaflets and lacing our boots to do some ecological political exercises. Why this apparent paradox?
>   . . . The human world is brought to this pass by an all-too-effective survival consciousness, which breeds anthropocentrism, nationalism, parochial localism, and other assorted self-centered uselessly narrow notions of identity. Throwing away these narrow notions of membership helps us to join the mammal world . . . the world of all animals . . . as well, the world of rocks, sand, clouds, and glaciers, the world of space, the world of emptiness.[31]

Snyder's "all-species perspective" does clarify Ginsberg's vatic verse and raises larger questions about the assertions of Eberhart, Bell, and Stafford about the poet as a "local animal" for whom "only local action will accumulate and connect" (Schley, 189, 190). At any rate, the moral and imaginative terrain on which contemporary poets in these years faced the nuclear age's edge of darkness was—and remains—divided by these eschatological boundary markers: mystical expansiveness and stoic humanism.

Snyder's assessment of the face-off between American Buddhism and the nuclear threat, besides articulating a vigorous defense of active transcendentalism (lacing on one's boots while declaring there is "no need to survive"), is a powerful prose piece. It appears in an interview in one of the anthologies issued in the 1980s. There have been many other opportunities for prosaic as well as poetic utterance from all the poets whose voices we have heard in this chapter. The meeting of Poets against the End of the World is one. So, too, are the political essays and speeches and their republication in collections—as well as the observations by scholars and critics whose political passion about nuclear issues infuses their literary and cultural critiques (as we shall see in the next chapter). Just as some readers find the boundary between free verse and prose difficult to establish, so, too, do writers of prose often express their concepts and convictions with almost poetic fluency and affect. Although genre has served as a convenient category and sociological rationale throughout this study, its permeable membranes are still much in evidence as we conclude by looking at two poets and a critic who in important respects epitomize the 1980s situation of imaginative writing in a culture of war.

Neither of the poet-citizens is as venerated as Robert Penn Warren nor as guardedly admired as Ginsberg (Kawada, 115–17). Yet for several decades Denise Levertov has been a model activist-artist, writing, speaking, demonstrating, and protesting in numerous antinuclear causes. Before joining the 12 other poets at Town Hall in 1982, she had marched and spoken at such symbolic sites as Seabrook, New Hampshire, Lafayette Park in Washington, D.C., and Sofia, Bulgaria, at an international peace congress. Her verses on Vietnam ("Advent 1966" [1965]) and Hiroshima ("On the 32nd Anniversary of the Bombing of Hiroshima and Nagasaki" [1978]) are widely known and often reprinted. They support but do not supplant her prose statements: "[A]s a published poet, I have an audience, and address that audience, in person and in print, on issues that engage my political concern . . . because the issues—justice and peace and 'the fate of the earth'—are always on my mind, they do enter my poems, and then I have the chance *through* poetry, to stir others' minds or to articulate what readers feel but have not found words for." Then she adds a personal note whose force is felt by many contemporaries:

> All I've said up to now is applicable to all "protest," "didactic," or "engaged" poetry. But it seems, as I read over what I've written to lack urgency. And was there ever a time as urgent? Never. Never have we faced extinction, the extinction of all future, all consciousness. Sometimes I wonder how we can write at all, under that shadow. Sometimes I wonder how we can write about anything else. But maintaining a sense of what life, nature, and spirit *are* is essential if we are to find the mind's resources to circumvent the results of the twentieth century's unethical infatuation with technology and the lust for power of its "leaders."[32]

Michael Daley is a younger, less famous, but no less anguished and determined poet-citizen. He also speaks literarily through both poetry and prose.

"Credo" (1983), a poem accompanied by commentary, can stand as a representative statement by a second-generation American *hibakusha*. It is, significantly, couched in negative terms—a typical mental and moral formulation of personal convictions for many late–twentieth-century Americans and others around the world. His poem confesses:

> Yet I do not believe—I who have ripened
> in Church—I do not believe that the unborn in my blood
> chanting whispers to polished remnants
> of my parents, are not to speak or name,
> not to call earth "Earth," the self "Self."
>
> Is it the death of zero we are planning?
> At the orchestra, at intermission, a man weeps
> for what will be no more. Passengers in the streets
> still ride to work, still read. How can we hold the idea?
> It is like metal. How can we not?[33]

What is not to be believed, then, is "the death of zero," the nuclear ground number signifying the disappearance of faith, family, descendants, art, the earth, our selves, in mass devastation. Already in many fatalistic minds, he suggests, zero thinking prevails. Still, the idea of civilized life persists, "like metal." This simple simile is double-edged, connoting durability yet, historically by nuclear association, also connoting bombs, rockets, Hiroshima. To this apparent paradox the poet retorts:

> I believe that when the morning star fires into the sky
> as from a mirror, the sun is empowered to deliver a message
> in code to earth. I believe we are that message. (Schley, 146)

In his prose commentary on this poem, Daley confesses his youthful ignorance.

> I have no experience to bring to writing about such things. Nor have I a memory of our first use of the Bomb. All the heinous crimes of government and military, whether of nuclear or non-nuclear powers, comes secondhand. So I must imagine, to write about them. . . . Nor can I adequately imagine my own death. Yet perhaps imagining death, on a planetary level, is part of the work of the poet, even, as Levertov suggests, in the daily freedoms of a civilized world. To imagine, let us hope, is to act, and to bring about action in our society. Perhaps we must imagine life as well, to make, as is the mandate from the Greek *poiein*, or to forge, as the old "apolitical" artificer once said, ". . . in the smithy of my soul the uncreated consciousness of my race." (Schley, 147–48)

Though Michael Daley did not stand with Levertov and the Town Hall poets (now seen perhaps as a generational gathering), his "Credo" does not conflict with any of the declarations of these older poets. Neither the black authors (Baraka, Jordan, Knight) nor the Native American Ortiz, nor the white men and women of diverse backgrounds and self-identities would, I believe, disagree with the younger poet's definition of the common task of poets living on the edge of postnuclear darkness.

Several years deeper into the 1980s ethos of fear and fragile hope, Terrence Des Pres published a scholarly study that resonated with many of the same ideas and emotions expressed by Levertov and Daley. *Praises and Dispraises: Poetry and Politics in the Twentieth Century* (1988) ends with a fervent call for a "changed poetics" (225). Des Pres, the author of *The Survivor* (1980), a riveting study of survivors of the Nazi concentration camps,[34] also admits that, like Daley, his backward and prophetic views of the relation between literature and society are not original. "It's an old story, except for the nuclear angle. For Thucydides it was Hellas going down. Now it's life on earth. . . . But being caught in the cross fire provokes interesting questions, in particular what we might still expect from poetry and fiction—enlightened feeling? finer sensibilities?—amid the *hysterico/passio* of nuclear Cold War politics" (225). To which Des Pres answers in a "credo" of his own:

> Between the self and the terrible world comes poetry with its minute redemptions, its lyrical insurgencies, its willing suspension of disbelief in tomorrow. These ministrations, I take it, compose our chances. I don't mean that poems can have a say in nuclear matters, or that through poetry we may expect a general change of heart. Power listens to none but itself; and the myth of progress through enlightenment, in my view, died in 1914. What I mean to say is that right language can help us, as it always helps in hard moments, with our private struggles to keep whole, can be a stay against confusion, can start the healing fountains. And whatever helps us repossess our humanity, able again to take place and speak forth, frees us for work in the world. ([1988], 228)

6

Critics and Historians of the 1980s Frame the First Nuclear Age

[T]he contemporary critic can assert both the historicity and the crucial role interpretation played in the events themselves. This is not to deny the historical facts of the Holocaust outside of their narrative framing, but only to emphasize the difficulty of interpreting, expressing, and acting on these facts outside of the ways we frame them.

James E. Young, (*Writing and Rewriting the Holocaust*)[1]

TERRENCE DES PRES IS TYPICAL OF THE CULTURAL HISTORIANS and literary critics who, in the last decade or so, have participated in, by interpreting, nuclear age events and expressions. Des Pres is morally and politically engaged in the central issues of the era primarily in and through his scholarly critiques. His is one more voice of a citizen impelled to alert fellow members of a dangerously warlike culture about a global situation whose immediate sources lie in World War II. Thus he echoes the focus, language, and moral perspective of many of the authors whose works I have been discussing—not only academics like Boyer and Lenz but also many novelists and short-story writers, nonfiction and children's literature specialists, and American poets. What unites all of these practitioners into a loose but discernible tradition has, I hope, become clear in these chapters. The connecting thread of their creatively critical writings is the fact of their being works of a literature of resistance. Profoundly humanistic in their shared concerns for the continuity of life, for peace and the fate of the earth, the writings of Hersey, Lifton, and Schell, of Merril, Bradbury, Miller, and Vonnegut, of Maruki, Vigna, and Strieber, of Bell, Levertov, Pratt, and Ginsberg, and more recently, of Johnson, O'Brien, and See, have taken on the cold war and explored the nuclear politics and cultural values that have decisively marked the era 1945–92. They do so in the common conviction that, in Des Pres's words, "right language" is a vital social resource. In "hard times," writers and readers must become aware of the fragility and preciousness of this resource. Only by re-creating, sharing, and criticizing nuclear experience and its varied expressions can postnuclear Americans in particular—as citizens of the instigator nation and superpower—step back from the edge of darkness.

There is another sense in which Des Pres speaks for others mentioned in this study. He stands on the common ground identified by the titles of his two books. If *Praises and Dispraises* echoes Hayden Carruth in urging poets and readers to embrace politics, *The Survivor* shows that public history and private memory come together, over the past half-century, under the joint historical signs of Auschwitz and Hiroshima. Thanks to Robert Jay Lifton and his successors, the survivors of the Nazi Holocaust and the *hibakusha* of Hiroshima and Nagasaki are now stamped on two sides of a fateful coin. Actual holocaust in Europe and actual urban devastations in Japan are, despite obvious differences, linked realities of the immediate past and foreshadowings of the world's problematic future. Certain scholars have explored the literary implications of this pair of awesome events more directly than has Des Pres; their arguments and insights will here be advanced as essential elements in the construction of a nuclear age history.

The onset and course of this historical period are topics that first must be arranged in an explanatory narrative. The actors and events, like their motives and consequences, do not by themselves make a meaningful sequence. Interpretation, as Young asserts in this chapter's epigraph, is essential. In beginning to do this, 1980s historians and literary critics are at last showing the way toward an inclusive cultural history. While struggling with the raw materials of nuclear experience, writers have learned to factor into their stories the intangible, private, and transnational dimensions alongside the documentable data about purely American actions, public institutions, and policies. Hiroshima's destruction, and the ineradicable fissure in secular time and world history that ensued, was not only a momentous military and geopolitical action but also led to an imaginative explosion in world consciousness. At the time, as surveys indicated, 98 percent of all Americans knew almost at once about the existence and deployment against Japan of the Bomb (Weart, 105). If in the half-century since many Americans (and others) have performed herculean feats of forgetting Hiroshima and its menacing implications, that psychosocial fact merely thickens the complexity of the event's monumental significance and the challenge of framing adequate literary accounts and reaching appropriate readerships.

Both historical narrative and various literary genres are involved, as we have seen, in this cognitive and emotional endeavor. The size of the problem demands the full range of expressive language, for historians, fiction writers, and poets now grasp a fact but dimly perceived by a few percipient minds in the 1940s: Hiroshima as fact and symbol possesses features and a force matched by few if any crucial events in our past. It can be argued that neither the American Revolution nor the Civil War, neither the Industrial Revolution nor the Great Depression, neither the automobile nor the computer, have affected so quickly and comprehensively the fate of the entire globe or delivered the means of wiping whole populations from its surface. "War *is* the culture of our age and the culture *is* war," ran the 1950 report of the Dun Commission, a conclave of leading clergymen (Boyer, 348). Four years earlier, Gen. Dwight D. Eisenhower anticipated a similarly sweeping truth when he observed: "[T]he problem of controlling and finally preventing, the use of atomic bombs (and other decisive weapons) thus becomes the problem of preventing war itself" (Gregory, 59). The clergymen and the general merely echoed Niels Bohr's wartime prophecy: "*We are in a completely new situation that cannot be resolved by war*" (Rhodes, 532). Present-day thinking, both civilian and military, repeats these assessments. Lisa Peattie's matter-of-fact description in 1984 is typical: the United States is a "warfare state," she writes, organized in "a certain mad orderliness" around nuclear weaponry (Gregory, 158, 156).

An alternative intellectual orderliness—one they hope is not as "mad" as nuclear America—has been attempted by the historians already named in these pages. Their first task has been to assign dates for the onset and stages of the first nuclear age. Both popular and working assumptions of scholars, of course, mark 6 August 1945 as the immediate beginning. Many among the 98 percent recognized on the spot that an epochal event had occurred. "The atomic bomb exploded over Hiroshima in the summer of 1945," wrote Margaret Mead in her autobiography. "At that point I tore up every page of a book I had nearly finished. Every sentence was out of date. We had entered a new age."[2] Even more dramatic was the remembered response of Daniel Berrigan. "In August of that year, I was a patient at Mercy Hospital in Baltimore, ill and exhausted. And one morning, a sister placed on my bed the daily newspaper, rolled up, a trumpet of doom. Doomsday, Hiroshima day: the Bomb had fallen. I read, turned to ice or stone. . . . A sense would come to me later with the force of a thunderbolt scoring its message on a wall, a sense of before and after: before Hiroshima, after Hiroshima."[3]

Behind the two explosions in Japan and these representative aftershocks in the minds of Mead and Berrigan stands a receding series of historical events, myths, and images that shaped and cloaked the ways other Americans would respond to the new age. This cultural prehistory is explored by two other 1980s scholars, H. Bruce Franklin and Jeff Smith. In the early chapters of Franklin's *War Stars: The Superweapon and the American Imagination* (1988), readers are reminded of the century-old tradition among American novelists and scientists anticipating a future event—the invention of an atomic bomb.[4] Behind these early prophets stood even older stories of a strange new world. In narratives like Mary Shelley's *Frankenstein* (1818) and H. G. Wells's *The World Set Free* (1914), plots and metaphors were originated, later to be projected onto Hiroshima.

Jeff Smith in *Unthinking the Unthinkable: Nuclear Weapons and Western Culture* (1989) adds an even longer prehistory to August 1945.[5] He traces the intellectual roots of the nuclear age to military events and literary texts that appeared in late medieval and early modern Europe, especially in Tudor and Stuart England. Two key events in those remote centuries that anticipate Trinity, SDI, and present-day nuclear dreams and fears are, first, the rise of the European nation-state, with total warfare as its instrument of dynamic expansion, and, second, literary articulations of the psychological tensions and moral implications of such a violent political history. Smith traces the connections between apparently quite disparate events and actors like the speech (in the Shakespearean play) of Henry V to his troops before Harfleur and modern discussions of Hiroshima by Ronald Reagan and the creators of *Dr. Strangelove* and *The Fate of the Earth*. Tenaciously held ideas and feelings, Smith contends, more than specific economic forces and political policies, have profoundly characterized Western cultural history. These deep causal patterns are best laid bare in literary texts and political rhetoric. Hence Henry V and Ronald Reagan are actors on similar stages: each mouths, in a different idiom, messages containing—and invoking—uncommon power for generating political and military evil. "I suggest that particular policies result directly from ideas, and thus only indirectly from material forces. Material forces produce particular policies only by taking certain cultural and intellectual forms rather than others, and it is these forms that must be looked at more closely," he asserts (xiv).

To be sure, neither Franklin nor Smith claims for literary imagery and political rhetoric the power to cause the nuclear age. "No text is going to turn cities into firestorms or bring on nuclear winter," Smith concedes. "But if those things happen they will be results of discourses and ideologies, and of the beliefs these generate at a given moment" (13). Deciding which "given moments" have proved decisive or propitious for ideas and emotions to be mobilized into which actions, words, and texts is a preoccupation of cultural historians. Historical choices of narrative order and sequence are just as necessary to a full understanding of the first nuclear age as interpretations by literary critics. Indeed, the two groups shared descriptions and analyses during the mid- and late 1980s. Two men led the way to a wider contextualizing of post-Hiroshima thought and feeling. Paul Boyer's *By the Bomb's Early Light* (1985) and Spencer Weart's *Nuclear Fear* (1988) have been repeatedly cited in these pages. Both extend (and qualify) the literary-historical formulations of Franklin, Smith, and others still to be mentioned or recalled. In complementary ways, Boyer and Weart show the need to *periodize* and *socialize* the war culture of these crucial decades.

Boyer was one of the first to mention the delays and long silences that alternate with periods of anxious attention to nuclear issues, his main theme. Though his periodization of the atomic age may seem to some rather old-fashioned pedantry, to his fellow 1980s scholars such structuring is essential. Fredric Jameson, for one, points out that defining any historical period is an important cultural construct. "Veterans [of any historic period]," he notes in an essay on the 1960s, "who have seen so many things change dramatically from year to year, think more historically than their predecessors." In fact, intellectuals in particular "find it normal to justify their current positions by way of a historical narrative."[6] Thus it seems plausible to assume that both scholars and survivors of history need to establish boundaries and assign names or categories to historical time.

To rehearse the particular pattern—used in this study—that Boyer has imposed on the age, we should recall the three periods he defines:

1. The Age of Excitement and Discussion: This period extends from 1945 to 1963 or 1964—that is, roughly from Los Alamos through the Cuban Missile Crisis, with the cold war, the H-bomb, Bikini, and Sputnik as periodic reminders of growing nuclear involvement. Other critics, like Michael J. Carey, term this early era (after W. H. Auden) the Age of Anxiety. Its highwater mark is the 1950s.

2. The Period of the Big Sleep: These years, 1964–79, are characterized by the continuing politics of deterrence, rosy hopes for nuclear energy, and carefully nurtured illusions of diminishing risks of nuclear war. Turmoil at home and the Vietnam War abroad combined to divert attention and encourage avoidance of nuclear threats and thinking, as détente failed and stockpiles grew.

3. The Age of Renewed Concern: Beginning about 1979 and continuing to the present (1985 for Boyer, the 1990s for us, perhaps), this period is marked by worldwide antiwar and antinuclear movements and heightened awareness at home of nuclear perils flowing from Reagan administration rearmament, anticommunism, and magical thinking. These years have been called in this book "America's reawakening" (see Boyer, 352–67).

This historical framework is useful as a preliminary ordering of literary texts and contexts, seen as responses in the wake of prior military and political acts. As works of the imagination, such responses are individual as well as retroactive, topical, or prophetic. Though private and idiosyncratic, certain literary expressions are nonetheless reflections and refractions of cold war concerns. As such, they refer to, anticipate, or ignore the received attitudes and values of the public or of other artists and intellectuals.

Boyer's pioneering work as orderer and interpreter of cultural responses to the Bomb is limited to the early years, roughly 1945–51. He examines a range of cultural materials, including government documents, editorials and sermons, cartoons, films, newspapers, and novels. His approach is to see all these expressions as direct reflections of, or oblique responses to, the new social and psychological situation. Derived from historical and literary records and texts, his focus generates two central conclusions. The first is "how quickly contemporary observers understood that a profoundly unsettling new cultural factor had been introduced—that the bomb had transformed not only military strategy and international relations, but the fundamental ground of culture and consciousness" (xix). A second and equally arresting hypothesis is that "all the major elements in our contemporary engagement with the nuclear reality took shape literally within days of Hiroshima" (xix). Thus he points out that, on 26 August 1945, the *Washington Post* mentioned the possibility that "some type of Star-Wars–like defense could be developed to destroy incoming nuclear missiles" (xix). This leads the historian, writing in 1985, to stress his and others' sense of déjà vu. In hindsight "once again the possibility of nuclear annihilation looms large in the national consciousness, and once again the agencies of culture and the media both resonate to and amplify that awareness. Indeed, the parallels are striking. Except for a post-holocaust 'Nuclear Winter,' every theme and image by which we express our nuclear fear today has its counterpart in the immediate post-Hiroshima period" (364).

For these reasons, Boyer sees the era's beginning as synecdoche. He is also encouraged by the archives to treat history and literature as unproblematically tied to social reality through representational language. His agenda, bringing together authors as diverse as William B. Laurence, Lewis Mumford, Edgar A. Guest, James Agee, and William Faulkner, is indeed comprehensive. But he assumes throughout that discourse itself is a relatively uncomplicated medium of communication, whether as denotation or connotation. Subsequent to the period he has selected, of course, many artists, critics, and indeed ordinary readers would come to question the powers of language to faithfully represent either social or psychic realities. Only later would the linguistic implications of Boyer's historiography emerge. Representation itself became a debatable capacity of language in the 1960s and 1970s as new ideas and theories reached the United States from Europe. To the formulations of literary deconstruction, structuralism, and various poststructuralisms were added new hypotheses about history and historiography. Thus to the European names of Roland Barthes, Gilles Deleuze, Jacques Derrida, Paul De Man, and a host of others were added the American names of scholars like Hayden White and Louis O. Mink.[7] Both groups challenged commonly held distinctions between denotative and connotative expression, between history writing and fiction or verse. The ensuing gap between word and world threatened very basic assumptions about representation and meaning. Language assumed an autonomy that, as we shall soon see, held profound implications for those seriously interested in the literature of Hiroshima and the Holocaust.

Despite Boyer's blind eye in the mid-1980s to this controversy over the linguistic nature of texts of all kinds, his analysis of the central challenge early writers faced after Alamogordo remains very perceptive. "The problem confronted all writers and artists," he declared.

> What was the appropriate aesthetic for the bomb? If an air raid on a small Spanish town could inspire one of Picasso's greatest canvases, or the individual brutalities of Napoleon's invasion of Spain Goya's most powerful work, how was one to respond imaginatively to Hiroshima and Nagasaki and, still more, to the prospect of world holocaust? The question haunted writers in 1945, and it would continue to do so. As one linguistic specialist asked in 1965: "Is it possible that in spite of our vast and ever-growing vocabulary we have finally created an object that transcends all possible description?" (250)

Though he emphasizes the overwhelming force of the historical referent, Boyer never acknowledges, in his reference to a linguist, the wider issue—the shift in theory and practice of literature and history that, already by 1965, had begun to make many aware of claims for the autonomy of language and the substitution of "images" and "texts" for "ideas" and "things." Fredric Jameson calls this intellectual revolution "a whole new problematic" (190).

Weart in *Nuclear Fear*, the second major cultural history of the 1980s, does not confront the new theoretical controversies any more directly than Boyer does, but he extends the latter's time horizon and widens even more his source materials. Weart's signal contribution, however, is to combine Boyer's zeal for documentation from the available archives with a greater appetite for exploring the liminal and subliminal depths of post-Hiroshima consciousness. Weart warns readers of the very real consequences of this sometimes bizarre history—involving "radioactive monsters, utopian atom-powered cities, exploding planets, weird ray devices"—that permeates readers' conscious and unconscious thinking. Though he once scoffed at such science fiction fantasies, he soon discovered fantasies and nightmares to be closely allied to waking fears about very serious dangers. Moreover, constructing a narrative of such "childish" responses to the Bomb confirms his conviction that "this is no story of things locked away safely in the past: the images are more powerful today than ever" (xi). By according cultural significance to ephemeral data like dreams and infantile fancies, Weart echoes and extends into the present day Smith's preoccupation with age-old feelings and legends. From his psychohistorical perspective, myth, private dream life, popular fad, and folk belief are still valid clues to collective cultural paranoia and aphasia.

Of this synthesis of conventional and innovative historical evidence Weart writes, "[T]he historian of images can take up a straightforward task: to look through materials of every description and find for a given group of people what pictures, symbols, beliefs, rational concepts, feelings, and emotions have become strongly associated with one another in a cluster that includes a particular subject, such as nuclear energy." Then this nuclear historian borrows from anthropology and sociology to "suggest how a particular social system would sustain a particular image structure. But the main sources of information," he adds, "are still the historian's, the records of the past, and particularly the written and visual images seen by many people. For experiments have proved what anyone would suspect: that such images do have lasting impact on the beliefs and opinions of their audience" (xii–xiii).

Hence *Nuclear Fear* rides on two premises that mark real advances over Boyer's more conventional historiography: first, "the images we cherish have a greater role in history than has commonly been thought," and second, "images do not just happen among people; they are built" (xiii). So he deploys data from many corners of culture and society: street-corner clichés, personalizations like "the Bomb," biblical language of apocalypse, newsreels, scientists' comments from Los Alamos and Bikini, cartoons, press releases, movies, and novels of all kinds. "There is no final way to prove that nuclear fear, or any other combination of emotions and imagery, played a specific role in history," he concedes of this eclectic approach. "What can be reliably said, based on a large sample of writings, films, polls, and so forth, is that this closely knit structure of associated emotions and images did pervade Cold War and McCarthyist discourse" (127).

As a framework for discussing popular and elite manifestations of secret and shared fears about the Bomb, Weart adopts Boyer's three historical periods. At the same time, he introduces subtle variations in Boyer's chronology. For example, the "Age of the Big Sleep" is carefully modified. "In the mid-1960s," he writes,

> the public, exhausted by war scares and longing to deny the threat hanging over them, turned their attention away from bombs; a great silence descended. Distrust of nuclear authorities remained, however, breaking forth during the 1970s in the movement against reactors. Civilian nuclear power had genuine problems, but these would not have inspired such furious opposition had there not been increasing misgivings about all modern civilization, including its structure of authority and even its commitment to technology and rationality. This was a gravely significant trend, and it was furthered by the dread of bombs. That dread persisted even when not spoken aloud. (422)

Weart's argument here precipitates discussion of transformational thinking—the psychic urge to escape completely from the atomic age by escaping completely from mortal life. In this thanatic response—one dramatized, as we have seen, in Norman Spinrad's "The Big Flash"—topical and timeless elements cluster closely together:

> The archaic symbols of nuclear legends resonate with universal anxieties and hopes. Peeking at forbidden secrets; punishment through abandonment or other victimization by an authority; a corresponding all-destructive rage; homicidal and suicidal urges and the accompanying guilt; struggle through chaos; heroic triumph over peril; miraculous life and regeneration of self; rebirth through a marriage of survivors; entry to a joyful community: these are the stages of transmutation imagery in ancient tradition, repeated in a thousand works on nuclear energy. (424)

This rich melding of ancient and postmodern imaginings of total disaster has been illustrated by the texts quoted in several different chapters of this book. Though he does not mention stories like Spinrad's, Weart anchors his analysis in many psyches—those of children, artists and intellectuals, and ordinary daydreamers. In recondite texts as well as comic books, magazine illustrations and photographs and Hollywood B movies, he traces the often hidden paths of fear and phobia. In such a context, the nuclear age is framed in terms of pervasive images, ideas, and ephemeral but explosive moods and emotions that, Weart argues, often affect public behavior and formal belief.

Boyer and Weart, like Franklin and Smith, agree that the minds of a wide range of American readers come together in the later nuclear era at the "untranscendable horizon" (in J. Fisher Solomon's language) of Hiroshima. Images originating in that historical memory continue to haunt many imaginations, feelings reactivated in the psyches of distant survivors and *hibakusha* alike. The 1980s critic who has delved most deeply into the dark (and blindingly bright) recesses of 6 August 1945 is, I believe, Michael Perlman. Now is the time to look somewhat more closely into *Imaginal Memory and the Place of Hiroshima* (1988), a seminal framing text for its subject. Here the author argues that the best way to deal with the Bomb as present threat and potential fate is for readers individually and collectively to reenter the past and immerse ourselves in the deaths and devastation of Hiroshima. In 1988, as it remains today, this imaginative journey is difficult but necessary. For as Robert Jay Lifton, the 1960s pioneer in this enterprise, noted in 1979, "[T]he great majority of people no longer experience—increasingly few remember—the original impact of nuclear killing."[8] Such ignorance or "forgetting" of an ever-present past is the "broken connection" of Lifton's book of that year, *The Broken Connection: On Death and the Continuity of Life*. So Perlman tries to transport us back to our age's profoundest point. To do so involves reminding us, first, of John Hersey's role in constructing its early framing. "*Hiroshima*," Perlman writes, "is thus an initiation into the more concretely memorable horror of the atomic bombs; the characters of the book are primary *imagines agentes* of the nuclear age" (189).

Like many of his fellow critics and authors who also return to Hersey, Perlman is personally committed to this act of reactivation. Yet in line with Boyer's earlier recognition that the politics of scare tactics did not succeed for the scientists and antinuclear activists of the 1940s and 1950s, Perlman wisely refrains from overdramatizing his narrative of fears and horrors. The announcement that *Imaginal Memory and the Place of Hiroshima* was written out of a "sustained cultural commitment to peace," without whose success he fears "being blasted into 'striking and unusual' shapes of death" (vii–viii) is no mere rhetorical flourish. It is rather an honestly personal conclusion drawn from the visual and verbal images of inexpungible horror that Hiroshima bequeaths to survivors' conscious and unconscious imaginations.

For Perlman, this message from the violent past speaks to present-day readers out of an ancient, common storehouse of myths, stories, images, legends. Unsurprising, therefore, is his interest in Greek as well as Japanese literature, the modern insights of Jung, Freud, and James Hillman, as well as recent writings and photographs from Hiroshima and Nagasaki. Past and present memories from many points are reciprocal expressions of human consciousness—and are therefore central to any cultural history. As the American present circles back through the world's past and returns, such interplay becomes more than a synchronic texture of myths, metaphors, and memories. New historical developments continually challenge former formulations. "The world, in its beauty, violence, pain and passion, must be taken literally *and* metaphorically," he declares (xi). To revisit Hiroshima in these terms is to conduct a life-giving and life-saving operation at the highest pitch of relevance. It challenges linguistic arguments asserting the impossibility of taking the world both literally and symbolically. This challenge, as we have seen, also falls with particular force on the imagination of poets like Maxine Kumin and Galway Kinnell. Nowhere else, Perlman believes, may present-day fears of total absurd death, and their place in the life of the soul, be found in denser psychosocial compression. The aim of his equally dense account is to help readers "build in memory a house of death" (5).

In dual awareness of both survival-transcendence *and* suffering and death, Perlman picks up (but also challenges) motifs in Hersey's book. The 1980s critic is more attuned than the *New Yorker* writer of the 1940s to the archetypal resonances of the Hiroshima story. "We who were not present at the bombings of Hiroshima and Nagasaki drink often of Lethe's safe waters," he declares, "and tend to consider the damage of these events to our individual and collective psychic lives as relatively superficial and minor, like Father Kleinsorge's cuts," adding, "this practice of imaginal memory involves a therapeutic perspective in which the emphasis is less on healing and health than on the 'un-healing' of the soul" (87). When Hersey dares to plunge into moments of pure psychic suffering, as we have seen him do in the scenes with Miss Sasaki and in Asano

Park through Father Kleinsorge's eyes, Perlman is deeply impressed. "Here we notice the psychological connections between woundedness, openness and depth. To be wounded is to be 'open,' with deeper structures and tissues laid bare" (88). Yet this imaginal viewpoint, clothed with somewhat academic overlays of Greek, Renaissance, and psychoanalytic imagery, demands a more learned as well as more unflinching reader than Hersey expected, either in 1946 or 1985.

Despite the cogency and mutual reinforcement of the arguments of Boyer, Weart, Jameson, Smith, and Perlman, all seem unwilling to confront fully the two cultural-intellectual problematics mentioned some pages back. The relation of postmodern literary theory and practice to the looming presence of the Bomb (always more safely and academically referred to as "the nuclear referent") remains problematic for scholars if not for popular audiences. In addition, the perplexing parallels and differences between Hiroshima and Auschwitz also pose epistemological as well as moral and political problems. These issues engage both historical and imaginative writing. Two recent attempts to come to grips with the gaps between theory and practice, and between one historical event and the other, are James E. Young's *Writing and Rewriting the Holocaust* (1988) and J. Fisher Solomon's *Discourse and Reference in the Nuclear Age* (1988). Though neither critic is particularly sensitive to periodization—an activity, as Jameson wryly observes, that is "theoretically unfashionable, to say the least" (178)—both recognize that fully adequate treatments of the Holocaust and Hiroshima must be interdisciplinary. The demands of literature, history, psychology, sociology, philosophy, and theology are involved in postmodern interpretations of nuclear discourse. "With the rise of contemporary literary and historical theory," Young declares, "scholars of the Holocaust have come increasingly to recognize that interpretations of both the texts and events of the Holocaust are intertwined. For both events and their representations are ultimately beholden to the forms, language, and critical methodology through which they are grasped. Religious meaning and significance, historical causes and effects, are simultaneously reflected and generated in Holocaust narrative—as well as in the names, periodization, genres, and icons we assign this era. What is remembered of the Holocaust depends on how it is remembered, and how events are remembered depends in turn on the texts now giving them form" (1).

Though directed to the historical tragedy in Europe, these shrewd comments are also applicable to the subsequent and smaller scale tragedies in Japan. "Images of nuclear energy," Weart observes, "like all modern thought, feel a tidal pull from the near extermination of the Jews of Europe. As the decades passed it became common for intellectuals to name Hiroshima and Auschwitz in the same sentence. Even the term most often used for the Nazi genocide 'the Holocaust,' was also used to describe a future nuclear war, as if the two things were akin. That association could add something essential to the concept of total war" (409). Perhaps the most prominent activist-intellectual exploring this linkage remains Robert Jay Lifton. His latest discussion is *The Genocidal Mentality: Nazi Holocaust and Nuclear Threat* (1990), written with Eric Markunen.[9] Yet both phenomena defy the constructs of postmodern critics determined to distance literary from historical and social experience or expression. Opposition to any such abstract theories is vital, Young asserts; readers must recognize that, no matter how hazily they grasp the language or assumptions of such theories, "the fear that too much attention [is paid] to critical method or to the literary construction of texts threatens to supplant not only the literature but the horrible events at the heart of our inquiry" (3). The very same danger threatens nuclear literature and criticism. "By seeming to emphasize the ways we know the Holocaust," Young continues, "to the apparent exclusion of the realities themselves, critics threaten to make the mere form of study their content as well. Instead of drawing closer to events, in this view, critics would impose an even greater distance between readers and events." The result is that for the community of scholars and common readers alike it becomes easier to believe "that all meanings of events created in different representations are only relative" (3).

The paradox here applies equally to Hiroshima. Though we depend on texts for knowledge of the past, that does not mean that texts are the only proper focus of literary historiography. Nonetheless, it also remains true that interpretations of texts "often reflect the kind of understanding of events by victims at the time; and as these 'mere' interpretations led to their responses, the interpreted versions of the Holocaust in its texts now lead us to actions in the world in light of the Holocaust. That is, by sustaining the notion of these interpretations' agency in events, the contemporary critic can assert both the historicity of events and the crucial role interpretation played in the events themselves" (3). Young's conclusion dovetails nicely with Perlman's about Hiroshima. The world, Perlman agrees, must be taken "literally *and* metaphorically." Or as Young puts the issue, "[T]his is not to deny the historical facts of the Holocaust outside of their narrative framing, but only to emphasize the difficulty of interpreting, expressing, and acting on these facts outside of the ways we frame them" (3).

Such a history of texts, readings, and rereadings raises other questions that are germane to nuclear textualizations and periodizations. To begin with, both events have been significantly recorded in fictional as well as nonfictional or historical accounts. In the process, fiction commonly invokes more openly than history certain metahistorical myths and imagery that, as Weart has found, occupy the dreams and anxieties of many people. Indeed, religious rhetoric in particular overlaps through its transcendent claims with the more mundane metaphors of history and fiction. Moreover, each mode of discourse—the "hard facts" of history, the "softer" idiom of fiction and poetry, and the spiritual language of religious myth—constitutes the accepted discourse of different readerships and their critics. Of this complex interweaving of texts, times, and traditions Young observes that, "while it is true that 'the image of the Holocaust' is indeed being shaped in fictional narrative, we might ask what the difference is between the 'historian's anvil' and the 'novelist's crucible.' Is it really between iron-hard history and the concoctions of the novelist's imagination? Are historical tracts of the Holocaust less mediated by imagination, less troped and figured, or ultimately less interpretive than the fictions of the Holocaust?" (6).

His reply is an emphatic no. Historical and fictional discourses do overlap, resemble, and correspond—as they do in everyday mental processes. These correspondences are due not only to common subject matter but to metaphorical language and metahistorical myth being inevitably involved in all narrative explanations of human behavior. Rather than seeking indisputably "factual" testimony, therefore, the historian or skeptical reader will need to be alert to the ways "facts" have been understood and arranged in a particular narrative, historical or fictional. Each reconstruction of the past—each framing, that is—employs literary strategies *and* observes historiographical conventions. Such eclecticism, moreover, emerges from, and is affected by, shifting social circumstances. By focusing on initial conditions of creation, publication, and reception, a given text may help explain the thought and behavior of persons involved in (or knowledgeably observing) early events. Interpretation may also facilitate later analysis of actions and reactions by readers who are also parents, citizens, leaders, and so forth. These transactions are extraordinarily densely determined by changing historical, social, and (as we have seen throughout this book) psychological factors. As a *literary* critic, Young—like Smith—understandably privileges close attention to the "poetics" of particular texts and genres. If I have often done the same in this study, it is out of a shared conviction that specific texts and literary forms afford fuller access than others to shared meanings and motivations as these cluster around momentous events like the advent of the Bomb.

Turning to Solomon's *Discourse and Reference in the Nuclear Age*, an immediate difference as well as convergences appear. Despite historical linkages asserted over the decades between Hiroshima and Auschwitz, the nuclear referent presents itself most pertinently as a potential rather than an actual past holocaust. Global, continental, or even national devastation did not, in fact, follow upon the initial explosions and deaths. By contrast, World War II concentration camps and the millions of victims are actual and unforgettable tragedies. One Holocaust happened, the other (despite the hundreds of thousands of casualties) is more insistently present as pointing to a possible holocaust. In a sense, this makes nuclear history (narrowly conceived) *less* relevant as history than the Nazi Holocaust but *more* powerful as political or imaginative reality. On the other hand, changing historical circumstances constantly alter these potentialities of nuclear warfare, making total or partial destructions more or less likely. This prospect is in constant relation to the actual history of Hiroshima and Nagasaki and serves to give nuclear criticism an immediacy and indeterminacy not quite so realistically shared by Holocaust survivors and scholars.

Whether these comparisons remain valid in the 1990s (given events in the Balkans and Middle East), the task of framing a contemporary critique of the atomic age remains formidable. While actual knowledge of Hiroshima, Bikini, and Chernobyl is growing (though still impeded by several governments), knowledge of the nuclear potential runs far beyond the factual. Both fictional and historical writers—as we have seen in the very different depictions of Vonnegut and Schell, for instance—often generate utopian or dystopian visions of a nuclear future of the planet. And as both Solomon and Jameson remind us, "utopian fancies [can] drive us toward *creative* political action even as we 'scientifically' or axiomatically present to ourselves the explanations for how conditions came to be as they are" (Solomon, 258). Therefore, the nuclear project demands theoretical justification in terms that equally respect history, the inescapable reality of the nuclear referent, and language in all its powerful forms of representation and distortion.

Solomon's search for adequate framing concepts is based on the sensible conviction that any linguistic or epistemological theory that denies the rational, intentional, and representational uses of discourse must be repudiated. He finds help from a very American source—the century-old pragmatic tradition in philosophy, which authorizes probable or potential references in language. "That is, we shall be searching for a ground for the rational discussion of the calculable probabilities for the behavior of physical entities and situations that exist outside of our discussion of them, outside our own archive" (35–36). Hiroshima, he argues, is the supreme "outside" entity of our literary epoch. Any grounding theory that dehistoricizes or reduces the Bomb to mere symbol or image is, quite frankly, a threat to human understanding and survival. "Such an epistemology," he asserts, "of course, does not in itself solve any of the political issues involved with the problem of the nuclear referent, but it can enable us to approach a nuclear present historically" (204). This pragmatic perspective on history and literature even makes room for suprarational ways of thinking and writing—as in fantastic imagery and narratives. The postnuclear person is therefore free "to define himself or herself in the world not only of the present but also of the future" (257). Any dialectical language system asserting independence of human historical experience must pose a profound threat in "a world held hostage by the hair-trigger mechanisms of computer-controlled strategic defense networks" (260). In the world we inhabit, "it is history and not the text that constitutes the untranscendable horizon of interpretation," so "it is to the extratextual reality of political experience that our narrative categories for historical presentation ultimately refer" (260–61).

Positioning himself and his assenting readers on this pragmatic ground,

Solomon summons key segments of the American social structure to meet. That is, he believes that "science, industry, and criticism"—the respective realms of believers in reason, believers in commercial and industrial progress, and the "irrationalists or romantics"—must unite. "[A]ll need to enter into dialogue in the face of real historical problems like those the nuclear referent presents, and the dialogue cannot be conducted as long as criticism claims that the only proper discourse is its own: the discourse of poetic ambiguity and uncertainty" (273).

This collection of historically minded scholars and critics is admittedly selective and imcomplete. Other names and points of view would sharpen and widen my analysis. Yet I believe that these fruitful approaches to the matter of Hiroshima can both complement and overlap each other; they have, for me, illuminated and helped to frame the preceding discussions of particular nuclear texts, genres, images, emotions, and ideologies. For their authors' common cause as responsible 1980s Americans in the late nuclear age is, I hope, clear. Writers of all sorts, readers, and their fellow critics need to cultivate the long-range consciousness displayed here by, for instance, Smith, Franklin, and Perlman. We must also learn to reawaken nearer memories and images of Hiroshima itself and its imaginative aftershocks in the minds of Americans as well as others. Doing so is facilitated by the work of Boyer, Weart, Perlman, Solomon, and Young. Indeed, their combination of imaginative and coolly rational responses cannot be limited to literary texts alone but must confront more general historiographical issues like narrative sequence, periodization, and comparison.

Whichever horizons of concern these critics alert us to—whether to Hiroshima, a remoter historical or mythic past, the immediate past decades, or a fragile or fantastic future—the common stance all endorse is personal, moral, and political commitment. Acts of social involvement are both preparation for and the desired consequence of literary transactions. This perspective embraces all writers and renders the cultural landscape a battlefield (a "Homeric" one, in Fredric Jameson's view[10]. Nuclear literature and criticism can thus play a vital role in current and future changes in society and polity. For as Jeff Smith asserts, "[N]uclear politics are not likely to seriously change until cultural imagery changes" (41). Writers, readers, and critics of all persuasions together create and re-create the common images, language, and rhetorical strategies that enable the citizenry (starting often as quite young children) to frame for themselves new and different responses to the Bomb.

One particular and recurring resource that nuclear writing offers us *hibakusha* are acts of commemoration. Books can be equivalents of the paper lanterns annually floating down the Ota River. Such responses are, in Michael Perlman's hopeful words, made "more lasting and forceful by Hiroshima's 'universality,' its imagination of obliterated boundaries, its utter inclusiveness. We are all within the bounds of the place of Hiroshima" (160). If recent events led the scholarly editors of *Nuclear Texts and Contexts* in 1992 to say goodbye to the first nuclear age, this act doubtless marks but a temporary framing of the epoch, not an end to cultural histories and literary discussions like the present one. The "future of immortality," Robert Jay Lifton reminds us, is now a permanent problematic in human history and demands continuous attention and analysis.

NOTES AND REFERENCES

Preface

1. Carolyn See, *Golden Days* (New York: Fawcett Crest, 1987), 4, hereafter cited in the text.

2. Jonathan Schell, *The Fate of the Earth* (New York: Avon Books, 1982), 105, hereafter cited in the text.

3. Robert Jay Lifton and Richard Falk, *Indefensible Weapons: The Political and Psychological Case against Nuclearism* (New York: Basic Books, 1982), 128, hereafter cited in the text.

4. Stephen Hilgartner, Richard C. Bell, and Rory O'Connor, eds., *Nukespeak: The Selling of Nuclear Technology in America* (New York: Penguin, 1983), 22.

5. Terrence Des Pres, *Praises and Dispraises: Poetry and Politics in the Twentieth Century* (New York: Viking, 1988), 228, hereafter cited in the text.

Chapter One

1. Einstein's letter is reprinted in *The Nuclear Predicament: A Source Book*, ed. Donna Gregory (New York: St. Martin's Press, 1986), 39–40, hereafter cited in the text.

2. Richard Rhodes, *The Making of the Atomic Bomb* (New York: Simon & Schuster, 1986), 536, hereafter cited in the text.

3. Michael J. Yavenditti, "John Hersey and the American Conscience: The Reception of 'Hiroshima,'" *Pacific Historical Review* 43 (February 1984): 48, hereafter cited in the text.

4. Paul Boyer, *By the Bomb's Early Light: American Thought and Culture at the Dawn of the Atomic Age* (New York: Pantheon Books, 1985), 209, hereafter cited in the text.

5. Spencer Weart, *Nuclear Fear: A History of Images* (Cambridge: Harvard University Press, 1988), 376, hereafter cited in the text.

6. *Hiroshima* originally appeared in the *New Yorker* 22 (31 August 1946); virtually the entire issue was devoted to it.

7. Michael Perlman, *Imaginal Memory and the Place of Hiroshima* (Albany: State University of New York Press, 1988), hereafter cited in the text.

8. David Bradley, *No Place to Hide* (1946; reprint, Hanover, N.H.: University Press of New England, 1984), xix, hereafter cited in the text.

9. Robert Jay Lifton, *Death in Life: Survivors of Hiroshima* (1967; reprint, New York: Basic Books, 1982), 479, hereafter cited in the text.

10. See, for instance, Erik Erikson, *Childhood and Society* (1950, 1963); *Identity: Youth and Crisis* (1958); and the two famous psychobiographies, *Young Man Luther* (1958) and *Gandhi's Truth* (1969).

11. Robert Jay Lifton, *The Future of Immortality and Other Essays for a Nuclear Age* (New York: Basic Books, 1987).

12. "Atom Eschatology," *Nation* 234 (27 February 1982): 228–29.

13. The paperback edition of *The Fate of the Earth* carried 20 endorsements, of which Hersey's is the ninth (ii).

14. Max Lerner, "Visions of the Apocalypse," *New Republic* 186 (28 April 1982): 26–29.

15. Anthony Rudolf, "Final Warning," *New Statesman* (4 June 1982): 21.

16. See Michihiko Hachiya, *Hiroshima Diary: The Journal of a Japanese Physician* (Chapel Hill: University of North Carolina Press, 1955); Yoko Ōta, *City of Corpses* (1950), in *Hiroshima: Three Witnesses*, ed. Richard H. Minear (Princeton: Princeton University Press, 1990); *Hiroshima and Nagasaki: The Physical, Medical, and Social Effects of the Atomic Bombings* (New York: Basic Books, 1981).

17. Ira Chernus, *Nuclear Madness: Religion and the Psychology of the Nuclear Age* (Albany: State University of New York Press, 1991), 177, hereafter cited in the text.

18. Neil Schmitz, "Anxiety and Its Displacement," *Nation* 234 (1 May 1982): 531.

19. In addition to works previously cited, see National Conference of Catholic Bishops, *The Challenge of Peace: God's Promise and Our Response: A Pastoral Letter on War and Peace* (Washington, D.C.: U.S. Catholic Conference, 1983); A. G. Mojtabai, *Blessèd Assurance: At Home with the Bomb in Amarillo, Texas* (Albuquerque: University of New Mexico Press, 1986), hereafter cited in the text.

Chapter Two

1. Gunther Anders, "Reflections on the H Bomb," *Dissent* 3 (Spring 1956): 146, hereafter cited in the text.

2. Jacques Derrida, "No Apocalypse, Not Now (full speed ahead, seven missiles, seven missives)," *Diacritics* 14 (Summer 1984): 23, hereafter cited in the text.

3. Thomas M. F. Gerry, "The Literary Crisis: The Nuclear Crisis," *Dalhousie Review* 67 (1987): 297.

4. Peter Schwenger, "Writing the Unthinkable," *Critical Inquiry* 13 (Autumn 1986): 33.

5. H. Bruce Franklin, "Strange Scenarios: Science Fiction, the Theory of Alienation, and the Nuclear Gods," *Science Fiction Studies* 13 (July 1986): 125, hereafter cited in the text as Franklin 1986.

6. David Ketterer, *New Worlds for Old: The Apocalyptic Imagination, Science Fiction, and American Literature* (Garden City, N.Y.: Doubleday Anchor, 1974), 123, hereafter cited in the text.

7. For bibliographical notations and annotations on the above, see Paul Brians, *Nuclear Holocausts: Atomic War in Fiction, 1895–1984* (Kent, Ohio: Kent State University Press, 1987), hereafter cited in the text. See also Joseph Dewey, *In a Dark Time: The Apocalyptic Temper in the American Novel of the Nuclear Age* (West Lafayette, Ind.: Purdue University Press, 1990).

8. See Mark Rose, *Alien Encounters: Anatomy of Science Fiction* (Cambridge: Harvard University Press, 1981), hereafter cited in the text; Robert Scholes and Eric S. Rabkin, *Science Fiction: History, Science, Vision* (New York: Oxford University Press, 1977), hereafter cited in the text; Thomas D. Clareson, *SF: The Other Side of Realism: Essays on Modern Fantasy and Science Fiction* (Bowling Green, Ohio: Bowling Green State University Popular Press, 1971), hereafter cited in the text; Eric S. Rabkin, *The Fantastic in Literature* (Princeton: Princeton University Press, 1976).

9. Michael J. Carey, "Psychological Fallout," *Bulletin of Atomic Scientists* 38 (January 1982): 21, 24.

10. Robert A. Heinlein, *Expanded Universe: The New Worlds of Robert A. Heinlein* (New York: Ace Books, 1980), 310.

11. "The 36-Hour War," *Life* 19 (19 November 1945): 27, hereafter cited in the text as *Life*.

12. See Tom Lehrer, "We Will All Go Together When We Go," in *Too Many Songs by Tom Lehrer* (New York: Pantheon Books, 1981).

13. Langston Hughes, *The Simple Omnibus* (New York: Aeonian Press, 1961), 201.

14. Walter M. Miller, Jr., and Martin Greenberg, eds., *Beyond Armageddon: Twenty-one Sermons to the Dead* (New York: Primus Books, 1985), 146, hereafter cited in the text.

15. Martha Bartter, "Nuclear Holocaust as Urban Renewal," *Science Fiction Studies* 13 (July 1986): 148–49, hereafter cited in the text.

16. Judith Merril, "That Only a Mother," *Astounding Fiction* (June 1948); see Brians, 260; Judith Merril, *The Shadow on the Hearth* (Garden City, N.Y.: Doubleday, 1950), hereafter cited in the text; Philip Wylie, *Tomorrow!* (New York: Rinehart,

1954), hereafter cited in the text; Pat Frank, *Alas Babylon* (Philadelphia: J. B. Lippincott, 1959), hereafter cited in the text.

17. Betty Friedan, *The Feminine Mystique* (New York: W. W. Norton, 1963).

18. Susan Sontag, "The Imagination of Disaster," in *Against Interpretation and Other Essays* (New York: Farrar, Straus & Giroux, 1965), 200–225.

19. Lewis Mumford, *In the Name of Sanity* (New York: Harcourt Brace, 1954), 3, hereafter cited in the text.

20. Michael J. Strada, "Kaleidoscopic Nuclear Images in the 1950s," *Journal of Popular Culture* 20 (Winter 1986): 179–98, hereafter cited in the text.

21. Michel Butor, "Science Fiction: The Crisis of Its Growth," in Clareson, 162.

22. Ray Bradbury, *The Martian Chronicles* (New York: Bantam Books, 1950, 1954, 1985), 167, hereafter cited in the text.

23. Darko Suvin, "Science Fiction and the Genological Jungle," *Genre* 6 (1973): 262.

24. Walter M. Miller, Jr., *A Canticle for Leibowitz* (New York: Harper & Row, 1959; New York: Perennial Library, 1986), 182; the Perennial edition is hereafter cited in the text.

25. Kurt Vonnegut, *Cat's Cradle* (New York: Dell Laurel Books, 1963, 1988), 113; the 1988 edition is hereafter cited in the text.

26. Edgar Lee Masters, "Knowlt Hoheimer," *Spoon River Anthology* (New York: Macmillan, 1916), 24.

27. W. R. Allen, ed., *Conversations with Kurt Vonnegut* (Jackson: University of Mississippi Press, 1988), 215.

28. Daniel L. Zins, "Rescuing Science from Technology: *Cat's Cradle* and the Play of Apocalypse," *Science Fiction Studies* 13 (July 1986): 176.

Chapter Three

1. Nicholas von Hoffman, "The Brahms Lullaby," *Harper's* 264 (February 1982): 50–59, hereafter cited in the text.

2. Harlan Ellison, "I Have No Mouth, and I Must Scream," in *The Fantasies of Harlan Ellison* (Boston: Gregg Press, 1979), 187, hereafter cited in the text; "A Boy and His Dog," in Miller and Greenberg, 332–73, hereafter cited in the text; Norman Spinrad, "The Big Flash," in Miller and Greenberg, 46–69. For bibliographic information on Ellison, see Brians (1987), 192–93 and 313–14 (Spinrad).

3. Eric S. Rabkin, ed., *Science Fiction: A Historical Anthology* (New York: Oxford University Press, 1983), 427, hereafter cited in the text.

4. Millicent Lenz, *Nuclear Age Literature for Youth: The Quest for a Life-Affirming Ethic* (Chicago: American Library Association, 1990), 261, hereafter cited in the text.

5. Patti Perret, *Faces of Science Fiction: Photographs by Patti Perret* (New York: Bluejay Books, 1984), n.p. (opposite Frederick Pohl photograph).

6. Joe Haldeman, "To Howard Hughes: A Modest Proposal," in *Infinite Dreams* (New York: St. Martin's Press, 1977), 61–77.

7. Thomas Bacig, "Norman Spinrad," in *Twentieth-Century Science Fiction Writers*, ed. Curtis C. Smith (New York: St. Martin's Press, 1981), 513, hereafter cited in the text.

8. Harlan Ellison, *Dangerous Visions* (New York: Berkeley Books, 1967); *Again, Dangerous Visions* (New York: Berkeley Books, 1972).

9. Kate Wilhelm, "Countdown," in *The Downstairs Room and Other Speculative Fiction* (New York: Doubleday, 1968); quoted here from Lenz, 35.

10. Kim Stanley Robinson, *The Wild Shore* (New York: Ace Books, 1984), vi, viii, hereafter cited in the text.

11. Ursula K. LeGuin, *The Left Hand of Darkness* (New York: Ace Books, 1983); Joanna Russ, *Picnic on Paradise* (New York: Ace Books, 1968).

12. Denis Johnson, *Fiskadoro* (New York: Vintage Books, 1985), 122, hereafter cited in the text.

13. Tim O'Brien, *The Nuclear Age* (New York: Dell Laurel, 1985), 4, hereafter cited in the text.

14. Grace Paley, "Digging a Shelter and a Grave," *New York Times Book Review* (17 November 1985): 7.

Chapter Four

1. Marvin Bell, "Because Writers Are Scared: This Writer in the Nuclear Age," in *Writing in a Nuclear Age*, ed. Jim Schley (Hanover, N.H.: University Press of New England, 1984), 188, hereafter cited in the text as Schley; John Berger, *Ways of Seeing* (New York: Viking, 1973), 7.

2. *Hiroshima-Nagasaki*, produced by Eric Barnouw for Columbia University Press (1970), narrated by Paul Ronder and Kazuko Oshima.

3. Frances FitzGerald, *America Revised: History Textbooks in the Twentieth Century* (Boston: Atlantic Monthly Press, 1979); Gordon Kelly, "Literature and History," *American Quarterly* 26 (May 1974): 141–59; Jack Zipes, "Second Thoughts on Socialization through Literature for Children," *Lion and the Unicorn* 5 (1981): 19–32, hereafter cited in the text.

4. Samantha Smith, in *Kids Who Have Made a Difference*, ed. Teddy Milne (Northampton, Mass.: Pittenbruach Press, 1989), 3–4.

5. Jane Tompkins, *Sensational Designs: The Cultural Work of American Fiction, 1790–1860* (New York: Oxford University Press, 1985), esp. chaps. 1 and 7; Philip Fisher, *Hard Facts: Setting and Form in the American Novel* (New York: Oxford University Press, 1987); Barbara Herrnstein Smith, "Narrative Versions, Narrative Theories," in *On Narrative*, ed. W. J. T. Mitchell (Chicago: University of Chicago Press, 1981), 209–32.

6. Paul Brians, "Nuclear Fiction for Children," *Bulletin of Atomic Scientists* 44 (July-August 1988): 24, hereafter cited in the text.

7. Whitley Strieber, *Wolf of Shadows* (New York: Alfred A. Knopf, 1985), hereafter cited in the text; Louise Lawrence, *Children of the Dust* (New York: Harper & Row, 1985); Gloria D. Miklowitz, *After the Bomb* (New York: Scholastic, 1984), hereafter cited in the text; Miklowitz, *After the Bomb—Week One* (New York: Scholastic, 1987), hereafter cited in the text; Gudrun Pausewang, *The Last Children of Schevenborn* (Saskatoon, Sask.: Western Producer Prairie Books, 1988), hereafter cited in the text.

8. Toshi Maruki, *Hiroshima No Pika* (New York: Lothrop, Lee & Shepard, 1980), hereafter cited in the text.

9. Judith Vigna, *Nobody Wants a Nuclear War* (Niles, Ill.: Albert Whitman & Co., 1986), hereafter cited in the text.

10. Dr. Seuss, *The Butter Battle Book* (New York: Random House, 1984); David Macauley, *Baaa* (Boston: Houghton Mifflin, 1985), hereafter cited in the text; Umberto Eco and Eugenio Carmi, *The Bomb and the General* (Orlando: Harcourt Brace Jovanovich, 1989).

11. "War Talk Can Overwhelm Children," *Iowa City Press-Citizen*, 16 February 1991.

12. James W. Carey, *Communication as Culture: Essays on Media and Society* (Boston: Unwin Hyman, 1989), esp. 23–36.

13. John E. Mack and William Beardslee, *Psychosocial Aspects of Nuclear Developments: A Report of the Task Force on Psychosocial Aspects of Nuclear Developments* (Washington, D.C.: American Psychiatric Association, 1982); Robert Coles, *The Moral Life of Children* (Boston: Atlantic Monthly Press, 1986), hereafter cited in the text.

14. "After the Cold War," *New York Times*, 1 February 1992.

15. Stephanie S. Tolan, "A Writer's Response to 'Members of the Last Generation,'" *Horn Book* 62 (1986): 358–62, quoted in Brians (1988), 24.

16. Pamela F. Service, *Winter of Magic's Return* (New York: Atheneum, 1985).

17. Hamida Bosmajian, "Conventions of Image and Form in Nuclear War Narratives for Younger Readers," *Papers on Language and Literature (PLL)* 26 (Winter 1990): 73–74, hereafter cited in the text.

18. Barbara and Scott Siegel, *Firebrats* series (New York: Archway, 1987); for Ahern's *The Survivalist* series, see Brians (1988), 108–11.

19. Whitley Strieber and James W. Kunetka, *Warday: And the Journey Onward* (New York: Warner Books, 1984), 495, hereafter cited in the text.

20. Carl B. Feldbaum and Ronald J. Bee, *Looking the Tiger in the Eye: Confronting the Nuclear Threat* (New York: Harper & Row, 1988).

21. Betty Jean Lifton, *A Place Called Hiroshima* (Tokyo and New York: Kodansha, 1985); R. Conrad Stein, *World at War: Hiroshima* (Chicago: Children's Press, 1982); Martin McPhillips, *Hiroshima: Turning Points in American History* (Morristown, N.J.: Silver-Burdett, 1985).

22. Gary B. Nash, et al., *The American People: Creating a Nation and a Society* (New York: Harper & Row, 1990), hereafter cited in the text.

Chapter Five

1. Denise Levertov, *Light up the Cave* (New York: New Directions, 1981), 60.

2. Rob Wilson, "Towards the Nuclear Sublime: Representations of Technological Vastness in Postmodern American Poetry," in *Prospects: An Annual of American Cultural Studies* 14 (1989): 407–39, hereafter cited in the text.

3. Richard Jones, ed., *Poetry and Politics: An Anthology of Essays* (New York: Morrow, 1985), 15, hereafter cited in the text.

4. Hayden Carruth, "Poets without Prophesy" *Nation* 196 (27 April 1963), 354–57, in Jones, 285.

5. See Kate Daniels, "Interview with Galway Kinnell," in Jones, 293–99, hereafter cited in the text as Daniels; and Jones, 300–316.

6. *Warnings: An Anthology on the Nuclear Peril* (Eugene, Oreg.: Northwest Review Books, 1984), hereafter cited in the text as *Warnings*; Morty Sklar, ed., *Nuke-Rebuke: Writers and Artists against Nuclear Energy and Weapons* (Iowa City: The Spirit That Moves Us Press, 1984), hereafter cited in the text; Joseph Kruchac, ed., *Breaking Silence: An Anthology of Contemporary Asian American Poets* (Greenfield, N.Y.: Greenfield Review Press, 1983), hereafter cited in the text; Gayle Peterson, Ying Kelley, and Patricia Carvin, *A Chance to Live: Children's Poems for Peace in a Nuclear Age* (Berkeley, Calif.: Mindbody Press, 1983), hereafter cited in the text.

7. Robert Penn Warren, "New Dawn," in Schley, 67.

8. See Peter B. Hales, "The Atomic Sublime," *American Studies* 32 (Spring 1991): 5–31.

9. David Mura, "The Hibakusha's Letter (1955)," in Kruchac, 200–201; Mura's "The Survivor," in Sklar, 160–61; Joy Kogawa, "Hiroshima Exit," *A Choice of Dreams* (Toronto: McClelland and Stewart, 1974), in Kruchac, 113.

10. See Hersey's *Hiroshima* for a possible inspiration for Mura's speaker's revulsion against red meat in Dr. Sasaki's hospital ordeal: "Tugged here and there in his stockinged feet, bewildered by the numbers, staggered by so much raw flesh, Dr. Sasaki lost all sense of profession. . . . [H]e became an automaton, mechanically wiping, daubing, winding, wiping, daubing, winding" (26).

11. Quoted in John Newhouse, *War and Peace in the Nuclear Age* (New York: Alfred A. Knopf, 1989), 41. See also the epigraph to Oyama's "The Day after Trinity."

12. William Stafford, "At the Bomb Testing Site" and "Indian Caves in the Dry Country," in *Stories That Could Be True: New and Collected Poems* (New York: Harper & Row, 1971), 41, 222.

13. Leonard Nathan, "One Vote," in Schley, 103.

14. Eleanor Wilner, "High Noon at Los Alamos," in *Sarah's Choice* (Chicago: University of Chicago Press, 1989), 66–67; also in *Warnings*, 47–48.

15. Maxine Kumin, "How to Survive Nuclear War," in *The Long Approach* (New York: Viking, 1985), 51–54, hereafter cited in the text.

16. Galway Kinnell, "The Fundamental Project of Technology," in *The Past* (Boston: Houghton Mifflin, 1985), 47–48; also in Schley, 40–41 (hereafter cited in the text).

17. Dennis Brutus, "Sadeko's [*sic*] Cranes Are Flying," in *Nuke-Rebuke*, 5.

18. Joseph Landauer, "When the Cranes Fly," in Peterson, Kelley, and Carvin, 16.

19. See Peterson, Kelley, and Carvin for Mollie Price,"Peace in a Big Field" (12) and "I Am Afraid" (26); Jude Hall, "When Nature is Dead" (28); Daniel Su, "One Thousand Cranes" (21); and Eliel Johnson, "The Bomb" (37).

20. June Jordan, "Who Would Be Free, Themselves Must Strike the Blow," in *Warnings*, 38.

21. William Pitt Root, "The Day the Sun Rises Twice," *Melt-down: Poems from the Core* (Full Count Press, n.d.), in Sklar, 103.

22. Carolyn Forché, "Imagine the Worst," quoted in Wilson, 418.

23. Minnie Bruce Pratt, "Strange Flesh," *NER/BLQ: New England Review and Bread Loaf Quarterly* 5 (Summer 1983), in Schley, 197–201, 199.

24. See Louise Kawada, "Enemies of Despair: American Women Poets Con-

front the Threat of Nuclear Destruction," *Papers on Language and Literature (PLL)* 26 (Winter 1990): 112–33, esp. on Pratt, 121–22, hereafter cited in the text.

25. Honor Moore, "Spuyten Duyvil," *Village Voice*, 15 June 1982, in Schley, 203–9, 209, ll. 185–94.

26. Quoted in *Panic Encyclopedia: The Definitive Guide to the Postmodern Scene*, ed. Arthur Kroker, Marilouise Kroker, and David Cook (New York: St. Martin's Press, 1989), 153.

27. Allen Ginsberg, "Plutonian Ode," in *Collected Poems, 1947–1980 (CP)* (New York: Harper & Row, 1984), 702–5, hereafter cited in the text; "Nagasaki Days (Boulder, Summer 1978)," in *CP*, 699–701.

28. Wallace Stevens, "An Ordinary Evening in New Haven," in *The Collected Poems* (New York: Alfred A. Knopf, 1961), 473.

29. Michael Schumacher, *Dharma Lion: A Critical Biography of Allen Ginsberg* (New York: St. Martin's Press, 1992), esp. 628–39, hereafter cited in the text.

30. Richard Eberhart, "Testimony," in *Warnings*, 136–38.

31. Phil Woods, "An Interview with Gary Snyder," in *Warnings*, 200–201.

32. Denise Levertov, "Poets against the End of the World," in Jones, 311–12.

33. Michael Daley, "Credo," *The Straits* (Empty Bowl, 1983), in Schley, 146–48, 146.

34. Terrence Des Pres, *The Survivor: An Anatomy of Life in the Death Camps* (New York: Oxford University Press, 1980).

Chapter Six

1. James E. Young, *Writing and Rewriting the Holocaust: Narrative and the Consequences of Interpretation* (Bloomington: Indiana University Press, 1988), 3, hereafter cited in the text.

2. Margaret Mead, *Blackberry Winter: My Earlier Years* (New York: Simon & Schuster, 1972), 271.

3. Daniel Berrigan, *To Dwell in Peace: An Autobiography* (New York: Harper & Row, 1985), 105.

4. H. Bruce Franklin, *War Stars: The Superweapon and the American Imagination* (New York: Oxford University Press, 1988), esp. chaps. 1 and 2, hereafter cited in the text.

5. Jeff Smith, *Unthinking the Unthinkable: Nuclear Weapons and Western Culture* (Bloomington: Indiana University Press, 1989), hereafter cited in the text.

6. Fredric Jameson, "Periodizing the 60's," in *The Sixties without Apology*, ed. Sonya Sayres, Anders Stephanson, Stanley Aronowitz, and Fredric Jameson (Minneapolis: University of Minnesota Press, 1984), 178, hereafter cited in the text.

7. For discussion, in nuclear terms, of the literary theorists cited, see Young, *passim*; Derrida, "No Apocalypse, Not Now"; and J. Fisher Solomon, *Discourse and Reference in the Nuclear Age* (Norman: University of Oklahoma Press, 1988), hereafter cited in the text. On historiography, see Hayden White, "The Historical Text as Literary Artifact," in *The Writing of History*, ed. Robert Canary and Henry Kozicki (Madison: University of Wisconsin Press, 1978), 41–62, and Louis O. Mink, "Narrative Form as Cognitive Instrument," in Canary and Kozicki, 129–49.

8. Robert Jay Lifton, *The Broken Connection: On Death and the Continuity of Life* [1979] (New York: Basic Books, 1983), 386–87.

9. Robert Jay Lifton and Eric Markunen, *The Genocidal Mentality: Nazi Holocaust and Nuclear Threat* (New York: Basic Books, 1990).

10. Fredric Jameson, *The Political Unconscious: Narrative as a Socially Symbolic Act* (Ithaca: Cornell University Press, 1981), 13.

A NUCLEAR BIBLIOGRAPHY

PRIMARY SOURCES

Bradbury, Ray. *The Martian Chronicles*. New York: Bantam Books, 1950, 1954, 1985. A seminal science fiction novel, stressing myth and fantasy over probability and history.

Bradley, David. *No Place to Hide* [1946]. Hanover, N.H.: University Press of New England, 1984. A popular personal account of the Bikini tests.

Briggs, Raymond. *When the Wind Blows*. London: Penguin Books, 1983. Ostensibly for younger readers, this illustrated book is graphic adult fare.

Brin, David. *The Postman*. New York: Bantam Books, 1985. Another sleeper—more thoughtful than most adventure stories.

Clarkson, Helen. *The Last Day: A Novel of the Day after Tomorrow*. New York: Dodd, 1959. A modest and powerful story.

DeLillo, Don. *White Noise*. New York: Penguin Books, 1985.

Ellison, Harlan. *The Fantasies of Harlan Ellison*. Boston: Gregg Press, 1979. Contains "I Have No Mouth, And I Must Scream" and other tales.

Frank, Pat. *Alas Babylon*. Philadelphia: J. B. Lippincott, 1959. A best-seller.

Ginsberg, Allen. *The Collected Poems, 1947–1980*. New York: Harper & Row, 1984. Contains "Nagasaki Days" and "Plutonian Ode," among other nuclear lyrics.

Heinlein, Robert A. *Expanded Universe: The New Worlds of Robert A. Heinlein.* New York: Ace Books, 1980. Fiction and nonfiction from the author of *Stranger in a Strange Land* (1961).

Hersey, John. *Hiroshima* [1946]. New York: Vintage Books, 1985. A reprint (with a new chapter, "The Aftermath") of the most popular nonfiction work by an American, one that reopened the atomic age for many in 1946.

Hoban, Russell. *Riddley Walker*. New York: Summit Books, 1980. Considered by many the finest postholocaust novel in English.

Ibuse, Masuji. *Black Rain*. Tokyo and New York: Kodansha, 1969. Probably the most influential of Japanese novels of nuclear destruction, written by a native of Hiroshima.

Johnson, Denis. *Fiskadoro*. New York: Vintage Books, 1985. A haunting story of life in the Contaminated Zone of South Florida after World War III.

Lifton, Robert Jay. *Death in Life: Survivors of Hiroshima* [1967]. New York: Basic Books, 1982. Reprint of the psychosocial account of *hibakusha*, history, and Japanese and American cultures after the Bomb.

Maruki, Toshi. *Hiroshima No Pika*. New York: Lothrop Lee & Shepard, 1980. A powerful illustrated book for eight-year-olds and up.

Merril, Judith. *The Shadow on the Hearth*. Garden City, N.Y.: Doubleday, 1950. One of the first suburban survival stories of the nuclear age.

Miller, Walter M. *A Canticle for Leibowitz*. New York: Harper & Row, 1959; New York: Perennial Library, 1986. Still regarded as the most powerful religious science fiction of nuclear survival in long historical perspective.

National Conference of Catholic Bishops. *The Challenge of Peace: God's Promise and Our Response: A Pastoral Letter on War and Peace*. Washington, D.C.: U.S. Catholic Conference, 1983.

O'Brien, Tim. *The Nuclear Age*. New York: Dell Laurel Books, 1985. An ambitious and moving survivor's story of growing up with the Bomb.

Pausewang, Gudrun. *The Last Children of Schevenborn*. Saskatoon, Sask.: Western Producer Prairie Books, 1988. A graphic story of a boy's initiation into the postnuclear world of death and dying.

Robinson, Kim Stanley. *The Wild Shore*. New York: Ace Books, 1984.

Schell, Jonathan. *The Fate of the Earth*. New York: Avon Books, 1982. A best-selling nonfictional anatomy of the nuclear situation and peril.

See, Carolyn. *Golden Days*. New York: Fawcett Crest, 1987. A pre- and postholocaust survivor's fable of California, the coast of dreams and death.

Shute, Nevil. *On the Beach*. New York: Morrow, 1957. Best-seller and centerpiece of the beach fiction of the nuclear era.

Strieber, Whitley. *Wolf of Shadows*. New York: Alfred A. Knopf, 1985. An animal and human survivors' story for younger readers.

Strieber, Whitley, and James W. Kunetka. *Warday: And the Journey Onward*. New York: Warner Books, 1984. A graphic documentary novel of postnuclear survivalism, for younger and older readers.

Vigna, Judith. *Nobody Wants a Nuclear War*. Niles, Ill.: Albert Whitman & Co., 1986. By comparison with Maruki, a safely suburban story for young readers having nuclear war nightmares.

Vonnegut, Kurt. *Cat's Cradle* [1963]. New York: Dell Laurel Books, 1988. A classic fabulist satire of nuclear life and death in the aura of the Cuban Missile Crisis.

Wylie, Philip. *Tomorrow!* New York: Rinehart, 1954. A savage satire and graphic depiction of nuclear attack on American cities, with a melodramatic conclusion underwriting the "winnable war" policies of the cold war.

ANTHOLOGIES

Kruchac, Joseph, ed. *Breaking Silence: An Anthology of Contemporary Asian American Poets*. Greenfield, N.Y.: Greenfield Review Press, 1983.

Miller, Walter M., and Martin Greenberg, eds. *Beyond Armageddon: Twenty-One Sermons to the Dead*. New York: Primus Books, 1985. An excellent collection of science fiction and other nuclear stories.

Milne, Teddy, ed. *Kids Who Have Made a Difference*. Northampton, Mass.: Pittenbruach Press, 1989. Samantha Smith and friends speak out.

Oe, Kenzaburo, ed. *The Crazy Iris and Other Stories of the Atomic Aftermath*. New York: Grove Press, 1985. Nine nuclear tales by Ibuse, Oka, and others.

Peterson, Gayle, Ying Kelley, and Patricia Carvin, eds. *A Chance to Live: Children's Poems for Peace in a Nuclear Age*. Berkeley, Calif.: Mindbody Press, 1983.

Schley, Jim. *Writing in a Nuclear Age*. Hanover, N.H.: University Press of New England, 1984. Fiction, poetry, and nonfiction by at least ten of the writers and critics cited in this book.

Sklar, Morty, ed. *Nuke-Rebuke: Writers and Artists against Nuclear Energy and Weapons*. Iowa City: The Spirit That Moves Us Press, 1984. Poetry, fiction, essays, artwork.

Warnings: An Anthology on the Nuclear Peril, ed. *Northwest Review*. Eugene, Oreg.: Northwest Review Books, 1984. Documents, photographs, fiction, poetry, artwork, essays.

Secondary Sources

Boyer, Paul. *By the Bomb's Early Light: American Thought and Culture at the Dawn of the Atomic Age*. New York: Pantheon Books, 1985. A pioneering cultural history, standard for the first years of the atomic age and a model for later studies.

Brians, Paul. *Nuclear Holocausts: Atomic War in Fiction, 1895–1984*. Kent, Ohio: Kent State University Press, 1987. Indispensable bibliographical guide to an extensive and international literature. Unfortunately, it stops just before the flowering of fiction and criticism, 1985 and after.

Chernus, Ira. *Nuclear Madness: Religion and the Psychology of the Nuclear Age*. Albany: State University of New York Press, 1991.

Clareson, Thomas D., ed. *SF: The Other Side of Realism: Essays on Modern Fantasy and Science Fiction*. Bowling Green, Ohio: Bowling Green University Popular Press, 1971. An international collection of fiction writers and critics discussing novels, films, and theories.

Dewey, Joseph. *In a Dark Time: The Apocalyptic Temper in the American Novel of the Nuclear Age*. West Lafayette, Ind.: Purdue University Press, 1990. Treats

Robert Coover, Don DeLillo, William Gaddis, Walker Percy, Thomas Pynchon, and Kurt Vonnegut.

Diacritics 14, no. 2 (1984). An issue devoted to nuclear literary theory.

Dowling, David. *Fictions of Nuclear Disaster*. Iowa City: University of Iowa Press, 1987.

Farrell, James J. *The Nuclear Devil's Dictionary*. Minneapolis: Usonia Press, 1985. Witty descendant of George Orwell and Ambrose Bierce; Farrell's succinct, provocative entries are dotted with cartoons.

Feldbaum, Carl B., and Ronald J. Bee. *Looking the Tiger in the Eye: Confronting the Nuclear Threat*. New York: Harper & Row, 1988. A general survey of nuclear history, written for high school and older readers.

Franklin, H. Bruce. *War Stars: The Superweapon and the American Imagination*. New York: Oxford University Press, 1988. Takes a century-long perspective on nuclear weapons, texts, and projects.

Gregory, Donna, ed. *The Nuclear Predicament: A Source Book*. New York: St. Martin's Press, 1986. A rich source of 44 excerpts and entire documents from public and private citizens.

Ketterer, David. *New Worlds for Old: The Apocalyptic Imagination, Science Fiction, and American Literature*. Garden City, N.Y.: Doubleday Anchor, 1974. Traces the ancestors of Vonnegut and company back to Charles Brockden Brown, Poe, Melville, and Mark Twain.

Lenz, Millicent. *Nuclear Age Literature for Youth: The Quest for a Life-Affirming Ethic*. Chicago: American Library Association, 1990. An earnest survey of all sorts of nuclear works, some not really aimed at children.

Lifton, Robert Jay. *The Future of Immortality and Other Essays for a Nuclear Age*. New York: Basic Books, 1987.

Lifton, Robert Jay, and Richard Falk. *Indefensible Weapons: The Political and Psychological Case against Nuclearism*. New York: Basic Books, 1982.

Minear, Richard H., ed. *Hiroshima: Three Witnesses*. Princeton: Princeton University Press, 1990. English translations of Hara Tamiki's *Summer Flowers* (1949), Ota Yoko's *City of Corpses* (1950), and Toge Sankichi's *Poems of the Atomic Bomb* (1952).

Mojtabai, A. G. *Blessèd Assurance: At Home with the Bomb in Amarillo, Texas*. Albuquerque: University of New Mexico Press, 1986. A valuable sociological study of the nuclear city, home to Pantex and many Christian fundamentalists happy about Armageddon.

Newhouse, John. *War and Peace in the Nuclear Age*. New York: Alfred A. Knopf, 1989. A thick companion volume to the PBS documentary series of the same title, aired in Great Britain and Japan as well as in the United States.

Papers on Language and Literature (PLL) 26 (Winter 1990). Contains 11 essays on aspects of nuclear literature and criticism.

Perlman, Michael. *Imaginal Memory and the Place of Hiroshima*. Albany: State University of New York Press, 1988. A rich study of Hiroshima images and memories in light of classic myth and Jungian psychoanalysis.

Rhodes, Richard. *The Making of the Atomic Bomb*. New York: Simon & Schuster, 1986. Long, detailed, balanced, thought-provoking; an essential work.

Schwenger, Peter. *Letter Bomb: Nuclear Holocaust and the Exploding Word*. Johns

Hopkins University Press, 1992. A provocative study of "what the nuclear referent could tell us about literature."

"Nuclear War and Science Fiction," *Science Fiction Studies* 13 (July 1986). An issue on nuclear literature edited by H. Bruce Franklin.

Smith, Jeff. *Unthinking the Unthinkable: Nuclear Weapons and Western Culture.* Bloomington: Indiana University Press, 1989. Argues for a long historical background to modern nuclear culture.

Solomon, J. Fisher. *Discourse and Reference in the Nuclear Age.* Norman: University of Oklahoma Press, 1988. A scholarly, closely reasoned argument for realism and potentialist hermeneutics as essential to nuclear texts and theories.

Strada, Michael J. "Kaleidoscopic Nuclear Images of the Fifties." *Journal of Popular Culture* 20 (Winter 1986): 179–98. A useful typology of popular, governmental, and science fiction imagery and ideas about the cold war.

Weart, Spencer. *Nuclear Fear: A History of Images.* Cambridge: Harvard University Press, 1988. A long cultural and psychohistorical survey of four decades of American emotions, individual and collective.

Wilson, Rob. "Towards the Nuclear Sublime: Representations of Technological Vastness in Postmodern American Poetry." *Prospects: An Annual of American Cultural Studies* 14 (1989): 407–39. Traces a major mode of poetic treatments of the Bomb and nuclear holocaust in the work of a dozen or more contemporary poets.

Winkler, Allan M. *Life under a Cloud: American Anxiety about the Atom.* New York: Oxford University Press, 1993.

Zipes, Jack. "Second Thoughts on Socialization through Literature for Children." *Lion and the Unicorn* 5 (1981): 19–32.

A CHRONOLOGY OF NUCLEAR HISTORY AND LITERATURE

1914	H. G. Wells, *The World Set Free*, pioneer atomic fiction.
1927	Pierrepont B. Noyes, *The Pallid Giant: A Tale of Yesterday and Tomorrow*, first American fictional treatment of nuclear fear.
1939	Albert Einstein writes to President Franklin D. Roosevelt, urging development of an atomic bomb.
1944	Niels Bohr writes to FDR, urging avoidance of postwar arms race.
1945	Trinity atomic bomb test, Alamogordo; Leo Szilard writes to FDR on plans to target Japanese cities; U.S. military drops an atomic bomb on Hiroshima on 6 August; second atomic bomb is dropped on Nagasaki on 9 August; "The 36-Hour War" (*Life*, 19 November); Langston Hughes, "Simple and the Atomic Bomb" (18 August).
1946	Tests Able and Baker, Bikini Atoll; John Hersey, *Hiroshima*; David Bradley, *No Place to Hide*; Ray Bradbury, "Million-Year Picnic."

1948	Berlin blockade and airlift; cold war starts.
1949	The Soviet Union tests its first atomic bomb; NATO is established.
1950	Korean War begins; Bradbury, *The Martian Chronicles*; Judith Merril, *The Shadow on the Hearth*.
1952	First H-bomb detonated at Elugelab.
1953	First Soviet H-bomb exploded; Arthur C. Clarke, *Childhood's End*.
1954	William Golding, *Lord of the Flies*; Philip Wylie, *Tomorrow!*; Edgar Pangborn, "A Master of Babylon"; *Them!* (film) (Gordon Douglas, director).
1955	*U.S.S. Nautilus*, first American nuclear submarine, is launched.
1957	Soviet Sputnik I and II orbited; Nevil Shute, *On the Beach*.
1958	Rachel Carson, *Silent Spring*.
1959	Helen Clarkson, *The Last Day*; Walter Miller, *A Canticle for Leibowitz*; Pat Frank, *Alas Babylon*; Mordecai Roshwald, *Level 7*; *Hiroshima, Mon Amour* (film) (Alain Resnais, director).
1960	U.S. U-2 spy plane captured; Paris summit conference fails.
1961	Robert A. Heinlein, *Stranger in a Strange Land*.
1962	Cuban Missile Crisis; Eugene Burdick and Harvey Wheeler, *Fail-Safe*.
1963	Limited test ban treaty signed; Kurt Vonnegut, *Cat's Cradle*; Peter George, *Dr. Strangelove* (novel).
1964	J. G. Ballard, "The Terminal Beach"; *Dr. Strangelove* (film) (Stanley Kubrick, director); *Fail-Safe* (film) (Sidney Lumet, director); Robert Lowell, "Fall 1961."
1965	Philip K. Dick, *Dr. Bloodmoney*.
1967	Robert Jay Lifton, *Death in Life*; Harlan Ellison, "I Have No Mouth, and I Must Scream."
1968	Nuclear nonproliferation treaty signed by many nations.
1969	Norman Spinrad, "The Big Flash"; Harlan Ellison, "A Boy and His Dog"; Doris Lessing, *The Four-Gated City*; Masuji Ibuse, *Black Rain*.
1970	With deterrence policy in full force, United States deploys MIRVs; *Hiroshima-Nagasaki* (documentary film) (Eric Barnouw, director).
1971	SALT I treaty signed by the United States and the Soviet Union.
1972	ABM treaty signed by the United States and the Soviet Union.
1974	David Ketterer, *New Worlds for Old*.

1978	New York City and Rocky Flats demonstrations; Allen Ginsberg, "Nagasaki Days" and "Plutonian Ode"; Vonda McIntyre, *Dreamsnake*.
1979	Ratification of SALT II treaty fails in U.S. Senate; United States deploys Pershing cruise missiles; accident at Three Mile Island nuclear power plant; *China Syndrome* (film) (James Bridges, director).
1980	Russell Hoban, *Riddley Walker*; Toshi Maruki, *Hiroshima No Pika*; *The Day after Trinity: J. Robert Oppenheimer and the Bomb* (documentary film) (John Else, director).
1981	Chaim Potok, *The Book of Lights*.
1982	Meeting of Poets Against the End of the World in New York; Jonathan Schell, *The Fate of the Earth*; Raymond Briggs, *When the Wind Blows*; Joy Kogawa, *Obasan*; Nicholas von Hoffman, "The Brahms Lullaby"; *The Atomic Cafe* (film) (Kevin Rafferty, director).
1983	President Ronald Reagan's "Stars War" speech on the Strategic Defense Initiative (SDI); nuclear freeze movement grows, peace marches proliferate; NATO deploys Pershing II missiles; *The Day After* (TV film) (Nicholas Meyer, director); *The Challenge of Peace*, pastoral letter issued by the National Conference of Catholic Bishops.
1984	Bhopal disaster; Kim Stanley Robinson, *The Wild Shore*; Whitley Strieber and James W. Kunetka, *Warday*; David Bradley, *No Place to Hide*, reissued; *Warnings, Nuke-Rebuke*, and *Writing in a Nuclear Age* (anthologies); *Threads* (film) (Mick Jackson, director).
1985	Mikhail Gorbachev becomes Soviet premier; Louise Lawrence, *Children of the Dust*; Paul Boyer, *By the Bomb's Early Light*; Whitley Strieber, *Wolf of Shadows*; David Brin, *The Postman*; Denis Johnson, *Fiskadoro*; Tim O'Brien, *The Nuclear Age*; Don DeLillo, *White Noise*; John Hersey, *Hiroshima*, reissued.
1986	Accident at Chernobyl nuclear power plant in the Soviet Union; 6,000 nuclear missiles deployed in West Germany; Judith Vigna, *Nobody Wants a Nuclear War*; Richard Rhodes, *The Making of the Atomic Bomb*.
1987	INF (intermediate-range nuclear forces) treaty signed; Carolyn See, *Golden Days*; Robert Jay Lifton, *The Future of Immortality*; Alan Moore and Dave Gibbons, *Watchman* (graphic or illustration novel).
1988	Spencer Weart, *Nuclear Fear*; Michael Perlman, *Imaginal Memory and the Place of Hiroshima*; J. Fisher Solomon, *Discourse and Reference in the Nuclear Age*; *War and Peace in the Nuclear*

Age (PBS TV series); Pausewang, *The Last Children of Scheven-born*, English translation; H. Bruce Franklin, *War Stars*.

1989   John Newhouse, *War and Peace in the Nuclear Age*; *Kids Who Have Made a Difference*; Jeff Smith, *Unthinking the Unthink-able*.

1990   Disintegration of the Soviet Union begins; glasnost and détente.

1991   President George Bush announces unilateral nuclear weapons reductions.

1992   President Bush and Russian President Boris Yeltsin sign START II nuclear arms agreement. *Nuclear Texts and Contexts* (schol-arly newsletter) announces farewell to the first atomic age.

INDEX

THE AUTHOR

Albert E. Stone is professor emeritus of American Studies and English at the University of Iowa. He has also taught at Yale, Emory, and abroad in Prague and Montpellier. His publications include *The Innocent Eye: Childhood in Mark Twain's Imagination* (1961), *Autobiographical Occasions and Original Acts* (1982), and *The Return of Nat Turner: History, Literature, and Cultural Politics in Sixties America* (1992). He is also the editor of nine volumes of *Singular Lives: The Iowa Series in North American Autobiography*, published by the University of Iowa Press.

In retirement, he and his wife live on a Maine island, seven miles as the seagull flies from Maine Yankee nuclear power plant.